'It is a violent overture, like the opening notes of an opera about war, a war between humans and the land.'

For many years and through many of the world's most remote regions Wade Davis has travelled in search of the rare places where cultural diversity survives, untainted by the influences of globalisation and modernisation. *The Clouded Leopard* brings together the extraordinary travels that have sprung from this quest. In Peru, Davis spends time with the San Pedro cult and their shamans, in the frozen north of Canada he hunts narwhal with the Inuit and in Haiti he unravels the complexities of the Vodoun religion and way of life. He describes the systematic destruction of the forests of Malaysia – far worse than that of the Amazon – and treks to the valleys of the Himalaya, where snow leopards and blue sheep still roam. His travels emphasise the fragility of the planet yet also illuminate the places and people where the bond between landscape and spirit is preserved. Beautiful and disturbing, tragic and yet hopeful, *The Clouded Leopard* sends out a timely message that cannot be ignored.

Wade Davis is Explorer-in-Residence at the National Geographic Society and was named one of its 'Explorers of the Millenium'. A Harvard-trained anthropologist and ethnobotanist, he has travelled widely and is the recipient of numerous awards, including the 2002 Lowell Thomas Medal, the Banff Mountain Book and Film Festival Award for adventure travel writing and the 2002 Lannan Foundation prize for literary non-fiction. In 2004 he was made an Honorary Member of the Explorer's Club. He lectures widely in the UK, US and Canada and writes for publications including *National Geographic*, *The New York Times*, *Outside*, *Harpers*, *Fortune*, *Conde Nast Traveller*, *The Wall Street Journal*, *The Washington Post*, *International Herald Tribune*, *Globe & Mail* and *National Geographic Traveller*. His books include the international bestseller, *The Serpent and the Rainbow*, as well as *Shadows in the Sun*, *Light at the Edge of the World* and *One River*. He is currently writing a book about the early British efforts on Everest in 1921–24.

'Davis has returned to the world of letters with *The Clouded Leopard*, a lovely collection of award-winning essays.'   *Globe & Mail*

'Davis's lovely, cubist, rich landscape portraits are also topographies of the spirit, conveying a sense of place, but perhaps even more, the music of place.'   *Kirkus*

'Engrossing . . . Davis's writing shines with warmth and moral concern. A rich celebration of what Davis fears is being lost to the homogenizing march of western culture.'   *Maclean's*

'A fascinating read. Davis's prose is richly descriptive, full of scientific detail that resonates with poetic meaning. Davis makes a compelling argument for the protection and conservation of the environment and the ways of indigenous peoples.'   *Quill & Quire*

'Consistently sensitive, yet unsentimental . . . Some of the most intelligent ecological travel writing available. Not only is *The Clouded Leopard* great fun to read, it's also a compelling plea to preserve the planet.'   *Vancouver Sun*

'To hear Wade Davis lecture is to be swept up and carried forward by a river of words. Reading him is a no less pleasurable experience. Surely one of the most enquiring minds of the century . . . he has made a garden of unearthly delights. If you think travel expands the mind, try travelling with Wade Davis.'   *Ottawa Citizen*

'So sensitively written its pristine language reflects the landscape it describes.'   *Library Journal*

Tauris Parke Paperbacks is an imprint of I.B.Tauris. It is dedicated to publishing books in accessible paperback editions for the serious general reader within a wide range of categories, including biography, history, travel and the ancient world. The list includes select, critically acclaimed works of top quality writing by distinguished authors that continue to challenge, to inform and to inspire. These are books that possess those subtle but intrinsic elements that mark them out as something exceptional.

The Colophon of Tauris Parke Paperbacks is a representation of the ancient Egyptian ibis, sacred to the god Thoth, who was himself often depicted in the form of this most elegant of birds. Thoth was credited in antiquity as the scribe of the ancient Egyptian gods and as the inventor of writing and was associated with many aspects of wisdom and learning.

THE CLOUDED LEOPARD

A Book of
Travels

WADE DAVIS

TPP

TAURIS PARKE
PAPERBACKS

Published in 2007 by Tauris Parke Paperbacks
an imprint of I.B.Tauris and Co Ltd
6 Salem Road, London W2 4BU
175 Fifth Avenue, New York NY 10010
www.ibtauris.com

In the United States of America and Canada distributed by
Palgrave Macmillan, a division of St. Martin's Press
175 Fifth Avenue, New York NY 10010

First published in 1998 by Douglas & McIntyre Ltd
Copyright © Wade Davis, 1998

Cover image: pilgrims at the Qoyllur Rit'i or 'Star Snow' Festival, in the
shadow of Ausengate, most sacred apu of the Inca © Wade Davis

ISBN: 978 1 84511 453 4

A full CIP record for this book is available from the British Library
A full CIP record is available from the Library of Congress

Library of Congress Catalog Card Number: available

Printed and bound in India by Rakesh Press

CONTENTS

For Tara and Raina

ACKNOWLEDGEMENTS

The travels and investigations referred to in this book have been made possible by the support of the Social Science and Humanities Research Council of Canada, the Canada Arts Council, the U.S. National Science Foundation, the Further Foundation, Future Generations, the Wenner-Gren Foundation for Anthropological Re-search, the International Psychiatric Research Foundation, the Inter-American Foundation, the Atkins Fund of Harvard University, the WILD campaign of the Western Canada Wilderness Committee, Rudy Haase and the Friends of Nature.

For editorial assistance on individual essays, I thank Bob Bender, Peter Biskind, Mark Bryant, Laurie Burnham, Lisa Chase, Dan Coyle, Keisuke Dan, Nancy Flight, Klara Glowczewska, Susan Lyne, Alicia Hills Moore, John Newton, Kazumi Oguro, Peter Petre, Tim Smith, Peter Stitt, Gary White, Tim White. Gail Percy reviewed and edited initial drafts of all these essays and her comments were invaluable. At Douglas & McIntyre I was very fortunate to work closely with editor Saeko Usukawa, whose insights were consistently thoughtful. Many thanks as well to publisher Scott McIntyre, who has been a supportive friend and colleague for many years.

For friendship and good company during my travels, and for ideas and insights touched upon in these essays, I am indebted to Caroline Alexander, Nabila Baraka, Nancy Baron, Elizabeth Beauvoir, Max Beau-voir, Rachel Beauvoir, Bernardo Bertolucci, Paul Bowles, Paul Burke, George Butler, Nilda Callañaupa, Syd Cannings, Michael Carlisle, Adriane Carr, Reg Collingwood, Ray Collingwood, Tara Cullis, Lavinia Currier, Simon Davies, Cindy Davies, White Dog, David Fisher, Bob Fleming, Chris Franquemont, Ed Franquemont, Peter Furst, Paul

ACKNOWLEDGEMENTS

George, Monique Giausserand, Ian Gill, Anna Gustafson, Diana Guyer, Stephen Guyer, Mariam Tyabji-Guyer, Herb Hammond, Thorn Henley, Rob Howard, Ernest Imle, Lee Jacobs, Alex Jack, Madeline Jack, Mike Jones, Ian Keane, Shane Kennedy, Grant Kennedy, Steve King, Lisa Kofod, Joel McCleary, Corky McIntyre, Dennis McKenna, Terence McKenna, Ian MacKenzie, Bruno Manser, Mimi Marshall, Nina Marshall, David Maybury-Lewis, John Mikes, Story Musgrave, Asik Nyelik, Dan Pakula, Tony Pearse, Marcel Pierre, Tim Plowman, All Poulson, Travis Price, Miles Richardson, Christopher Sawyer-Lauçanno, Richard Evans Schultes, Asma Sidi Baba, Hélène Simon, Herard Simon, Gary Snyder, Calvin Sperling, Vittorio Storaro, David Suzuki, Jesse Taylor-Ide, Daniel Taylor-Ide, John Tichenor, Mutang Tuo, Etta Turner, Anderson Mutang Urud, Annie and Bill Vanderbilt, Lyall Watson, Andrew Weil, Johannes Wilbert, Elizabeth Wing and Jim Yost. Finally, I thank my family, Gail, Tara and Raina, for their laughter and constant love.

Wolf Creek, Summer 1998

INTRODUCTION

Americans look west for heroes, but Canadians look north. When winter came to the St. Lawrence, and ice storms shut down the schools in the town where I lived just west of Montreal, my friends and I would gather around a coal-fired stove in a shack on the riverbank and listen as the old priest who tended the fire spoke of his life in the Arctic, in the barren lands of Keewatin, a place, as he put it, of serious cold. He told us of the early years of the country, tracing our history in stories of the *coureurs de bois*, the runners of the woods, the fur traders who traversed a continent in sixty days in canoes made of tree bark. As a boy I memorized their routes and could recite the portages as effortlessly as an American kid might name ballplayers. When I was ten, I paddled for two weeks across northern Quebec with a teacher who had been mauled by a bear. His strength and knowledge of the bush impressed me as much as the dreadful scars on his legs.

Growing up in Canada, first in Quebec and later in British Columbia, meant, at least then, that a young person would almost inevitably be drawn to the wild. Summers in the mountains fighting fires, cutting trail or logging were the backdrop of our lives. My first encounter with a larger world came in 1968 at the age of fourteen, when my parents sent me to Colombia, a trip that instilled a love of Latin America that has never faded. In the mountains above Cali, on trails that reached west to the Pacific, I encountered the warmth and benevolence of a people charged with an unfamiliar intensity, a passion for life and a quiet acceptance of the frailty of the human spirit. At twenty I returned to South America as a student of ethnobotany, inspired by the great Amazonian plant explorer Richard Evans Schultes, the man who

1

sparked the psychedelic era with his discovery in the late 1930s of the sacred mushrooms known to the Aztec as *teonanacatl*, the flesh of the gods. On a journey made possible by Schultes, inspired by him and infused at all times with his spirit, I travelled the length and breadth of the Andes, studying a plant known to the Inca as the divine leaf of immortality, coca, the notorious source of cocaine.

After eight years of intermittent field work, mostly along the eastern flank of the Cordillera and in the Northwest Amazon, I was sent by Schultes to Haiti to seek the formula of a folk poison reputedly used by sorcerers to make zombies, the living dead. Arriving in Port-au-Prince, I expected to stay for a few weeks. Instead, the study consumed four years. In the end I found myself swept into a complex worldview utterly different from my own—one that left me demonstrating less the chemical basis of a popular belief than the psychological and cultural foundation of a pharmacological possibility. The zombie phenomenon in all its ramifications could not be extricated from the social, religious and political matrix of the Vodoun society.

Haiti is a land of transformation, a culture and a people deeply imbued with a sense of the spirit. Living among a dozen tribes in South America, working with shaman, ingesting their sacred plants, had opened my mind to the poetics of culture. Haiti completed the process, shattering the rigidity of my scientific perspective. In later journeys to Borneo and the high Arctic, Tibet and the forests of northern Canada, the swamps of the Orinoco delta and the deserts of the Middle East, I found myself increasingly drawn to the wonder of cultural diversity, and especially to those societies that have yet to succumb to the forces of modernization.

Indeed, one of the intense pleasures of travel is the opportunity to live among peoples who have not forgotten the old ways, who still feel their past in the wind, touch it in the stones polished by rain, recognize its taste in the bitter leaves of plants. Just to know that nomadic hunters exist, that jaguar shaman yet journey beyond the Milky Way, that the myths of the Athabaskan elders still resonate with meaning, is to remember that our world does not exist in some absolute sense but rather is only one model of reality. The Penan in the forests of Borneo, the Vodoun acolytes in Haiti, the wandering holy men of the Sahara, teach us that there are other options, other possibilities, other ways of thinking and interacting with the Earth. This idea has always filled me with hope.

Yet the very ease with which we move about this small planet confronts us with a terrible irony. We journey to learn, yet in travelling grow each day farther and farther from where we began. When the American poet Gary Snyder was once asked to discuss at length how individuals could best help resolve the environmental crisis, he responded with two words: "Stay put." Only by rediscovering a sense of place, he suggested, a commitment to a particular piece of ground, will we be able to redefine our relationship to the planet. For many people around the world, particularly those few still living in small communities unaffected by the frenzy and disappointments of the industrial age, this notion of belonging has never been forsaken.

In the winter of 1982, I was fortunate to live among the Quechua in a small village in the southern Andes of Peru. Though the highland flora was spectacular and the agricultural skills of these descendants of the Inca nothing short of genius, what impressed me most was the daily round, the accumulation of gestures that together spoke of an intimate and profound reverence for the very soil upon which the village lay. The village, of course, was not merely the warren of adobe and thatch houses clustered around the small church. It was the totality of the existence of the people—the ancient ruins that ran away from the village and hung like memories at the edge of the cliffs overlooking the river, the fields cut into the precipitous slopes of the sacred mountain Antakillqa, the lakes on the *pampa* where the sedges grew, and the waterfall where no one went for fear of meeting Sirena, the malevolent spirit of the forest.

For the people of the village, every activity was an affirmation of continuity. In the morning, before the labour in the fields began, there were always prayers and offerings of coca leaves for Pachamama, the Great Mother. The men worked together in teams forged not only by blood but by reciprocal bonds of obligation and loyalty, social and ritual debts accumulated over lifetimes and generations, never spoken about and never forgotten. Sometime around midday, the women and children would arrive with great steaming cauldrons of soup, baskets of potatoes and flasks of *chicha*. The families feasted together every day, and in the wake of the meal the work became play, the boys and girls taking their place beside their fathers—planting, hoeing, weeding, harvesting. At the end of the day the women scattered blossoms on the field, and the oldest man led the group in prayer, blessing the tools, the seed, the earth and the children.

This spirit of place, this sense of life as community, manifests itself in ways that are both exquisite and profound. Every February, for example, at the height of the rainy season, the fastest young man in the village dresses up as a woman and, pursued by virtually the entire population, races around the boundaries of the community's land. It is an astonishing physical feat. The distance travelled is only 30 kilometres, but the route crosses two soaring Andean ridges. The runners first drop 300 metres below the village to the base of Antakillqa, then ascend 1200 metres to the summit of the mountain before descending to the valley on the far side, only to climb once more to reach the high pampa and the trail home. It is a race, but also a pilgrimage, and the route is defined by sacred places, crossroads and rock cairns, waterfalls and trees, where the participants must stop to make ritual offerings. Warmed by alcohol, fuelled by coca leaves, the runners fall away into trance, emerging at the end of the day less as humans than spirit beings who have fought off their adversaries and reaffirmed for yet another year the boundaries of their land. It is their way of defining their place, of proclaiming their sense of belonging.

This loyalty to the land is perhaps the single most powerful distinction between indigenous peoples and those of us whose ancestors grew up on distant continents across the endless oceans that for so long isolated the Americas. I once attended a public hearing in northern Canada where a number of different organizations and individuals, both Native and non-Native, had come together to speak out against a proposed hydroelectric development. At the climax of a tumultuous meeting, just after an old Native trapper promised to use his pension to buy dynamite to blow up whatever it was the company intended to build, a young white settler stood up and spoke passionately against the proposed dam. "If they build this thing," he proclaimed in what he took as a gesture of solidarity, "I'm just going to have to leave this country." The next speaker was a Tahltan Indian. With quiet dignity, he turned to the previous speaker. "Partner," he said, "that's the difference between you and me. If they build this dam, I'll still be here."

The essays and stories in this book, though distilled from travels in widely separated parts of the world, are fundamentally about landscape and character, the wisdom of lives drawn directly from the land, the hunger of those who seek to rediscover such understanding, and the consequences of failure.

CACTUS OF
THE FOUR WINDS

Over two thousand years before the Inca Empire grew to embrace Tawantinsuyu, the Four Quarters of the World, the first of the great Andean civilizations was born in a small Peruvian valley on the edge of mountains where the rivers run together and fall away to the forests of the Amazon. In a flowering of culture and art unprecedented in South America, the people of Chavín produced textiles of stunning beauty, sophisticated architecture and allegorical stone carving which, in its fluidity and drama, would never be surpassed in the Andes. All of this implied a new level of political complexity, and the ability to marshal resources and concentrate labour in a manner which had never occurred before. But more than anything, Chavín represented the triumph and subsequent dissemination of a religious idea. Shrouded in mystery, the cult of Chavín arose from an oracular shrine, a temple of stone which cradled and then brought forth a new belief, a spiritual conviction of unknown character but of such immense authority and power that within a century its worship had spread north and south, encompassing all the central Andes and reaching west as far as the sea.

The inspiration for the cult may be found today in a pyramid at Chavín de Huántar, a ruin in the shadow of the Cordillera Blanca, excavated by the Peruvian archaeologist Julio César Tello in the 1920s. Though a landslide later covered much of the site, access to the pyramid was not affected. From a sunken plaza, a broad stairway leads to a portal of white granite and black stone columns swirling with carved birds. Within the structure is a labyrinth of tunnels, and a tall chamber where four narrow passageways converge in the darkness. There, in the centre, piercing the floor like a dagger, is a slender monolith twice the height of a man. Known as the Lanzón de Chavín, it is an image of the Smiling God, the First Creator of the World, a being crystallized in stone at the beginning of time and only later enveloped by the temple walls which now shield it from the sun. Its face has the fangs of a jaguar, hair woven with serpents, and upturned eyes lost in trance.

A clue to the origin of its ancient vision, and a possible explanation for the sudden florescence of the Chavín cult, may be found inscribed in low relief on one of the flat stone carvings which once lined both the sunken plaza and the base of the pyramid. Dated to 1300 B.C., the image is again a god, an anthropomorphic creature with serpentine hair, raptor's claws, the fangs of a cat and a belt of a double-headed serpent. The symbols are of the lowland forest, jaguar and anaconda. The claws are those of a harpy eagle, monkey hunter and killer of wayward children. In this carving they grasp a stalk of cactus, four-ribbed and depicted in an unexpectedly literal fashion which leaves no doubt as to its botanical identity. It is *huachuma*, Cactus of the Four Winds, a magical plant native to the mountains, loaded with mescaline and recognized by botanists as the night-blooming *Trichocereus pachanoi*.

Although no one knows how the plant was used over eight centuries by the people of Chavín, there are certain indications in the archaeological record. In weavings discovered on the south coast and dating to the first millennium B.C., the cactus appears erect and spineless, surrounded by feline motifs and images of hummingbirds, symbols today of a shaman's ability to withdraw negative forces from the body of a patient. Other depictions in ceramic associate the plant with deer; swift and elusive animals that represent the agility by which the healer detects and combats malevolent spells. A motif appearing on several Chavín vessels dated to about 700-500 B.C. portrays a spotted jaguar flanked by stalks of huachuma, all surrounded by stylized spirals. These may be no more than simple abstractions, but it is possible that they represent the vortex of colour induced by the plant and the visions which carry the initiate into the world beyond.

As Chavín expanded, absorbing under its influence all the diverse tribes and deities of the mountains and coast, changing forever the pattern of tribal isolation in the Andes, the cult in turn was influenced by local religious ideas. And when finally the power of Chavín waned in the fourth century B.C., its sacraments remained. The cactus, known today by the Spanish name San Pedro, most commonly grows between

18oo and 2700 metres, but it may be planted on the coast and almost certainly was in ancient times. Mummy bundles of the Nazca civilization (100 B.C.-A.D. 500) have been found with pieces of huachuma projecting from the shoulders, symbols of the ability of the deceased to be born again out of darkness, just as the cactus blossom emerges in the early hours before dawn. Moche water vessels from approximately the same period depict an old *curandera,* half woman and half owl, draped in a shawl and leaning forward in the act of healing with a stalk of the plant. In the pottery of Chimú, the kingdom that displaced Moche and ruled the Peruvian coast until overwhelmed by the Inca in A.D. 1475, this image of a female healer survives and is seen blowing the spirit of the cactus onto the earth as a blessing.

With the coming of the Spaniards, a whirlwind of disease and brutality devastated the northern coast and all the lands where the cactus was revered. In Europe in the late fourteenth century, the Black Death killed a third of the population in four years. In the immediate wake of the Conquest, the death rate in Peru was two-and-a-half times as great. The fertile desert valleys of the north, together with adjacent areas of the highlands, were virtually depopulated. Aqueducts and narrow canals which brought life to the deserts fell into disuse or were deliberately destroyed. It would be 450 years before Peruvians would manage to place as much land under irrigation as existed in 1528, the year Francisco Pizarro first saw the desert bloom at Tumbes.

In the midst of this holocaust, the taking of huachuma was driven underground, and its sacred role transformed in ways which remain unclear to this day. Its use was certainly widespread at the time of contact and continued throughout the colonial era. As the Church attempted to purge all vestiges of ancient beliefs, missionaries came upon evidence of the power and persistence of the cult. "The principal caciques and curacas of this nation," wrote Father Oliva in 1631, "in order to know the good or bad ... drink a beverage they call Achuma which is a water they make from the sap of some thick and smooth cacti that they raise in the hot valleys." Some twenty years later Father Cobo identified the cactus as "the plant with which the devil deceived the Indians of Peru in their paganism, using it for their lies and super-stitions. Having drunk the juice of it, those who drink lose conscious-ness and remain as if dead; and it has even been seen that some have died because of the great frigidity of the brain. Transported by this drink, the Indians dreamed a thousand absurdities and believed them

7

as if they were true." A Church document published by the Bishop of Cajamarca describes the arrest and trial in 1782 of a shaman accused of conducting a healing ceremony with a potion derived from *gigantón,* yet another name used to describe the cactus.

For the next 150 years, the plant disappears from the written record. Then, in 1945, an anthropologist found stalks of the cactus being sold in markets along the northern Peruvian coast. A number of academic papers followed, confirming the existence of an extraordinary healing tradition, a fundamental feature of which was the nocturnal ingestion of the hallucinogenic cactus. In the late 1960s, research by several anthropologists, most notably Douglas Sharon, then a fellow graduate student of Carlos Castanedas at UCLA, began to unveil the wisdom of the contemporary cult. In a series of articles and books, Sharon wrote of his apprenticeship to Eduardo Calderón, a remarkable folk healer from the coastal city of Trujillo.

By ingesting the magic plant, Sharon reports, Eduardo learns to see, to transcend the ordinary, to attain the clarity of vision that enables him to diagnose and treat disease. According to Eduardo, the plant induces "a numbness in the body and afterward a tranquillity. And then comes detachment, a type of visual force in the individual inclusive of all the senses: seeing, hearing, smelling, touching—all the senses, including the sixth sense, the telepathic sense of transmitting oneself across time and matter ... to a distant dimension." In treatment, a healer facilitates revelations, allowing patients to bloom, to "open like a flower" that they too may be "set free from matter." By taking San Pedro, Eduardo informed Sharon, "one is transported across time, matter, distance in a rapid and safe fashion."

As the soul takes flight, the healer soars into metaphysical realms where time and space have no meaning. Thoughts become destinations. Often, in the months after Eduardo first became a *curandero,* his soul alighted high in the Andes, at the edge of a series of sacred lagoons known as Las Huaringas. These lakes, he informed Sharon, were home to the greatest of the curanderos, and along their shores grew the most powerful of the healing plants. In his work, Eduardo generally had no difficulty divining the cause of a patient's predicament and prescribing a cure. But occasionally it would be necessary to dispatch a patient to the lakes, a journey of metamorphosis and spiritual regeneration believed by all the healers to be profoundly curative. Some patients were adept enough to travel through trance. Most took the bus, along a road that climbs into the mountains to the highland town of Huancabamba, the spiritual centre of the San Pedro cult. From there, a trail weaves through the valley and rises beyond the clouds to the lakes on the *puna* where no trees grow.

The rains had come early to the mountains of Peru in the winter of 1981, but the rivers of the coastal desert remained inexplicably dry. Two years later El Niño would bring disastrous floods, melting the mud homes of the poor, tearing away bridges, destroying crops, scouring the stony banks of the Piura and Chira Rivers as broad sheets of water turned the Sechura Desert into a sea of rolling grass. Opportunistic merchants would truck cattle from the high Andes to graze on lands suddenly flush with growth. Now, the worry was drought, and such a transformation of the desert was impossible to imagine. On the outskirts of the oasis city of Piura, where I stayed for two days gathering supplies for my journey to Huancabamba, goats grazed in the branches of leafless trees, and the grass mat shacks of the dispossessed high-landers stretched amid endless dunes. Those who knew the desert scavenged for the succulent roots of *yuca de caballo* and gathered the long green pods of *algarroba*, with which they fed both their children and their livestock. Immigrants from the highlands, many of them women still wearing three and four layers of woollen skirts in the searing heat, sent their families into the city to survive, husbands to work as porters, hollow-eyed children to beg or steal in markets where goat heads dried in the sun and the wives of fishermen sold snakeskins and charms, deer bones and shrivelled embryos of llamas.

For the first 65 kilometres, the route from Piura to Huancabamba follows the Pan-American highway, a narrow ribbon of asphalt that runs the length of the coastal desert. Seven years before, I had passed this way with my good friend and colleague Timothy Plowman. For well over a year Tim and I had journeyed throughout the Andes studying coca, a plant known to the Inca as the Divine Leaf of Immortality. It was during those travels that I had first encountered the San Pedro cactus, planted incongruously in the patio of a local bank in a small town in Ecuador. A few months later, after leaving Peru and crossing the *altiplano* to Bolivia, Tim and I made a casual excursion south of La Paz to a highly eroded canyon, a badlands of fantastically contorted rock and pillars of cracked clay known locally as the Valley of the Moon. There, we stumbled upon a wild relative of San Pedro, a curious cactus known as *Trichocereus bridgesii*. Though the plant had never been reported as a hallucinogen, an old Aymara woman told us that it made one drunk with visions. So we tried it, and indeed it was true. What now drew me to Huancabamba was a desire to study and collect this most powerful of plants, and to observe its use by traditional healers whose lineage could be traced to the dawn of Andean civilization.

The road to Huancabamba left the main highway and followed a rough track across the flank of the mountains, running in and out of dry riverbeds for 95 kilometres to Canchaque, a small town at the foot of the Andes. From there, it rose unnaturally up the face of the mountains, climbing 3000 metres in less than 50 kilometres. Until the 1940s there was no road from the west, and to reach the coast the people of Huancabamba walked overland, two weeks on a narrow trail. Today a bus can make the journey in eight hours, provided the road holds up. Once the rains begin, even the most garrulous of drivers merely shrug when asked to predict an arrival time. On the day I travelled, it took eleven hours to reach the height of land, and three more to coast down into the gentle basin of the Huancabamba River.

The vegetation gradient is among the most dramatic in South America. At the base of the slope, skirting the desert's edge, are small copses of mesquite and *palo verde,* a forest of leafless trees and shrubs, with stones and sand as ground cover. Then, as elevation is gained, moisture gathers in small pockets, supporting a richer flora, blue and red salvias, the bright flowers of composites and wild mustards, hardy calceolarias growing among opuntias and tall columnar cacti wrapped around with the vetch-shaped leaves of a sprawling *Mutisia.* There are two different species of *Jatropha,* one with red and the other with white flowers. These, I was told, were *huarnarpo macho* and *huarnarpo embra,* the male and the female, and the bus driver assured me that the slightest prick of their thorns would leave a man or a woman crazed with sexual desire.

Suddenly, or so it seemed, we entered a layer of mist and soft rain. The light changed, and for a moment it was difficult to tell whether the leaves were simply greener, or the plants different. Then it became obvious. The fog heralded the beginnings of a cloud forest, a narrow band of vegetation perched overlooking the barren desert. After a month on the coast, I was astonished to see orchids and aroids, mosses and ferns, *Fuchsia* and *Iochroma,* purples amidst the bright orange corollas of *Bomarea* and the red blossoms of the heath family. It was so unexpected, yet so graphic, a lesson in geography lifted from the pages of a book. The warm humid air of the Pacific condensing into clouds as it flows over the cold Humboldt Current. The clouds falling as rain on the ocean. The dry winds over the desert picking up moisture once more as they rise against the mountains, forming new clouds which hover above the radiant heat and make possible the growth of tibouchinas, clusias, rhododendrons and all the other species of the cloud forest.

The passengers huddled against the cold and damp, oblivious to the changing panorama of species and colour. Two were sisters, both from Lima and, judging by their appearance, reasonably well-off. One complained of being too fat, the other too thin. A fourteen-hour bus ride makes anyone feel like family, and it did not take long to learn the real story. The older sister, the one with the matching lipstick and shawl, and the enormous silver crucifix trapped between her breasts, explained that her father's spurned lover had cursed the entire clan. Her younger sister had not eaten a real meal in a month. She, on the other hand, could not stop eating. They were prepared to pay as much as 100,000 soles, roughly $200, to have the spell broken. It would be well worth it. She showed me a carefully typed list of all the people affected by the curse, and there were enough names on it to fill a neighbourhood. The other sister reached into her bag and withdrew a silk glove belonging, she said, to her enemy.

"*Una mujar sin vergüenza,*" she sighed, "a woman without shame." Even from a distance one could smell the perfume of the accused.

Beyond the coastal divide, the vegetation changed once more. The land, though green and lush with the seasonal rains, became considerably drier, and the trees of the summit—*Polylepis, Buddleja,* and alder —gave way to eucalyptus and agave and dense thickets of blackberry, lantana and *Eupatorium.* Corn grew in the fields, and as the road fell 900 metres to the valley of Huancabamba, the spirit of the landscape became that of the Andes. During the time of the Inca, the mountain highway linking Cuzco and Cajamarca with Ecuador ran along the Río Huancabamba, passing close to the modern town. Known as Capac-ñan, the beautiful road, it bound the region both physically and culturally to the north-south axis of the empire. The river itself, rising less than 160 kilometres from the Pacific, flows east, draining into the Marañon and thence to the Amazon. Until the construction of the road over the summit to Canchaque, modern Huancabamba was effectively cut off from the coast. Its orientation was to the mountains, and like all Andean communities it looked to the lowlands of the east and west with some trepidation, a source of wondrous products, and a repository of magic and power.

"*Allí esta*" exclaimed the bus driver, "*la ciudad que camina*. The city that walks." From a distance, the town appeared like any other, an enduring Andean settlement laid out like a white cross in a field of green. But the land is unstable, and the entire town is slowly sliding into the river that runs through it. Every so often townspeople go to sleep, only to wake up the next morning and discover that they have new neighbours.

The people of Huancabamba, I soon discovered, were proud of the town's tradition and displayed little of the contempt with which *mestizos* normally view all things Indian. The reason for this became clear as I wandered around, collecting a few plants along the banks of the river, a wild tobacco and later a beautiful kalanchoe growing between the red tiles of the rooftops. I saw from the faces of the children that Huancabamba, unlike every other pueblo I had visited in the mountains, was not an Indian town. The language in the street was Spanish, not Quechua. In the fields that ran up close to the edge of town, solitary farmers grew wheat and worked teams of oxen yoked to wooden scratch plows no different from those used in southern Europe at the time of the Conquest.

When later in the morning I met the mayor, he gladly provided a list of the most eminent healers, as well as the names of several guides for the trip to the lakes. For him, Huancabamba was Lourdes, the curanderos the main industry. He had little sense that their healing art was linked in any way to indigenous beliefs and practices that went back 3500 years. It was precisely this misconception which allowed him as a mestizo to be proud of the town's number-one attraction. But he could not have been more wrong. The aboriginal roots of the cult are apparent in virtually every phase of the healing ritual, as I discovered two days later at the home of Pancho Guarnizo, one of the most venerable of the Huancabamba curanderos.

A muddy brown trail wove past agaves swollen in flower and arrived at an open verandah, flanked on three sides by the adobe walls of the farmhouse. Four patients sat passively on rough benches along one side of the enclosure. At their feet lay the offerings each must bring to the ceremony: a bottle of alcohol, a bag of white sugar, and one bottle each of *agua florida* and *agua cananga,* scented water and red perfume. Some had been living at the compound for several days, others had arrived that morning. Each had already consulted Don Pancho, or the *maestro* as they called him, and the healing process had begun at that first encounter. The long hours of waiting served as a passage, a time of reflection which separated them as individuals from the mundane cares of their ordinary lives. In isolation, they waited for the night and the possibility of revelation.

The four of them exemplified the eclectic troubles treated by the maestros. A one-eyed father and his daughter had come from Mendoza, near Chachapoyas in the Marañon valley. Until recently, the girl had been paralysed, and though partially treated by a lowland shaman, she still suffered severe back and stomach pains and a general psychological depression. A mysterious ailment had reduced the family cattle herd from fifty-eight to six. Then, to make things worse, an aunt had gone mad. As she was too sick to travel, the father had come in her place, with hex stones and coins to present in proxy. Another patient was a businessman from the coastal city of Sullana who wanted to discover the identity of the culprit who had embezzled 800,000 soles, roughly $1500, from his company. The final patient was mentally ill. Several weeks before, he had discovered his wife in the arms of another man. The forsaken husband had gone for a gun, but the lover was quick of tongue. He cursed the husband, warning him that a murder would be avenged in heaven; in the meantime, he would face life in a Peruvian jail. According to Don Pancho, the words had fallen "like clumps of sod across a hollow coffin." The husband had collapsed in convulsions, from which he emerged insane.

The maestro appeared shortly after ten that night, wearing a dark poncho and an enormous straw hat that covered all of his face save his chin, which protruded like the toe of an old boot. Holding a kerosene lamp, he announced simply that it was time to begin. His wife, a short and shadowy figure, led the patients to a sheltered alcove on the far side of the house and directed us to sit before the *mesa,* a ceremonial altar outlined on the ground by an arc of seven colonial swords driven into the earth. The maestro took his place beside the altar and began the slow and deliberate process of laying out the mesa. From several cloth bags, he withdrew a strange assortment of whale bones, deer antlers, quartz crystals, pre-Columbian ceramic shards, brass lions, plastic toy soldiers and silver plate. All no doubt had symbolic meaning, but in the moment it was less the objects than the steady concentration of the maestro that bound the patients to his will. One sensed his ability to reach through time and space, to appropriate elements of the coast and lowland forests: murex shells, wild boar tusks, wooden staffs of *membrillo, chonta* and *ajohaspi,* all plants of the jungle. As if to pay homage to history, he added a colonial knife, a pair of dice, a statue of the Virgin, and several images and figurines of Catholic saints. He then placed before the altar a single item chosen from the offerings of each patient. It was again an act of inclusion. Once their destinies were linked to the field of fate represented by the objects of the mesa, the ceremony could begin with the maestros invocation.

"Long may we have luck, work and good fortune," he sang, his voice softening into a low chant. "I am slowing down the world that I may drift into another, one of good times and wondrous moments. With the grace of God and the most Holy Virgin I pray that this tobacco will provide my patients with all their solutions, with my good tobacco, and the good mountains and lakes, the good herbs and my good tobacco—leaf for leaf, vein for vein, root for root, shoot for shoot, whether in Piura, in Lima or in Cajamarca where died our King Atahualpa—pieces of gold, bells of silver. Likewise shall ring out my name, the name of my family, my luck, my work, my fortune and my business, with the grace of God and the most Holy Virgin."

Having finished the prayer, the maestro announced that it was time for the patients, including me, to make a first offering. One by one we stood before the altar and bowed as he blew a fine mist of alcohol and perfume over our heads. Then, in a similar fashion, he saluted the cardinal points. Following this *pago,* or offering, a large bowl appeared in which leaves were soaking in an aromatic solution. Placing the bowl on the ground, the maestro poured in a bottle of *aguardiente* and slowly massaged the contents with his hands.

He stood up, dipped a scallop shell into the dark liquid, and lifted it to his nose. The first dose was inhaled sharply through the left nostril. A second dose, perhaps 30 millilitres in all, followed immediately through the right nostril. He called this a *florecimiento,* a flowering and an opening of the heart. He instructed each of us to do as he had and then to walk to the open end of the verandah, shake our bodies and "release the force." I wondered if the leaves were tobacco. I hoped they were not datura, a potent and toxic hallucinogen. The solution burned my nose and trickled down my throat. I walked outside and stood for a moment in the cold air. I looked back, saw the warm glow of the lamps, and realized that here was the interface between the inner and outer, the shrine as sanctuary, the world beyond a place of darkness and spirits. The next hours were a series of invocations and litanies, followed invariably by disagreeable snorts of aguardiente and perfume. After thirty minutes I determined by default that the leaves in the solution were tobacco. Had they been datura, I would no longer have possessed awareness, let alone memory.

Finally, midnight arrived, and the maestro instructed us to stand as a large cauldron containing an infusion of San Pedro cactus was brought into the room. A small calabash passed in a clockwise direc-tion, and each patient drank three cupfuls of the tea. The taste was familiar, smoky and strong, the flavour of plants not meant to be eaten. By now it was growing late and the temptation to sleep touched us all. Curled up on the dirt floor in our blankets, with a leaden sky covering the moon and lamplight flickering across the brass crucifix on the mud wall above the altar, we fought against a natural desire to rest. The maestro talked incessantly, beseeching us to stay awake. I waited expec-tantly for the potion to take effect. When finally it did, I felt only a vague sense of clarity and stimulation, a tease of colour, a purplish hue, faint and fleeting.

The maestro went about his work, speaking with each of the patients, divining the source of their afflictions, diagnosing a path to recovery. His gestures were sincere, the cadence of his voice deep and comforting. He moved from body to body, touching the temples of the young girl, sucking on the chest of the man who was mad, speaking quietly in turn with the others. An hour passed, and the patients lay around the edges of the altar. If any were affected by the cactus, there was no evidence of it. Despite the dire warnings, we all dozed off, including the maestro himself.

Just before dawn, the businessman leapt to his feet and rushed with a pair of wooden staffs to the edge of the verandah. "Away evil," he yelled, "away things of the night! We are soldiers! We are soldiers! We now have the power through the grace of Don Pancho Guarnizo and so away things of the night!" The maestro awoke suddenly, clearly embarrassed. Cursing himself for sleeping, he struggled to his feet and slowly made his way outside, where the businessman was still howling at the fading stars. I could just make out his shadow in the dim light. A long series of grandiose accusations, boasts and threats echoed through the house, all accentuated with violent thrusts of the staffs. At last, having shamed us all with his rigour and piety, the man returned to the mesa. He then called for more aguardiente and perfume. Before dawn we had each inhaled through the nostrils several portions of the dark liquor.

Another purification began at first light. With stones and sticks lifted from the mesa, the maestro rubbed each patient, massaging the limbs, pulling on the joints of the fingers. Then, one at a time, he spun us clockwise, a whirling, dizzying illusion shattered by the violent thrash of a whip on the back, blows that sent each of us tumbling to the end of the verandah, as his detached voice demanded that we shake off the forces of the night. Two young apprentices then took over, rubbing each patient with round black stones, white rocks, quartz crystals and melted glass. A second massage followed, with wooden staffs and steel swords. Finally, with the aid of two staffs placed across the chest, the stronger of the apprentices swung each of us off the ground, violently shaking our limp bodies. Then, with a gentle hand, he led us over a cross formed on the ground by the swords. Having passed this threshold, we returned to the light of day. There were more florecimientos, followed by ritual sprays of perfume, aguardiente, sugar and talc. After a final benediction, the ceremony ended, and each participant was presented with a *seguro*, a small perfume bottle filled with magical protection, water and herbs gathered at the sacred lakes of Las Huaringas.

For the next seven days, the rains came each afternoon and evening, soaking the fields and flooding the banks of the river. With the road to the coast washed out, the telegraph lines down, the trails in and out of the valley almost impassable with mud, a blanket of isolation fell upon the town. For once there was a lull in the spiritual life of the maestro, and he had time to see to his crops. The patients remained at his home, eating his food and sleeping in the alcove where the ceremony had been held. With their ailments diagnosed but not fully treated, they lived suspended in time, incapable of retreating from the revelations of the mesa, yet unable to go forward until the weather changed and they could experience the curative power of the holy lakes.

Each morning before the clouds gathered, I would meet the maestro in his field and talk about herbs. He was a generous man, not at all difficult, but he seemed weary. His son José, by contrast, was alive with a love of plants and fired by the promise of the cult. The botanist of the family, and an active member of the Asociación de Naturalistas Evangelicas del Peru, he had documented the names of over three thousand medicinal plants, mostly native to the high puna.

There had been healers in the Guarnizo clan for a dozen generations. Originally from Ecuador, the family had moved to Huancabamba a century before, with one branch taking land near the shore of the Laguna Negra, the Black Lagoon, one of the many lakes of Las Huaringas. Pancho Guarnizo's grandfather had been a famous curandero, a guardian of the lakes, and the maestro himself had lived on the puna for much of his life. Only in the last years, as he grew old and arthritic, had he escaped the cold and settled in the valley. The family still had land in the mountains, and José's wife and children were there, tending the herds while he worked with his father. It was his task to guide the patients to the lakes, along the narrow trail that climbed several hundred metres above the valley and fell away to the windswept high-lands, where careless wanderers were turned into stone.

As we waited for a break in the weather, José guided me through the lower valley and shared his remarkable knowledge of plants. One thing I wanted to find was San Pedro in flower. The cactus blooms by night, the blossoms are ephemeral, and it had been largely overlooked by botanists. Since first being described in the 1920s from material discovered in Ecuador, collections had been few. Despite its importance, there were no complete botanical specimens at either Harvard or the Field Museum of Natural History in Chicago, the largest and most important repository of Peruvian plants in North America.

One morning, in the hills that rise to a hamlet known as Cataluco, a young boy led us to a beautiful stand, growing close to his aunt's house. The cactus stood 4.5 metres tall, and emerging from several of the stalks were lovely white blossoms, 20 centimetres long and similar in aspect to those of a night-blooming cereus. The trunk was spineless, and most of the stalks had seven rays. The cut flesh stained orange, thus indicating, according to José, that the plant was especially powerful. It was a lucky find. At one time San Pedro grew commonly throughout the valley. By 1981, it was relatively rare and found almost exclusively in association with house sites, the property of individual families. With the popularity of the healing cult increasing, demand for the plant ran high. In coastal markets, a 30-centimetre section of about 20 centimetres girth sold for as much as a dollar. A cactus the size of the plant at Cataluco could feed a family for a month.

There was one other mystery that had drawn me to Huancabamba. Although San Pedro was the most celebrated of the healing herbs of the valley, dozens of other medicinal plants were used, often in curious combinations which had never been fully investigated. Anthropologists had written a great deal about a magical potion known as *cimora*, but no one knew precisely what it was. As early as 1967 Richard Evans Schultes, the world authority on hallucinogenic plants, had written that the proper identification of cimora represented "one of the most challenging problems in the ethnobotany of hallucinogenic plants, and one which would not be difficult to investigate thoroughly." Indeed, it was not. To find a solution, I needed to go no further than José Guarnizo's garden.

In the early afternoon we returned to the valley, reaching the Guarnizo farm just as the clouds broke over the mountains. After showing the specimens to the maestro and sharing a few drinks, José and I spent the hours of the storm in a small shelter overlooking his garden. The term *cimora*, as it turned out, invoked a range of possibilities. It was, on the one hand, the name for a plant or a group of plants. At the edge of the garden grew three tree daturas, all *Brugmansia candida*, which José identified as *cimora galga, cimora toro curandero* and *cimora oso*. He also mentioned three other plants that I did not see, *cimora aguila·, cimora leon* and *cimora restrera*. From his description, these too were most certainly tree daturas, either *Brugmansia candida* or one of three other species that had been reported from the valley, *B. insignis, B. suaveolens* and *B. versicolour*. But cimora was not just a name, it was a concept, the embodiment of *algo malo*, "something bad." It was a label for certain plants, but it also invoked a condition, the state of emptiness and dread induced by the magical properties within these plants. According to José, the tree daturas, also known as *mishas*, were only rarely added to San Pedro teas. Instead, they were taken alone, with all their power, by solitary healers confronting impossibly difficult medical cases. The result would be a different set of visions—chaotic, confused, frightening— and the maestro would approach them not as a man of knowledge who might interpret and manipulate his spirit world but rather as a supplicant who, in just touching the realm of madness unleashed by the plants, might attain revelation.

The days went by and the rain showed no sign of letting up. In the mornings I continued to explore the valley, collecting along the hedgerows and on the steep slopes where cattle could not graze. On the face of Cerro Colorado, a great mound of red rock and earth rising over the town, I found a small garden of unusual species, spindly *Ephedra*, *Notholaena* ferns, a beautiful *Peperomia* growing in dense clusters on the bare stone. In the midst of the rainy season, these wild plants provided a window onto the dusty months of summer, when the land is parched and brown, and the Andean sun relentless. Among them was a tall segmented cactus, with six to eight pronounced ribs and moderate spines. Its name was *pishicol*, and though it grew in some abundance on Cerro Colorado, it turned out to be an extremely rare endemic, *Armatocereus laetus*, originally described in the 1940s without reference to a type specimen. Reported from only four localities, all in northern Peru, it had never been collected.

Beyond the flank of Cerro Colorado, the trail passed an old graveyard of cement and brick tombs, crumbling and overgrown with wild tobacco and nightshades. The San Pedro cactus takes its name from the Christian notion that St. Peter holds the keys to heaven. I entered the cemetery, curious whether I might find the plant growing as a guardian over the dead. I saw no sign of it. But there were beautiful red passionflowers entwined in iron crosses and a row of young eucalyptus trees, fragrant in the light rain. One of the graves had been recently cleaned, and the one plant left standing by it was a thorn apple, a true datura, *Datura stramonium*. This was Jimson weed, a spindly plant native to eastern North America and named for the witches of James-town, Virginia, who reputedly ingested it during demonic gatherings. For the Algonquin and other Indian peoples, datura was a toxic medicine, a ceremonial hallucinogen used during initiation rites. Confined in a longhouse and fed exclusively a ritual diet of the plant, young men would be kept in a state of raving madness for three weeks, thus ensuring that they would emerge into life having lost all memory of being boys.

When later I showed the faint purple blossoms to José and his father, they recognized the plant immediately as *chamico* and noted that it was a very effective treatment for asthma. I knew this to be true, but I was surprised that neither one of them commented on its hallucinogenic properties. Nor did they associate the low shrub with its close botanical relatives, the tree daturas, which they recognized as the various cimoras. Apparently, it was not pharmacology alone that determined the magical potential of a plant. Provenance played a role. Chamico is an introduced weed, and as such has no place among the sacred plants of the maestro's repertoire. The cimoras are of the Andes, as are huachuma and, for that matter, pishicol, the unusual cactus growing on Cerro Colorado. Pancho Guarnizo knew it well and maintained that it was just as effective as San Pedro. He even provided a recipe: take a 180-centimetre branch, slice it transversely, place it in a 20-litre can of water and boil for five hours. What had begun as a casual foray had yielded a rare endemic and a new hallucinogen, one that the maestros had long employed in their preparations.

When, after a week, Pancho Guarnizo remained reluctant to dispatch his patients to the lakes, I decided to proceed alone on foot, with the hope that I might meet José and the others later on. To carry specimens and gear, I hired a mule from Romulo Seminario, a fellow recommended by the mayor, and arranged for one of his sons, Jorge Eduardo, to come along as guide. We left early one morning, just after dawn, and followed the banks of the river until the trail began to climb steeply into the sierra. For the first few hours, the route passed through cultivated land, and in almost every field there were men and women working the soil, husbands directing the wooden plows, wives a few steps ahead keeping the oxen in line. The animals struggled against slopes so precipitous that when the teams turned, ready to begin a new furrow, it appeared as if oxen and plow might at any moment simply fall off the mountain.

It seemed strange, this valley, where so much of Spain had been grafted onto the Andes. I thought of Cuzco, its churches and cathedrals built atop the ancient Inca temples, and how with every earthquake the original architecture is revealed, solid and enduring. A similar theme was evident in the work of the maestros. Their prayers to the Virgin were sincere and true, as was their fidelity to the cross. But the essential act of faith is physical movement through space, a walk across landscape, a pilgrimage which brings the supplicant from the realm of human society to the bleak reaches of the puna and the endless possibilities for redemption or madness inherent in every encounter with the wild. This is not a notion born of Christianity.

Las Huaringas, the name of the lagoons, is derived from two roots. *Huari* in Aymara means "the god of force." *Inga* is the colonial word for Inca, meaning "lord" or "king." Thus the holy lakes are the Lords of Life, of Power, the Baths of the Inca. Their connection to the valley is literal. The Río Huancabamba rises in the Shimbe lagoon, the White Lake. But the relationship is also highly symbolic. The lakes and streams carry the milk of Pachamama, the Great Mother. In falling to the valley, the river becomes the thread of life, the umbilical cord that links the magic of the lagoons to the fields of the living and beyond, past the final ridge of the mountains and down into the endless forests of the Amazon.

As the pilgrims struggle up the slope, leaving behind the silver blue agaves, the opuntias, alders and eucalyptus, the journey becomes a passage. It is a long arduous walk, a climb of 1800 metres in a day, across an endless series of switchbacks etched into the flank of the mountain. The goal is the lake. The effort is the sacrifice, a term that does not mean to give but rather to make sacred. This is the key to the maestros' art of healing. It is not enough just to identify a symptom and eliminate it, with either medicinal plants or the intervention of positive magic. To heal the body, one has to seek realignment, not only with the supernatural realm but with the Earth itself, the source of all life. It is movement through sacred geography that makes atonement possible. This is the true meaning of healing. To make whole. To be holy. To give of oneself to the Earth and thus rediscover balance, the foundation and essence of well being. As much as any aspect of the contemporary cult, it was this pursuit of equilibrium that linked the maestro to the ancient traditions of the Andes.

At one point, perhaps three or four hours after our departure, I was walking across an open hillside through coarse grass, well above tree line. The trail was heading for a draw that rose onto the open puna. I glanced to my right and saw clouds gathering, and rain showers sweeping across the floor of the valley far below. A glint of sunlight fell upon the wing of a bird, a condor soaring just a metre away. Its eyes were like small seeds, black and shiny, and I could hear the air pushing through its feathers.

The wind dragged clouds across the puna, and with the sun moving in and out of shadow, the landscape expressed a dozen moods. Seasons came and went, cold rain, bright sun, sudden bursts of hail. It was astonishing to see crops at such an elevation, scattered fields of fava beans interplanted with tubers native to the Andes, not potatoes but *lisas* and *oca*. The soil was dark and volcanic, but even the richest of the fields seemed out of place, cut like patchwork into the hillsides of wild grass. Soon even these few signs of human activity fell behind, and the trail faded into the open tundra. For perhaps 8 kilometres, we followed the flight of caracaras and the quick darting movements of a curious Andean fox until finally coming upon an isolated homestead, exposed on the open puna. The mud house was surrounded by three empty corrals, walled in stone and brush, and a couple of hundred metres down the slope was a field, recently plowed.

The house belonged to José Guarnizo, and we were greeted at the edge of the yard by his wife, Angelita, and several snapping dogs. It was not a happy scene. The woman was pregnant and sick, and had not seen her husband in a month. Given the circumstances, the fact that I had been working with the Guarnizo family did not impress her. Still, the air was cold and damp, rain threatened, and we had been walking since first light. With the sun going down and darkness at hand, Angelita told Jorge Eduardo where to graze the mule and then led me into her home for the night. Approaching the door, I found my way blocked by an emaciated dog. The woman turned and kicked the poor creature so hard that it spun off the porch and landed limp on the ground.

The room was dark and smoky. A low fire burned in the hearth, and beside it was a pile of fuel, blocks of green sod cut from the puna. The walls were mud and straw, unpainted and hung with tools, aluminum pots, bunches of herbs and the dried carcass of a sheep. The only bed was a raised platform of adobe, covered with sheepskins. Sprawled across it were four sleepy children, aged two to perhaps eight, though it was difficult to tell. A small baby slept in a neat wooden crib by the fire. It had begun to cry as we came in and Angelita moved quickly to the child's side, gently rocking it back to sleep as she reached for a cauldron of soup and placed it on the fire. Farther south I had seen cooking fires kindled above tree line with *tola*, a plant of the heath so resinous that it burns well, even when green. But this sod put out more smoke than heat. I laid out my bedroll on the dirt floor by the door and looked forward to sleep.

The following morning I woke stiff and cold, and stumbled out into the light. The sun was up, but mist obscured the sky. At the foot of the porch, the dog lay dead where it had landed. During the night something, probably one of the other dogs, had chewed away most of its flank. When I later mentioned this to Angelita, she shrugged and surprised me by laughing. She was not a cruel woman, but it would take more than a dead dog to move her. Breakfast was a bowl of soup, hot and saltless, a thin broth of mutton and *tarivi*, the seeds of a poisonous lupine. It was this plant that got her family through difficult months. Unlike the tuber crops, tarwi could be sown at any time and harvested after just four months. By soaking the seeds for a week, discarding the water and boiling them three times, it was possible to remove the toxic alkaloids and render the plant edible.

Angelita was not happy to learn that I intended to visit the Laguna Negra. Her concern was not that my presence might violate the sanctity of the lakes. She just didn't want the responsibility of explaining my disappearance to the police. What possible protection did I carry? What would keep me from becoming *encantada*, enchanted by the wind songs and turned into stone? The very thought of exposing oneself without the guidance of a maestro appalled her. I showed her my seguro, the small bottle of herbs and red perfume that her father-in-law had given me the morning after the ceremony. She was not impressed. Neither was Jorge Eduardo. But after a brief argument, he at least offered to go, provided I did not expect him to enter the lake. I agreed and the two of us headed off.

The trail from Angelita's house at Talaneo passed for an hour over the open grasslands and through a series of moist fens and marshes before coming down on a small alpine lake, jet black and sunk in a depression at the base of a rocky escarpment. Clouds moved low over the water. The wind was picking up and rain blew in great gusts over the lake. It was very cold, our clothes were wet, and the ground underfoot was sodden. Jorge Eduardo wrapped himself in a magenta poncho and sought shelter in the lee of large boulder. I moved closer to the lakeshore. To please Angelita, I held my seguro in my hand but felt rather silly doing so. The lake, in its solitude, seemed utterly ordinary. The shoreline covered by brown tufts of ichu grass, the stones luminescent with lichens. Patches of *Polylepis* running up the creeks that drained into the far shore. The mountain spurs soaring above. Gentians, madders, violets and heathers here below. In between, the windswept surface of a simple lake.

The water was freezing. I tried to imagine pilgrims from the jungle and coast approaching such a place, stripping to their underwear and standing in the cold drizzle as the maestro poured perfume and alcohol into the palms of their hands. A long invocation, the potion inhaled through the nose, their movement into the water, the ritual tossing into the lake of silver coins and sweet limes sprinkled with sugar. Plump matrons and young children, shaking with cold, drying off with damp rags, waiting for the blessing of the maestro before getting back into wet clothes. A spray of white powder. A cleansing with the maestros swords. A ritual purification with amulets. A madman kneeling alone by the water, perhaps in the very spot where I stood, blowing sweet wine and perfume over the lagoon. The maestro ending the ceremony by again invoking the power of the lake, calling its protection down upon the patients and blessing each one with a final libation, a herbal tincture poured from his seguro and made from the plants that grew at his feet.

There was a yell, and I turned to see Jorge Eduardo, exposed amidst the tussocks, waving for me to get away from the shore. I walked over and found him huddled behind the boulder. He said it was time to leave. I told him to wait a few more minutes, then returned to the lake, stripped off my clothes and entered the water, for no other reason than to wash. It was very cold, and I was soon back on shore, shivering in the wind. Jorge Eduardo was horrified that I had entered the waters without proper protection, and I tried to make it up to him by walking directly back to Talaneo, not pausing in the rain to collect any plants. I recognized the gulf that lay between us. For me, the Laguna Negra was a mountain lake. For him, it was a repository of spiritual power of a decidedly ambivalent nature. Neither one of us was more correct than the other. We just came from different worlds.

When Jorge Eduardo told Angelita about my bath, she was not pleased, but she did smile. Though that night she continued to complain about her husband, over the next day or two she softened some-what, and before long her children were scattered all over the meadows gathering herbs for the collections. In the evenings, or in a lull between storms, Angelita hovered over my work and taught me about the healing plants. Generally, they fell into one of two overlapping categories. On the one hand were the spirit plants employed as medicinals, many of which were no doubt pharmacologically active. An infusion of the ground leaves of *pegapega* mixed with honey was a strong remedy for respiratory ailments. A decoction of *chagapa morada* in aguardiente was taken specifically for yellow fever. For more general treatment of fever, they used its cousin *chagapa roja*, a different species of the same genus. There were scores of such medicines, employed in various combinations.

But for Angelita, the boundary between the material world and that of the spirit was imprecise. A delicate member of the rush family, *la hierba de dominacion*, the herb of domination, lay a shroud of protection over the living, insulating the forces of white magic from the power of evil. Other plants of the lakes were employed magically as admixtures to San Pedro. The most important of these was *hornamo*, a powerful purgative taken when the power of the cactus ran wild and brought turmoil to the dreams of the pilgrim. There were dozens of plants known by this name, each with a specific epithet—the purple hornamo, the white form, the hornamo of the horse, the hornamo of the fox. All, it turned out, were species of *Valeriana*, a natural sedative. Taken in excessive dosage, they bring on hallucinations and blind spasms of excitation.

After five days at Talaneo, during which I had scarcely begun to explore the botany of the lakes, the time came to return to Huancabamba. Angelita spent the last morning dictating orders for me to deliver to her husband: the children were hungry, the fields not planted, the fire cold. I listened to her every lament, made a number of promises and then walked away on the trail which flowed like mercury back to Huancabamba. The flat passage across the puna, the effortless descent into the forests of the sheltered draws, the switchbacks on the face of the valley, the route of foxes and sheep. Rain and cold wind, always rain.

Seven hours down the mountain, Jorge Eduardo and his mule were walking ahead, eager for town. I too was tired and ready for a good meal. By then the vegetation was familiar, agaves and eucalyptus, the standard plants of the Andes. As we walked around a bend, passing over a section of trail I had covered but had no memory of, I glanced to my left and saw what I took to be an illusion. We were only 5 kilometres from Huancabamba. But there, growing beside a house of red tiles and adobe, was a stand of San Pedro so large I could not judge its distance from the trail. I called to Jorge Eduardo, telling him to stop. He ignored me and kept walking.

I put down my pack and dropped off the trail, heading for the cactus. There was a noise, and I turned to confront a wiry and frantic *campesino*. I greeted him and asked if I might borrow his machete. Together, we cut through dense thickets of baccharis and wild blackberry, and walked into the shadows of the cactus. It was an astonishing sight, a single clone of San Pedro covering perhaps 1000 square metres, individual shoots towering to 14 metres, fallen branches 30 centimetres in diameter. These dimensions were twice as large as anything reported for the species in the literature. It was like walking through a forest. Every stalk was in flower, and though the hour was late, the scent was overwhelming. I sliced into several trunks and passed the specimens to my new companion. He took them and slowly eased his way toward the edge of the stand. Then, as he gazed behind me, he suddenly yelled and flung himself face first to the ground. Somewhat unnerved by his behaviour, I hurried to complete my collection.

Later, upon reflection, I wondered why the stand, growing a mere five minutes from the main trail to Las Huaringas, had not been harvested. San Pedro was selling for a dollar for 30 centimetres, yet here was a single clone of literally tonnes of the cactus. The next morning, when I broached the subject with Pancho Guarnizo, he gravely asked how far I had ventured into the stand. When I replied that I had merely made some collections on the periphery, he sighed in relief. In that case, the maestro said, I would not die but merely suffer a horrible pestilence. The land belonged to a Señor Cortes. But the keeper of the cactus was an enormous serpent living at the centre of the stand. The snake did not attack intruders but rather, as spirit guardian of the plant, caused repugnant diseases to break out—a plague of foul growths all over the body. The flesh of this clone was exceedingly powerful, but no maestro dared to use it. Hence, in a hundred years the stand had never been disturbed.

For another week, I remained in Huancabamba, waiting for the coast road to open. Pancho Guarnizo had finally sent his patients to the lakes. José had gone with them, no doubt to relieve his wife, and in his absence I continued to work in the valley. The memory of the encounter in the cactus grove remained strong. The centre of power, the image of the serpent. But what of the disease, this curse of pestilence? Since nothing had come of it, I was not sure what to make of the maestros warning. Perhaps it was a magical notion, spewed venom of a guardian snake. But possibly it was real and had caused outbreaks in the past. My thoughts turned to the dreaded *verruga*, Carrión's disease, a terrible affliction found only between 760 and 2800 metres in the foothill valleys of the western Andes.

Caused by an endemic bacterium carried by tiny flies, it produces an eruption of wartlike nodules, heavy with blood and easily pierced, mainly on the face but often covering the entire body. During the Conquest, Pizarras men suffered a severe outbreak of the disease in their assault on the mountains east of Tumbes, 160 kilometres northwest of Huancabamba. In his *Royal Commentaries* published in Lisbon in 1609, the Inca Garcilaso de la Vega described their plight:

> They thought at first that these were warts, because at the beginning they looked like warts. But as time passed, they grew larger and began to ripen like figs, of which they had both the size and shape: they hung and swung from a stem, secreted blood and body fluids, and nothing was more frightful to see or more painful, because they were very sensitive to touch. The wretched men afflicted with this disease were horrible to look at, as they were covered with these purpleblue fruits hanging from their foreheads, their eyebrows, their nostrils, their beards and even from their ears; nor did they know how to treat them. Indeed some died of them while others survived. Then it suddenly disappeared the way it had come, as do bad attacks of the grippe.

So perhaps the serpent of the grove had an ally, a microscopic pathogen vectored by insects too small to be seen. But what of the other defences of the cult? What was it about the maestro that left him so guarded? For nearly a month I had tried to pry from the surface of his faith the rich overlay of Catholic belief and imagery. Twice more I had participated in the mesa, drinking the San Pedro tea, enduring the florecimientos. Still nothing happened. No one became intoxicated. Anthropologist Douglas Sharon had written that "much more than the psychoactive cactus is at work in learning to 'see.' To see, to attain vision beyond what we would call the real world requires hard work, lengthy training and most important a very special kind of psychological predisposition combined with cultural conditioning."

This made sense, but only to a point. No doubt the ability of a traditional healer to interpret the hallucinogenic experience is a highly evolved skill. In ceremony, it is the shaman who gives form and meaning to the bombardment of visual and auditory stimuli, and it is through his ritual knowledge that the participants may be partially insulated from the raw and ambivalent potential of such powerful preparations. But rarely does a shaman limit or restrict the experience of the seeker. On the contrary, one of the explicit goals of shamanic practice is the release of the individual's wild genius, direct contact with the divine, all facilitated by the magic plants. In other words, the complete package.

Twice I had experienced the raw power of the cactus. In the spring of 1975, soon after finding *Trichocereus bridgesii*, a close relative of San

Pedro, in the Valley of the Moon outside of La Paz, Tim Plowman and I had travelled east beyond the edge of the Andes to search for wild coca in the forests of the *montaña*. A month later, coming back toward the mountains, we traversed the Coroico Gorge, and in our exhaustion came upon a waterfall at the edge of rock walls that fell away 300 metres to the canyon below. We camped just off the road, in the cloud forest at the base of a dozen pools. In the evening I brought out a hemp bag, and we each ate a handful of the dried cactus.

An hour passed. We sat face to face on wooden crates in a small clearing surrounded by tree ferns. Neither dared look at the other. Both of us felt queasy, a faint trace of nausea that could be the first wave of intoxication, or the onset of poisoning. The light changed, and over the canyon came flights of swallows. Wind carried up the draw and swept over the silver foliage of the *Cecropia* trees. The earth began to undulate in slow waves, the forest to speak, whispering as the light turned to amber. A truck passed, and a dozen laughing Aymara women, as if sensing our delight, tossed fruit our way, mangos and avocados and bananas that left faint traces in the air.

Climbing a small ridge overlooking the gorge, we came upon an old shrine marked by a fallen wooden cross and surrounded by cinchona flowers. As the moon rose, we watched in the silver light as sphinx moths alighted on the fragrant blossoms. Halos formed around their wings, a warm glow which spread into the still night air and fell upon our dog, Pogo, curled up on the dry earth, waiting for the morning. When it came, we discovered that we had found not only a new hallucinogen in *Trichocereus bridgesii* but also a rare cinchona, source of the drug quinine, and an unknown species of coca, a delicate shrub growing on either side of the broken cross.

Leaving the mountains for the coast, we found ourselves a week later in the desert just south of Lima, camped upon on a rocky bluff that sheltered an isolated cove, a crescent beach of white sand curled around a small island speckled with guano. It was noon, and the sun had burned off the sea mist. Knowing that the cactus was benign and eager to experience its full potential, we let an hour or two pass until the light softened somewhat, and then each ate several handfuls. For a few moments we waited, sitting quietly on the sand, watching the waves crash upon the shore. Soon, perhaps too soon, I thought, I felt that strange, unmistakable sensation, a warmth in the belly, a faint intimation of what lies ahead. The wind breathing in the air, a bird in flight, silent and composed. The waves came in, falling on the sand, spitting up white froth. Suddenly, the wave was within, the ebb and flow pulsing, moving physically into the body.

We stumbled toward the sea and became lost in the life on the rocks, starfish and crabs, amphibious lungfish crawling onto the land, being flung back by the surf, struggling back to cling to the wet volcanic stone. Their black primordial skin glistened in the sun. The light on the water splintered into diamonds. In the sky, a vault of colour, a red rain. On land, transparent veils of mauve and rose fused the sand with the sky and softened the cliffs beyond.

A surge of energy carried us up the face of a cliff, bare feet touching rock, dark stones bursting into blossoms. The wind blew off the ocean, lifting us onto a broad promontory beyond which lay the entire desert. Every gesture brought forth a reaction in the dry air, a wave of colour that ran away to the horizon. The air took form, became tactile. It was like swimming in a pool of soft pastel light. I turned and saw Tim silhouetted against the sea. Overhead, the confusion of a dazzling sky. Around the sun were figures flying in circles: wild creatures with red breasts, blue serpents for hair, and eyes like saucers of light spinning in tighter and tighter circles.

The sky opened. A dome of the deepest blue gave way to black, with small crystals of light flaring on all sides. I looked down and saw the brown earth receding. We were caught upon the wings of birds, passing through space, through emptiness, over lands of purple sand and rivers of glass running to the sea. From the desert, shapes emerged, castles and temples, enormous lizards draped over dunes, totemic figures etched onto the sand, a mere semblance of known things. Flying along the wild face of mountains, in the wind the touch of clouds upon feathers. They were our feathers, sprung from the skin. The eye of a hawk. The beauty of water carving veins in the earth. The wind carrying us away into the night sky and beyond the scattered stars.

A distant voice came from far below. A well of darkness. The pale face of a smiling child. I turned and saw a raptor arched across a morning sky, flying on, its beak aimed at the centre of the sun. There was no sound, just the image of a soaring bird heading for oblivion. And then a slow spiralling descent that seemed to draw the earth to my feet. And once again the ground. Slowly, I stood up and walked to the point overlooking the sea. The sun was down. Hours had passed. I looked back and saw Tim sitting on a stone at the centre of a pool of velvet light.

The moon had turned slowly through the sky and the desert was coming alive. The light changed and silver traces flashed by in the rough wind. Soon the dawn was fully upon us and the clouds to the east took on a luminous tone in an empty sky. Every colour of the sunset returned in an infinitely more subtle hue. A great rolling wall of mist swept over the shore, and by the time it dissipated, there were fishermen on the beach, combing the surf for bait.

In the moment all things seemed possible. Collective visions, movement through time and space, metamorphosis—these were no more illusory or wondrous than the beauty of a dry blade of grass sprouting from beneath a rock in that barren desert. Spirals of colour, primordial images etched upon the earth, birds soaring into the jaws of celestial jaguars—these were no longer metaphor. They were real or, at the very least, they represented reality as unveiled by the cactus. Here perhaps was the key to understanding the origin of the first great civilization in the Andes, the mystery of Chavín, the source of the religious impulse that had swept the mountains four thousand years before. The Cactus of the Four Winds, a plant so powerful that it could annihilate consciousness, transform body into spirit, crack open the sky.

In Huancabamba, something quite different was going on. It struck me that the maestro, though himself no doubt familiar with the visionary world illuminated by the cactus, retained firmer control of access to that spiritual realm than had been commonly assumed. His role seemed less like that of a shaman than a Roman Catholic priest, the only conduit through which the believer can partake of the body of Christ. The tea certainly did not realize the pharmacological potential of the cactus. Instead, like the wafer of the Eucharist, the cactus had been reduced to a symbol of the divine. This, more than any other feature of the contemporary cult, suggested the triumph of the Catholic Church in the valley of the serpent. Certainly, ancient themes still resonate in the maestro's faith. The belief in spirit guardians, the concept of healers doing battle with malevolent forces, the conviction that the land itself is breathed into being by consciousness. But what was missing, at least for the participants at the mesas I had attended, was the key to a world beyond order and ceremony, beyond ritual. This was not something metaphysical, but a simple matter of dosage.

HUNTERS OF THE
NORTHERN ICE

Olayuk Narqitarvik is a hunter. As a boy of twelve, he killed a polar bear at close quarters, thrusting a harpoon into its soft underbelly as it lunged toward him. That same year he took his first whale. In winter darkness, when temperatures fall so low that breath cracks in the wind, he leaves his family each day to follow the leads in the new ice and kneel motionless, for hours at a time, over the breathing holes of ringed seals. The slightest shift in weight will reveal his presence; in perfect stillness he squats, knowing full well that as he hunts he is hunted. Polar bear tracks run away from every hole. If a seal does not appear, Olayuk may roll over, mimicking the creature to try to attract a bear so that predator may be reduced to prey.

Ipeelie Koonoo is Olayuk's stepfather, second husband to his mother. Revered as an elder, he too is a hunter. When he killed his first bear at nine, with a harpoon made for him the night before by a favourite uncle, he could not stop smiling. His first seal was taken when he was still too small to lift it from the ice. But he knew that the animal had chosen to die, betrayed by its thirst for fresh water. So he followed his uncle's teachings and dripped fresh water into its mouth to placate its spirit. If animals are not properly treated, they will not allow themselves to be taken. But if they are not hunted, the Inuit believe, they will suffer, and their numbers will decrease. Thus the hunt is a reflection of balance, a measure of the interdependence of all life in the Arctic, a polar desert cloaked in darkness nine months of the year and bathed in intense luminosity for the short weeks of *upinngaaq*, the summer season of renewal and rebirth.

Simon Qamanirq is both artist and hunter, the youngest of the three men, nephew of Oyaluk's wife, Martha, the matriarch of the extended family. On his accordion, he plays Scottish reels adapted from those of ancient mariners and whalers, and with his firm hands turns soapstone into exquisite figurines of animals, all depicted so powerfully that they seem to move within the stone. "You can't be a carver," he explains, "if you are not a hunter." For some time, Simon lived down south, attended vocational school and played drums in an Inuit rock-and-roll band named "The Harpoons." But he grew tired of the confused ways of people whose "heads were full of a thousand words." So he returned north. "I got nothing more interesting than hunting," he says. "Down in Canada I'm always cold. My body needs blood. Even their meat has no blood."

Three men, three generations of Inuit hunters. Seeking caribou on the open tundra during the cold months of fall, taking narwhal from the ice in July, they replicate through movement a seasonal round that recalls a distant time when all our ancestors were nomads. In living by the hunt, they remain apart, utterly different. Every idea and thought, every notion of culture and society, every impulse, belief and gesture reflects the consciousness of a people who have not succumbed to the cult of the seed. Ideas that we take for granted—private ownership of objects and land, laws and institutions that place one person above another in a hierarchy of power—are not just exotic to the Inuit, they are anathema. If implemented, they would doom a way of life. This is something the Inuit know. "We hunt," Olayuk explains, "because we are hunters."

For most of the year, these men and their families live in the small community of Arctic Bay, a fiercely self-sufficient and independent clan, survivors of a century that has seen untold hardships unleashed upon their people. But for a brief time in June, in the fortnight leading up to the solstice, they make camp on a gravel beach at Cape Crauford, on the western shore of Admiralty Inlet, the largest fjord on Earth, a vast inland sea that cleaves the northern shore of Baffin Island 800 kilometres north of the Arctic Circle. There, beneath the dark cliffs of the Brodeur Peninsula, on a promontory overlooking Lancaster Sound, the richest body of water in the Arctic, they invite outsiders into their world.

The journey north begins before dawn in Ottawa and ends nine hours later on the seasonal ice off the shore of Olayuk's camp. It is a five-hour flight just to the weather station and settlement of Resolute Bay, the highest point in the Arctic serviced by commercial jets, where we switch from a 727 to a de Havilland Twin Otter. North of Resolute lie another 1600 kilometres of Canada. It is a place, the pilot remarks, where Canada could hide Britain and the English would never find it.

We fly across Barrow Strait, then over Lancaster Sound. From the air, the ice fuses with the snow-covered land. Ringed seals appear as dark specks on the ice. There are no polar bears to be seen, only their silent tracks wandering from seal hole to seal hole. At the mouth of Prince Regent Inlet, east of Somerset Island, the ice gives way abruptly to the black sea. Beyond the floe edge, scores of white beluga whales move gracefully through the water. A small mesalike island rises out of the sea. The plane banks steeply past the soaring cliffs, and in its wake tens of thousands of birds lift into the air. The Prince Leopold sanctuary is just 78 kilometres square, but on it nest nearly two hundred thousand pairs of migratory birds: thick-billed murres, northern fulmars and black-legged kittiwakes. Baffin Island lies ahead, and within minutes the plane roars over the beach at Cape Crauford, turns into the wind and lands on skis on a smooth stretch of ice 800 metres offshore.

In the brilliant sunlight we stand about, nineteen strangers drawn together by the promise of the journey. As an anthropologist, I want to take a firsthand look at ecotourism in action. The leader of the expedition is Johnny Mikes, outfitter and legendary river guide from British Columbia. It was Mikes who first encouraged Olayuk's family to establish a guiding operation. On a warm day in September 1989, while on a kayaking expedition in Admiralty Inlet, Mikes stumbled upon a bay where hundreds of narwhals were feeding in the shallows. On the shore was an Inuit encampment, with narwhals hauled up on the beach. Olayuk's brother Moses had just killed a bearded seal, and in the blood-stained waters Greenland sharks lingered. Mikes had never seen the raw edge of nature so exposed. As he spent time with the Inuit, he came to understand that for them blood on snow is not a sign of death but an affirmation of life. It was something he thought others should experience. And then Moses introduced him to Olayuk, and Olayuk told him about the floe edge and the ice in June.

There are places and moments on Earth where natural phenomena occur of such stunning magnitude and beauty that they shatter all notions of a world of human scale. It is such an event that draws Olayuk and his family to their June camp at Cape Crauford.

Every winter in the Arctic, virtually all of the sea between the islands of the Canadian archipelago lies frozen, a single horizon of ice that joins the polar icecap and eventually covers 15.5 million square kilometres, twice the area of the United States. As temperatures drop to as low as minus 60 degrees Celsius, of marine mammals only the ringed seals remain, dependent on breathing holes scratched through the ice. Polar bears survive by stalking the seals throughout the long Arctic night. Other marine mammals—belugas, bowhead whales, walrus and narwhals—head out through Lancaster Sound to the open waters of Baffin Bay and Davis Strait, between Canada and Greenland. Only small populations overwinter, surviving in rare pockets of open water kept ice-free by the action of winds and currents.

In spring the animals return, wave upon wave, hovering against the retreating ice edge. The winter population of a hundred thousand mammals soars in the summer to 17 million. Foraging in the rich waters, they await a chance to disperse to feeding grounds scattered throughout the Arctic. In the long hours of the midnight sun, brown algae bloom beneath the ice, billions of shrimp and amphipods flourish, and millions of Arctic cod thrive upon the zooplankton. A quarter of a million harp, bearded and ringed seals feed on the fish, as do thousands of belugas and narwhals. They, in turn, fall prey to roving pods of killer whales. A third of the belugas in North America gather here, and three of every four narwhals on Earth.

By June, the waters of Lancaster Sound are free of ice. But those of Admiralty Inlet, 48 kilometres wide at the mouth, remain frozen. From the camp at Cape Crauford, using snowmobiles and sleds, it is possible to travel along the floe edge, where the ice meets the sea, and listen as the breath of whales mingles with the wind.

Snowmobiles and a dozen Inuit kids descend on the plane. An old Inuk man motions us to split up and pile our gear and ourselves onto one of the sleds, which he calls *qamatiks*. He speaks no English, and the soft sounds of Inuktitut, the Inuit language, delight and astonish.

The camp is a line of canvas outfitter tents, arrayed in military precision along the high shore. At one end is the cooktent, at the other the guides' tents. The foreshore is a clutter of sleds and snowmobiles. Tethered on the ice are three dog teams. They yelp and howl, and the air is pungent with the scent of seal meat and excrement. One of the young Inuit, Olayuk's son Eric, explains his preference for snowmobiles: "They are fast, they don't eat meat and they don't stink."

We divide ourselves up two to a tent and stretch our bedrolls on caribou hides on the ground. Johnny Mikes then distributes insulated boots and bright orange survival suits. They are awkward and stiff, but essential. Chances of survival in Arctic waters plummet after a minute of exposure. In the cooktent we are introduced to the Inuit— Olayuk, Ipeelie, Simon, Olayuk's brother-in-law Abraham and, most important of all, Olayuk's wife, Martha, and her older sister, Koonoo Muckpaloo, who run the kitchen. Both are beautiful women, especially Martha, whose face is radiant and kind, quick to laugh. Someone asks Olayuk how many children they have. He looks pensive and begins to count on his fingers. "Ten," he concludes. Martha elbows him and spits out a quick phrase. Olayuk looks sheepish. "Eleven," he adds.

Over a dinner of narwhal soup, bannock, arctic char and caribou, I learn that Olayuk and Martha were the first of their generation to marry for love. They planned to elope and were willing to court death by setting off over the ice, when finally the families agreed to the match. They are still in love. One sees it in their every gesture: Martha carefully drawing a comb through his thin beard, Olayuk gently nestling her hand in his. Martha is asked whether it bothers her to be cooking dinner at such a late hour. "I am used to it," she responds, "my husband is a hunter." Olayuk is asked how many seals a polar bear kills in a week. "That depends," he explains, "on how good a hunter he is."

There is no night and no morning, only the ceaseless sun. At some point we sleep, with blinders and earplugs. The camp never rests. Winter is for sleep, and the summers are ephemeral. We wake and head off in five sleds, travelling south up Admiralty Inlet to get around a body of water before returning north to reach the edge of the floe. The ice by the shore is a tangle of pressure ridges, but farther on it becomes smooth, glasslike. The spartan landscape rolls on, empty and desolate, and all one can think of is survival. On the horizon, islands, ice and sky meld one into the other, and the black sea is a dim mirage.

A dense fog descends, muffling the roar of the engines as the snowmobiles drag us, three or four to a sled, over the ice. The drivers push on, watching for patterns in the ice, small ridges of hard snow that run parallel to the prevailing winds and reveal where you are. When clouds obscure the sun, Simon explains, the Inuit study the reflection of the ice on the underside of low clouds. Open water appears black, the sea ice white, and ground covered in snow and traces of open tundra appear darker than the sea but lighter than snowless land. Upon the clouds lies a map of the land. Not one of our guides can remember ever having been lost.

A pair of ringed seals are killed to feed the dogs back at camp, and moments later we reach the edge of the floe. Olayuk peers out over the water, sensing the wind in his face. It's from the north, which is good. Should a fissure appear in the ice behind us, a southerly wind could push our entire party out to sea, without our knowing it. Just two weeks before, a party of schoolchildren and teachers had misread a lead in the ice, and were set adrift on an ice floe. It was a new moon, with high tides and gale force winds that prevented rescue. For eight days they drifted, reaching all the way to Baffin Bay before finally being saved by military helicopters. There was no panic. The elders prepared food and kept the children calm with stories.

The only sign of life at the edge of the ice is a cackle of glaucous and Thayer gulls, fighting over the carcass of a narwhal killed by a hunter. One of the guides slits open the narwhal's stomach and examines the contents—chitonous beaks of squids and octopus, the carapaces of crustaceans, the ear bones and eye lenses of fish. The ligaments running the length of the back are salvaged for rope. The deep red meat is too rich to be eaten. The skin and blubber, a delicacy eaten raw, has already been harvested.

Suddenly, a shout from the floe edge. I look up to see the marbled backs of four female narwhals barely crest the surface before slipping once again into the dark sea. As we wait, hoping the animals will return, Mikes asks Olayuk to say a few words about his life. A thin, somewhat reluctant account follows. Clearly, Olayuk finds the moment awkward. Later, Abraham, university educated and remarkable in his ability to move freely between worlds, explains Olayuk's reticence. "In your culture, the goal is to excel and stand out, flaunting your excellence in public. Here, the greater your skills, the more you want to fade into the background. You must never reveal what you know, for knowledge is power. If you step forward, you show yourself to your enemies. In the old days it might be a shaman who waited outside a camp and watched before casting spells on the strongest man. This is something the whites have never understood. The only time you can reveal your stories is when you no longer have the power. In old age."

The next evening we encounter a polar bear and give chase on the ice. After long hours of searching in vain for wildlife, the drivers are eager to get as close as possible to the animal. The bear is run ragged. No one objects. For a brief moment, each client succumbs to the thrill of the hunt. "If you think that was fun," Abraham later tells the one vegetarian on the trip, "you ought to try it with a tag" (that is, a hunting permit).

When asked who had first seen the bear, Abraham replies, "Simon did. Well, actually, it was Olayuk, and Simon saw it in his eyes. Oyaluk said nothing."

There are ancient graves above the camp, stone mounds erected centuries ago. The bones from those that have been breached lie covered in lichen and moss. Around the gravesite is a circle of life—purple gentians and dwarf willows, small plant communities established long ago on the rich nutrients of the dead. A ring of flowers around an eider's nest, a seedling growing out of the droppings of a gull, lichen slowly eating away at rock, two centimetres of soil taking a century to accumulate. One marvels at the art of survival. Bears hunting seals, foxes following the bears and feeding on excrement. Inuit cutting open animals, feeding on clam siphons found in walrus stomachs, lichens and plants concentrated in the gut of caribou, mother's milk in the belly of a baby seal, a delicacy much loved by the elders. Meat taken in August is stored in skins and bladders, cached in rock cairns where it ferments to the consistency and taste of blue cheese to be eaten in winter.

Beyond the graves, 800 metres from the shore, the land rises to a high escarpment 400 metres or more above the sea. An hour of scrambling on steep scree takes me to the ridge and a promontory overlooking all of Lancaster Sound. The sense of isolation and wonder is overwhelming. Gravel terraces on the shore reveal the beach lines of ancient seas. Icebergs calved from the glaciers of Devon Island, and the sea ice covering the mouth of the inlet, are awash in soft pastels—pinks, turquoise and opal. On the underside of distant clouds are streaks of dazzling brightness. Every horizon shimmers with mirages. Low islands seem towering cliffs, ice floes appear as crystal spires. The land seduces with its strange beauty. In the entire annals of European exploration, few places were sought with more passion, few destinations were the cause of more tragedy and pain.

The Northwest Passage, which begins at the mouth of Lancaster Sound, was always less a route than an illusive dream. Hopes of fame and riches drove those who sought it, and certain death found the many who came ill-prepared for the Arctic night. By 1631, the voyages of Martin Frobisher, John Davis, William Baffin and Luke Foxe had made clear that no practical commercial sea route to the Orient existed south of the Arctic Circle. Incredibly, by the early nineteenth century these journeys had passed into the realm of myth and the discoveries had become suspect. Brilliant feats of navigation and cartography were supplanted by fantasies of a northern polar sea, ice-free water at the top of the world.

The real impetus for seeking the Northwest Passage was provided by Napoleon. In the wake of his defeat, the British navy reduced its conscripted force from 140,000 to 19,000. But it was unthinkable in class-conscious England to lay off a single officer. Thus by 1818 there was one officer for every three seamen. The only way for advancement was to accomplish some stunning feat of exploration. And so they sailed for the Arctic. Edward Parry and John Ross's was the first of dozens of expeditions to be flung against the ice, each met by Inuit who spoke to the ships as if they were gods. The entire endeavour, spanning the better part of half a century and culminating in the search for John Franklin and his gallant crew, was coloured by a single theme: those who ignored the example of the Inuit perished, whereas those who mimicked their ways not only survived but accomplished unparallelled feats of endurance and exploration.

The British mostly failed. They wore tight woollens, which turned sweat to ice. The Inuit wore caribou skins, loose, with one layer of hair toward the body, another turned out to the wind. The British slept in cloth bags, which froze stiff with ice. The Inuit used the heat of one another's naked bodies on sleeping platforms of ice covered with caribou hides, in snow houses that could be assembled in an hour. The British ate salt pork and, to prevent scurvy, carried lime juice in glass jars that broke with the first frost. The Inuit ate narwhal skin and the contents of caribou guts, both astonishingly rich in vitamin C. Most disastrous of all, the British scorned the use of dogs. They preferred to harness their young men in leather and force them to haul ridiculously heavy sleds made of iron and oak. When the last of Franklins men died, at Starvation Cove on the Adelaide Peninsula, their sledge alone weighed 300 kilograms. On it was a 360-kilogram boat loaded with silver dinner plates, cigar cases, a copy of *The Vicar of Wakefield*—in short, everything deemed essential for a gentle traveller of the Victorian age. All of this they planned to haul hundreds of kilometres overland in the hope of reaching some remote trading post in the endless boreal forests of Canada. Like so many of their kind, they died, as one explorer remarked, because they brought their environment with them. They were unwilling to adapt to another.

At one end of camp is a recently erected wooden cross marking the grave of a woman who died delivering a child in the midst of winter. Asked about her fate, Olayuk responds, "She decided to have a baby." This lack of sentiment confused and horrified the early British explorers. To them, the Inuit were brutal and callous, utterly devoid of human kindness. How else to explain a language that has no words for hello or good-bye, or thank you? Or a people who would abandon an elder to die, or allow the body of the newly dead to be dug up and gnawed by dogs? What the English failed to grasp was that in the Arctic no other attitude was possible. The Inuit, a people of patience and resilience, laughed in the face of starvation and confronted tragedy with a fatalistic indifference because they had no choice. Death and privation were everyday events. In our camp is an old woman who remembers the last time her people were forced to eat human flesh. It occurred in the late 1930s, during a season when "the world became silent." All of the animals were gone. So one of her extended family had designated himself to die, and he was killed. "Someone must survive," she said, "and someone must die." After the event, the women in the group cut off their long braids, a symbol for all others that they had been obliged to sacrifice their kin.

Fear of going native, of succumbing to such impulses, blinded the British to the genius of the Inuit. In dismissing them as savages, they failed to grasp that there could be no better measure of intelligence than the ability to thrive in the Arctic with a technology limited to what could be made with ivory and bone, antler, soapstone, slate, animal skins and bits of driftwood that were as precious as gold. The Inuit did not endure the cold, they took advantage of it. Three arctic char placed end to end, wrapped and frozen in hide, the bottom greased by the stomach contents of a caribou and coated with a thin film of ice, became the runner of a sled. A sled could be made from the carcass of a caribou, a knife from human excrement. There is a well-known account of an old man who refused to move into a settlement. Over the objections of his family, he made plans to stay on the ice. To stop him, they took away all of his tools. So in the midst of a winter gale, he stepped out of their igloo, defecated, and honed the feces into a frozen blade, which he sharpened with a spray of saliva. With the knife he killed a dog. Using its rib cage as a sled and its hide to harness another dog, he disappeared into the darkness.

Sitting with Ipeelie by his tent early one morning, I thought of the Inuit ability to adapt. His gear was scattered about, some of it draped over the cross of the young mother who had died. He was cleaning the motor of his snowmobile with the feather of an ivory gull. Earlier that day on the ice his clutch had failed, and he needed to drill a hole in a piece of steel he intended to use as a replacement. Placing the metal on the ice, bracing it with his feet, he took his rifle and casually blew a circle in the steel.

Gradually and effortlessly, we work toward a nocturnal schedule, when the light is soft and the animals more active. Out on the ice by late afternoon, long pounding runs in the sleds across the edge of the floe, midnight by amber sea cliffs on the far side of the inlet, where northern fulmars nest by the tens of thousands. Breakfast at noon, dinner at four in the morning, a few hours of sleep in between. There is a hallucinatory quality to the endless sun. All notions of a diurnal cycle of light and darkness fade away, and everyone is cast adrift from time. By the third morning, not one of my companions is certain of the date, and estimates of the hour vary to an astonishing degree.

The wildlife sightings are far fewer than expected. In the first seven days of a nine-day sojourn on the ice, we see birds and ringed seals by the score, but only one other polar bear, four narwhals, one bearded seal, and a fleeting glimpse of walrus and belugas. The numbers are there, but the landscape is so vast that it absorbs the multitudes. The other clients don't seem to object. A psychiatrist from Seattle speaks of the land in religious terms and is content to sit on his collapsible seat for hours at a time, glassing the sea for birds. Others are brash and irritating and find it impossible to be quiet, a trait that makes them appear willfully dense. At one point, during a discussion of Inuit clothing, Martha passes around a dark sealskin boot with a beautiful design of an eagle sewn into the hide. One especially garrulous woman examines the stitching and asks, "How do you find fur with such an interesting pattern on it?" Later in the evening, talk passes to all the places she has been—an impressive list that includes the Amazon, the Galápagos, Nepal, Antarctica and now the Arctic. When she mentions Borneo, a place I know well, I ask what she did there. After a confused moment, she says, "I don't really remember. But it was all very interesting."

Such conversation is discouraging and gives the impression of travel reduced to commodity, with the experience mattering less than the credential of having been somewhere. By the economics of our times, anyone can purchase instant passage to virtually any place on the planet. Ecotourism has become a cover for a form of tourism that simply increases the penetration of the hinterland. But have any of us earned the right to be there? Whatever the shortcomings of the early explorers, they gave something of themselves and paid a real price for their experiences.

One night I escaped the camp shortly after midnight and returned to the mountain ridge, where I walked for several hours. Gazing out over the sound, I thought of what some of the early explorers had endured. One who stands out is Frederick Cook, an American physician and explorer who tried to reach the North Pole. In 1908, lost in the barrens, he and two companions walked 800 kilometres, living on meat scraped from the carcasses of their dogs. When forced to winter on the northern shore of Devon Island, a mere 160 kilometres from our camp at Cape Crauford, he had only four rounds of ammunition left for his rifle, half a sled, a torn silk tent and the tattered clothes on his back. For five months of darkness they lived in a shallow cave hollowed by hand from the earth. With tools carved from bone, they killed what they could, using blubber to fire torches to thrust into the jaws of the bears who stalked them. At the first sign of light in February, they made their escape. Living on rotten seal meat and gnawing the skin of their boots, they walked some 500 kilometres across the frozen wastes of Baffin Bay to rescue in Greenland.

Another astonishing story of survival is the ordeal of the Danish explorer Peter Freuchen. In 1923, while on expedition on the west coast of Baffin Island, Freuchen became separated from his party in a blinding blizzard. Seeking shelter, he dug a shallow trench in the snow and pulled his sled over top. Exhausted, he collapsed in sleep. On waking, he had no feeling in his left foot. When he tried to move, he found that his sled was frozen above him. He considered sacrificing one of his hands, deliberately allowing it to freeze in order to use it as a spade. But he feared it would break too easily. Instead, he chewed on a piece of bearskin, which froze hard as iron. Using this as a tool, he managed to scrape a small opening in the snow. He stuck out his head, and the moisture around his mouth froze his face fast to the metal runner of the sled. He tore it away, leaving a mass of hair and blood. Breaking free at last, he crawled deliriously through the storm and, by chance, was saved by an Inuit hunting party. When his foot thawed, gangrene set in, and the flesh around his toes fell away until the bones protruded. The Inuk shaman treating him wanted to remove the toes with his teeth to prevent dark spirits from entering the body. Freuchen chose instead to knock them off himself with a hammer.

Someone has brought a copy of *New Age Journal* on the trip. In it is an advertisement for post cards featuring the faces of endangered species, prominent among them the harp seal. There are 5 million harp seals in the eastern Arctic, and their numbers have never been higher in this century. There are 7 million ringed seals, and it is upon this species that the Inuit have traditionally relied. When in 1983 the Europeans banned the import of sealskins, they did not distinguish one species from the other, and Inuit families on Baffin Island saw their *per capita* annual income drop from $16,000 to nothing. Simon asks, "How can they love a seal more than a human being?"

One evening, after a long day on the ice, there is a demonstration of dogsled-mushing. Everyone is to have a ride. Though the sound of runners passing over ice and snow is sublime, the event is a fiasco. Harnesses become tangled, dogs bellow and snarl at their drivers, riders are left behind on their duffs as sleds dash off in all directions. It is a far cry from the days when a dogsled musher, with a quick snap of the whip, would cut off the tip of a stubborn dog's ear and bring the team into line. On the way back to camp, some of the clients grumble about "loss of tradition." One asks Abraham if the people ever wear their traditional clothes. Abraham gestures to the modern coat on his back. "Yes," he says pointedly, "I wear my parka all the time."

For the Inuit, the first fundamental break with their past occurred in the early years of this century. Along with European diseases that left only one in ten alive came missionaries whose primary goal was the destruction of the power and authority of the shaman, the cultural pivot, the heart of the Inuit relationship to the universe. The missionaries discouraged even the use of traditional names, songs and the language itself. The last avowed shaman in Olayuk's community of Arctic Bay died in 1964.

By then the seduction of modern trade goods had drawn many of the people away from the land. As Inuit concentrated in communities, encouraged by Canadian authorities to relocate, new problems arose. In the late 1950s, the wife of a Royal Canadian Mounted Police constable was mauled and killed by a sled dog. Thereafter, all dogs had to be tethered outside the settlements. Any dog found without a vaccination certificate for rabies was summarily shot. A distemper outbreak rationalized wholesale slaughter. In exchange, the RCMP offered snowmobiles. The first arrived in Baffin in 1962. No technology since the introduction of the rifle did more to transform Inuit life.

In 1955, the decision was made to screen all Inuit for tuberculosis. Medical teams accompanied by RCMP constables dropped by helicopter into every nomadic encampment, whisking away every man, woman and child for a compulsory X-ray examination on a hospital ship named the *C. D. Howe*. Anyone who showed signs of the disease was held forcibly on board and sent south to sanitaria in Montreal or Winnipeg. One out of five Inuit suffered such a fate. Although the intentions of the medical authorities were good, the consequences for those ripped from their families were devastating.

Other initiatives were less benign, even in conception. As recently as the 1950s, the Canadian government felt compelled to bolster its claims in the North American Arctic by actively promoting settlement. Inuit were moved to uninhabited islands. Others found work constructing the DEW (Distant Early Warning) Line and other Cold War installations. Family allowance payments were provided but made contingent on the children's attending school. Nomadic camps disappeared as parents moved into communities to be with their young. Along with the schools came nursing stations, churches and welfare. The government conducted a census, identified each Inuk by number, issued identification tags, and ultimately conducted Operation Surname, a bizarre effort to assign last names to individuals who had never had them. More than a few Inuit dogs were recorded as Canadian citizens.

After half a century of profound change, what, indeed, is tradition? How can we expect a people not to adapt? The Inuit language is alive. The men are still hunters. They use snares, make snow houses, know the power of medicinal herbs. They also own boats, snowmobiles, television sets and satellite phones. Some drink, some attend church. As anthropologist Hugh Brody points out, what must be defended is not the traditional as opposed to the modern but, rather, the right of a free indigenous people to choose the components of their lives.

Canada has at long last recognized this challenge by negotiating an astonishing land-claims settlement with the Inuit of the Eastern Arctic. On April 1, 1999, an Inuit homeland known as Nunavut will be carved out of the Northwest Territories. Including all of Baffin Island and stretching from Manitoba to Ellesmere Island, with a population of just twenty-six thousand, the area will be almost as large as Alaska and California combined. In addition to annual payments of $840 million over fourteen years to fund start-up costs and infrastructure and to replace current federal benefits, the Inuit will receive direct title to over 350 000 square kilometres, an area larger than New Mexico. Within Nunavut, all political control will effectively be ceded to a new government completely staffed and administered by Inuit. It is arguably the most remarkable experiment in Native self-government anywhere to be found.

In the meantime, like any other people, the Inuit will grow and change. The threat to their culture is not the delight that Olayuk's young daughters show as they turn up their Walkman and blast their ears with the latest rock and roll but rather the underwater noise from ships' engines and propellers that chase away the narwhal, or the plans to grant a score of oil and gas drilling permits in the mouth of Lancaster Sound. Or the global spread of contaminants that raise the levels of industrial toxins in the milk of Inuit mothers five times above those of white women further south. Or Ipeelie's lament that the weather has become wilder and the sun hotter each year, so that for the first time Inuit are suffering from skin ailments caused by the sky. These are things that do threaten the Inuit, just as they threaten us.

Day by day the ice melts. Blue pools yield to a dark bay, the bay fills with broken ice, and the leads in the ice spread to broad channels. The frozen airstrip where we landed but a week ago is now open water, and it is here, a day before our scheduled departure, that the narwhals and belugas finally arrive. Olayuk sees them first, and Abraham rustles up the camp to a fever pitch. Movement over the ice, first by sled and later on foot, is precarious. Olayuk walks ahead, testing the path with a harpoon. It is at precisely the time when the ice is most dangerous that the Inuit hunt narwhal. As we move cautiously forward, with a blazing noonday sun overhead and the ice bending under our weight, someone asks Simon what it is like to camp out on the floe for days at a time when everything is in flux. "You wake up in the morning," he replies, "and run like hell."

A hush falls upon the group as we hear the first sighs of the belugas as they breach and see the vapour of their breath. There are hundreds of the beautiful creatures, white as pearls, moving in small groups, ebbing and flowing with the current. The narwhals swim among them, diving in unison to great depths, driving schools of cod to the surface at such a rate that the fish lose consciousness and lie stunned upon the surface of the water. A feeding frenzy is underway, though it occurs in slow motion, as each massive animal rises and falls with astonishing agility and grace. Only the frantic flight of gulls as they dip and dive toward the water betrays the excitement of the hunt.

A smile comes to Olayuk's face as the tusk of a male narwhal breaks the surface at our feet. It appears like a creature from a bestiary, and in an instant one understands how it inspired the legend of the unicorn. Throughout the Middle Ages, narwhal ivory sold for twenty times its weight in gold. In all of Europe, only fifty complete tusks were known, and they were a source of endless mystery. The beautiful animals still are. Nearly blind, their entire sensory world is based on sonar reflection, a clatter of clicks by which they communicate. Of their behaviour and ecology, the patterns of their migration, we understand little, for they live most of the year beneath the polar ice. No one knows where they go or what they eat in winter. There is something wonderful in this, a chance to be with a creature that has defied science and all our obsessions with systematizing the world.

Olayuk knows only that the narwhals come in the spring, as they always have and always will. From him, we have learned something of a hunter's patience and are grateful to encounter the animals before leaving. Patience is perhaps the most enduring trait of the Inuit. There is a story from Greenland about a group of Inuit who walked a great distance to gather wild grass in one of the few verdant valleys of the island. When they arrived, the grass had yet to sprout, so they watched and waited until it grew. I see patience now in Olayuk's face, as he observes the arrival of the first wave of a migration that is one of the highlights of his life. I ask him if he will hunt tomorrow, after we are gone. His eyes sparkle. "Oh yes," he says. "We will be here."

PASSION IN THE DESERT

As a young girl, she dreamed of vanishing into Arabian sands. At twenty she did. Emerging from the Nile, sick and feverish, she hacked off her hair with a pocketknife and set off into the Sahara on a journey of annihilation. Months later, barefoot and dressed in rags, she arrived at the door of her great aunt's palace in Sidi Bou Said, Tunisia. The servants were sent for debusing powder. The phone lines to New York, London and Paris hummed with news of her condition. It was not what the Baroness D'Erlanger expected of a niece. But it was typical of Lavinia Currier, whose only disappointment was that she had not been embraced in the desert by a living saint and the full wonder of Sufi mysticism. Asked eighteen years later in the Jordanian desert what had become of her fantasy, she glances around at a small army of extras working in searing temperatures that melt Polaroids and drive actors to despair, and says, with a smile, "This *film* is what became of the fantasy."

Five years in the making, and the first feature shot primarily on location in Jordan since *Lawrence of Arabia*, *A Passion in the Desert* is Currier's original adaptation of a famously controversial love story by Honoré de Balzac. Set in Egypt during the ill-fated Napoleonic campaign of 1798, it tells of the metamorphosis and descent into madness of a French officer, Augustin Robert. Assigned to escort an eccentric painter, Venture de Paradis, one of the artists travelling with the armies to catalogue the ancient monuments, he loses his way in a sandstorm. Consumed by thirst, Venture commits suicide. Augustin, adrift in the desert, stumbles upon and then flees a Bedouin encampment. Chased into the hills, he finds shelter in a damp cave and awakens the following morning in the arms of a beautiful creature. Her name is

Simoon, and for months she protects him, revealing the ways of the desert. Passionate, sensual, explosive, their tryst has all the drama of a great cinematic love affair, with one exception. Simoon is an African leopard.

While studying theatre, Ben Daniels, the thirty-year-old English stage actor making his first screen appearance as Augustin, did a lot of animal work, hanging out in the London Zoo, mimicking the gestures, absorbing in a totemic way the characters within. But he had no idea it would lead to this—a rose-coloured chamber carved into the ancient sandstone of the lost Nabataean city of Petra, snows outside swirling in the Jordanian night, a film crew shivering in a nest of rocks while at his feet lies his co-star, Mowgli, one of three leopards raised since birth to play Simoon. The challenge is enormous. If the film is to succeed, this relationship must work. For an hour, it will be Daniels and the cats, alone. There is no blueprint. In every scene, he must watch for some gesture, some clue, some indication from the leopards. "Its like improvising," he explains, "with another actor who doesn't know he's acting. And who can kill you in an instant."

The tension in the cave is palpable. The skeletal crew includes only Currier, her Russian cinematographer, Alexis Rodionov, who shot *Orlando*, two camera units, and animal trainer Rick Glassey, who hovers off-camera constantly talking to Mowgli. Everyone else is outside, including a Jordanian medical team, equipped with blood for transfusions. At the mouth of the cave are Glassey's wife, Judy, and sixteen-year-old daughter, Brooke, both trainers and the only people besides Rick capable of handling Mowgli if he bolts. Anything can happen. At one location, the leopard snapped a restraining belt, escaped up a chimney of rock and was caught just moments before running into a horde of stunned Israeli tourists visiting the ruins. On another occasion, he sprang from the cave, right past Rodionov's head. The laconic Russian, by all accounts, barely flinched. "The leopards are no problem," he says. "They are just like insane people."

It's not quite so simple. Perhaps with lions or tigers, but leopards are so idiosyncratic, so unpredictable, that they have never before been used in this way by a major production. Rick Glassey has worked with big cats for twenty years. "There is no such thing as taming a leopard," he explains, "and the more you try to train them, the less physical contact you can have. If you offer them meat, you're putting pressure on them, and the more pressure you put, the less contact you can have. With leopards, you have to earn everything."

Even were it possible, Currier had no interest in domesticating the cats. Her challenge was the opposite. "We had to be able to untrain them to the point where they have the curiosity and freedom needed for this picture. The Disney approach, sentimentalizing animals, turning them into people with inner voices, would never have worked with a leopard, and it would have been totally wrong for this film."

A Passion in the Desert is a $7-million roll of the dice, Currier's personal gamble that she will be able to induce meaningful performances from wild animals. "The leopards," notes Michel Piccoli, the legendary French actor who plays the artist Venture, "are the most important characters. They are the real stars of the film."

When Jean-Jacques Annaud made *The Bear*, he prepared 1,700 storyboards a year in advance, trained a dozen mimes to impersonate bears, had mechanical animals constructed at a cost of several hundred thousand dollars. Nothing was left to chance. Currier's approach is completely different. She allows a real relationship to unfold between actor and cats, with the hope that the magic of the moment will translate onto film.

"The leopards alone have this impassive power and beauty," says Currier. "That, we can capture. Their charisma. When they look at you, you see right through their eyes, and you feel like you've been photographed. And you have. They forget nothing. If you turn your back, they're upon you in a second. Once in the middle of a shot, one of them became unhappy. She spat and hissed and did their equivalent of a roar, a snarly raspy sound. I have been around them since they were born, but in that moment I shivered to the core of my being. That's when I understood why the leopard is the animal most feared by humans. It is the night, the perfect image of transformation, the avatar of the wild."

In an industry of pampered stars, it is remarkable to encounter a young actor willing to risk his life for a scene. Daniels, who approaches the role with a disarming combination of dry humour and fatalism, has nevertheless had his moments. "They don't purr," he says, "and you can never tell if they are happy until they bite you or roll over and let you rub their fur. We lost one scene when Mowgli, the male playing the female Simoon, was all over me and then turned to camera to reveal a glorious erection."

The most perilous scenes are those which require Daniels to play emotions that naturally excite, frighten or confuse the leopards, and thus provoke an instinctive aggressive response. In other words, the very shots Currier must have if the relationship is to work. Daniels recalls his initial experience with Mowgli. "I was playing the fear of waking up in the cave for the first time. Mowgli was sitting by the entrance. I was behind. I became scared as the character, and she looked around and saw this wide-eyed, trembling face and thought . . . prey. I saw her eyes go round, and the pupils became really small, yellow, like looking into the centre of the sun. She started to skulk around the back of the cave and then came up to me. Her mouth opened on my leg. Rick told me to say 'cut' if I felt the teeth. Then she moved off and came back with an even more peculiar look, and clambered on top of me. I said 'Cut, that's it.' "

"Largely because of Ben," Glassey notes, "we've gotten things on film that nobody in their right mind would try. He's damn courageous. Any time you put a wild animal with an actor, and you as a trainer are some distance away, and you're not controlling the animal, it's always dangerous. Leopards are the worst. They're nature's most efficient killing machine. When we began, the odds were very high that these cats would never work with the actor. And it could still happen. If Ben makes a wrong move, it's over. He could be dead. And even if he wasn't hurt, the cats would never be able to work with him again."

On camera, Daniels is himself utterly feline, with long thin blond hair, wispy beard, eyes darkened with kohl that causes the whites to shine and the blue to appear like skylight. Cowering against a sandstone wall, knees pressed up against his chest, his officer's tunic torn and tattered, he looks every bit as wild and crazed as the nervous cat pacing along a ledge a metre or so above his head. The scene calls for him to gnaw on the legbone of a gazelle. The scent of meat attracts Mowgli, who begins a slow stalk. Daniels stays in character. Rick Glassey moves as close to frame as he can without ruining the shot. His voice remains deep and confident. Daniels unexpectedly lifts the leg-bone toward the cat. Mowgli clamps his jaw around one end. A gentle tug of war ensues. For Mowgli, who has been well fed, it is a playful gesture. On film, it will reveal intimacy, trust, character. So Currier and Glassey let the scene unfold. Then, prompted by clues impossible to define, Glassey moves suddenly into camera, positioning himself between Daniels and the cat. Once Mowgli is safely restrained, Glassey glances at Currier, who knows nothing more will be shot that day. Nevertheless, she is pleased with Mowgli's performance.

"He works best at night," she remarks. "He's more sure of himself, more confident around his hunting time. During the day, he justs want to sleep."

As Currier walks over to compliment Daniels, her assistant director, Waldo Roeg, son of Nicholas Roeg who did second unit work for David Lean on *Lawrence*, orders the set wrapped. "Only film I've ever been on," he grumbles, "where the shooting schedule is determined by the diurnal cycle of a fucking cat."

Lavinia Currier's childhood was one of gardens and lakes, a beautiful mother's love, and carriage rides through lush corn fields with a father whose innocent dream had transformed a Virginia farm into an idyllic estate. All of this died the morning she learned that her parent's plane had disappeared on a routine flight over the Bermuda Triangle. Despite the most extensive military search ever mounted, ordered personally by then President Lyndon Johnson, no trace of their small aircraft was found. It took years for Currier to come to terms with the tragedy.

"After losing your parents as a small child, you never quite trust the tangible reality of the world. Anything can fall apart."

Her first film, *Heart of the Garden*, is a haunting autobiographical tale of a young girl searching through shadows for memories of Eden. *A Passion in the Desert* returns to the theme of paradise lost. The leopard, embodiment of nature, is the only creature capable of saving Augustin. The soldier falls in love, but his passion yields to aggression, fear, impulsiveness and jealousy as he attempts to contain her. Ultimately, his desire to control and possess destroys them both.

"As a storyteller," Currier explains, "I had no interest in depressing statistics on rates of destruction of species or habitat. Nobody wants to hear it. But I felt that if I could tell a love story between a human and an animal, I might draw people across that boundary, away from themselves, to the realization that every species has a right to exist.

"The image of Augustin at the beginning and end of the film is that of a man poisoned by madness and grief. That's what I want people to feel. I want to capture on film the feeling of emptiness, regret and true sorrow that we will all have when it dawns on us that the last of the great animals of Africa has disappeared. We're all in mourning at some level. We're sick with grief at what we've made of the planet."

For Currier, these are not idle sentiments. Those who know her describe a regnant Diana, a woman emerging from the wild like a deer at the edge of a clearing. It was in Paris that she first learned of Balzac's tale of love between man and animal. Her impulse was to do a short silent film—no words, simply gestures isolated in the desert. She travelled to Africa, rode camels to Lake Turkana and wrote a story of a gunrunner set in modern times, to be shot in a contemporary style, *cinéma vérité* with intense footage of desolation and destruction. After three or four drafts, she drifted back to the simplicity and beauty of Balzac. She then went looking for paradise.

The sands of Namibia were too red, the landscape too dramatic to pass for Egypt. An oasis in Tunisia felt like a stage set. Morocco was overused. Everywhere, she encountered the detritus of other productions. In Oman she found a salt oasis still visited by leopards, but the sultan, discouraged by an English advisor, withdrew permission at the last moment, apparently convinced that the film might prove a celebration of bestiality. "With the French," he was told, "and especially Balzac, you just never know." After two years of scouting locations, Currier woke to the depressing realization that there was no pristine nature left.

"I couldn't even find a place to do the movie. Like Augustin, humans everywhere had tied down the leopard and killed it." Finally, she settled on Jordan, enchanted by the landscape and resigned to the fact that she would have to shoot her film in a desert devoid of wild things.

The rising sun at Wadi Araba touches the flank of the mountain, casting long shadows that quiver for a moment and then give way to a river of sunlight that pours impartially over every slope. At the foot of the ridge, along the ancient route that once brought frankincense and myrrh to Gaza, light falls upon a troop of Napoleonic soldiers encamped on white sand amidst monuments and ruins. From the pristine condition of the uniforms, it is clear that their ordeal has just begun. In time, desert storms will tatter their clothing, their eyes will seal shut with pus, plague will rot their skin, and they will trample one another and kill for a few drops of water. None will suffer more than Augustin, who watches the morning dawn from his perch on top of the styrofoam sphinx that dominates the set.

"The desert is like another member of the cast," Daniels explains. "The heat informs your character, and the silence tunes all the senses."

When Daniels first landed in Jordan, Currier dispatched him directly from the airport to Wadi Rum to live among the Bedouin.

"I arrived in the country at night," he recalls, "and she left me with a bag of food and a blanket at their tent. I didn't see anything until sunrise the next day. I then spent a week sitting on a rock, slipping in and out of consciousness. It was as near to hallucinating as I've ever come. I've been drawing on that experience for the entire film."

On the set, in the soft light, the closest thing to an apparition is the line of Mameluke calvary silhouetted against the sky at the crest of an immense dune. A caste of warriors from the Caucasus, the Mameluke ruled Egypt for five hundred years, replenishing their numbers each year by buying boys from their original homeland. Torn away from their parents, raised to kill, they knew no fear and had no attachments. All their fantastic wealth was worn as finery. In battle, they conquered or died. Their scimitars could slice a musket in half, but in the end their Arabian horses proved no match for cannon and Napoleonic squares. On the banks of the Nile, French soldiers bent their bayonets into grapples to retrieve and loot the bejewelled bodies of the Mameluke dead.

At the base of the sphinx, stunt co-ordinator Stuart St. Paul rehearses the extras for the coming battle. Communication is a problem. There are twenty or more nationalities on the set. Some are hopeless as fighters, others disturbingly good, like the Iraqis and Chechen exiles scarred by wounds, and the Sudanese who smiles as he recalls the day he was forced to drive a truck across a Kuwaiti plaza blanketed with corpses.

Nothing has come easy on this film. At Petra, snow fell in October, and bad weather on the set was so predictable that local farmers looked forward to the return of the film crew as a certain sign of rain. The leopards adjusted poorly to the move to Jordan and took a nervous dislike to the sound of Arabic. Elaborate sets broke apart in desert sandstorms, actors and crew became lost on the way to locations, a location was scratched when the crew discovered they were shooting on ground peppered with land mines. The pace of filming has been slow. A grain of sand can ruin a shot.

Despite the heat and painful delays, morale on the set remains high. There is still talk about the death scene of Venture, a stunning nine-minute performance by Michel Piccoli, a single take that caused the entire crew to burst into spontaneous applause. The presence of the veteran actor, whose explosive power and charisma on camera are often compared to that of Sean Connery, lends weight to a production that in so many ways is charting unknown territory. As one person close to Currier put it, "If you did this by the book, you'd never do it. No one would have funded this. It's too difficult. Too uncertain."

To prepare for the film, Currier spent months in Paris, reading journals and memoirs of the campaign, examining the collections of armaments and uniforms at Les Invalides, all the while guided in her efforts by her grandmother Evangeline Bruce, author of the best-selling biography *Napoleon and Josephine*. The attention to historical detail is remarkable. The coconut canteens were cast from an original carved in the desert by one of Napoleon's soldiers. The woollen uniforms, stained with sweat, are missing buttons, which were used as currency during the invasion. The costumes of the Mameluke are a blaze of silk and sparkling jewels. The Arabian horses, provided by Crown Prince Hassan, are the finest in Jordan.

At the base of the hill, Currier and Rodionov huddle with Daniels. The charge down the dune, and the subsequent battle, will be shot from three angles. There are twenty-six horses, as many as can be fed and watered in the desert, and the task is to make them appear on film like a hundred. Neither the horses nor the riders will be keen on doing the scene more than once. Cameras roll, and pandemonium erupts on the set. Cannon shot blasts the face off the sphinx. Soldiers dash to form ranks. From dust clouds burst the Mameluke. The fighting is fierce for five minutes, until Currier stops the action. Everyone is pleased. Gerard Naprous, the veteran horse master whose recent credits include *Braveheart, Rob Roy* and *First Knight,* turns to his son Daniel, who has led the charge. "It's going to look very big," he says, "very big indeed for a picture that began so small."

In the end it comes down to this. An untested director, a compelling script, a woman of poetic vision taking on a story said to be impossible to film. In moments of doubt, Currier remembers the advice of her mentor, Yoichi Matsue, Kurosawa's producer on *Dersu Uzala* and other films. When she first brought the story to him, he told her it might take a decade to complete. She gasped, certain that it would be finished and out of her life in a year. Three years later, as production was finally to begin, Currier hesitated. The locations weren't right. The script was flawed. But everyone associated with the film told her she had passed the point of no return. Actors had been hired. Contracts signed. Then she remembered Matsue had told her that beauty emerges from patience, that Kurosawa can spend weeks painting a single storyboard. From Antigua, she called Tokyo. Matsue responded to her concerns with five words: "Bad Wind. We don't sail." So she didn't.

"I suppose, had I known how difficult it would be," she says, "I might not have done it. Several times I thought of quitting. But the story kept picking me up. Somebody had to speak for the animals. And that's ultimately what this film is about. The idea that the wild has a right to be."

It is this conviction, softly spoken and pursued without compromise, that has earned Currier the affection of cast and crew alike. In a career that has spanned four decades, Michel Piccoli has appeared in thirty-seven films, working with Louis Malle, Luis Buñuel, Robert Bresson. Asked on a terrace overlooking the Red Sea why he has chosen now to work with Currier, he replies gracefully, "To begin, it was Balzac, then it was a chance to work with a young American director interested in Balzac, then the script, and then Lavinia. When she smiles, she has the eyes of a child."

DREAMS OF A
JADE FOREST

My plane to New York had been delayed four hours and that's how long Bruno Manser had been waiting in the lobby of the Regency Hotel. He was dressed in a sleeveless wool vest, faded trousers and sandals. His arms were bare, save for dozens of blackened Penan dream bracelets that hung at his wrists. Short and sinewy, with dark hair shaved by his own hand and rimless spectacles hugging the bridge of his nose, he really did look like Gandhi, just as the Malaysian press had reported.

He was hungry, but without a dinner jacket he had been barred from the hotel restaurant. Here was a man who had disappeared for six years into the rain forest of Borneo, relinquishing all contact with the modern world to live as a hunter and gatherer with the nomadic Penan. Here was the Swiss shepherd whose vision of a world without greed collapsed in the face of the most rapine deforestation known on Earth. Here was the reluctant warrior who brought the Penan to barricade the logging roads, electrifying the international environmental movement and stunning the Malaysian government, which placed a reward on his head and hunted him down with police and military commandos. Apprehended twice, he escaped and, protected by Penan, eluded capture for three years. Dismissed in Malaysia as a latter-day Tarzan, the man became a lightning rod for all the forces gathered in the struggle for the world's most endangered rain forest. But in New York, without a jacket, he couldn't enter a restaurant.

Anticipating the problem, a friend arrived for dinner with an extra coat which made Bruno appear absurd enough to satisfy the maître d'. It was Sunday night and the restaurant was empty. The meal passed calmly until, just as it was time to pay the bill, a rat appeared and scampered the full length of the restaurant. Within moments three waiters and the maître d' hovered at our table, spewing apologies. Bruno raised his glass. "It was a Norway rat," he said to them, "and it wasn't wearing a jacket."

The mouth of the Baram river is the colour of the earth. To the north, the soils of Sarawak disappear into the South China Sea and fleets of empty Japanese freighters hang on the horizon, awaiting the tides and a chance to fill their holds with raw logs ripped from the forests of Borneo. The river settlements are settings of opportunity and despair— muddy logging camps and clusters of shanties, their leprous façades patched with sheets of metal, plastic and scavenged boards. Children by the river's edge dump barrels of garbage which drifts back to shore in the wake of each passing log barge. For 150 kilometres the river is choked with debris and silt, and along its banks lie thousands of logs stacked thirty deep, some awaiting shipment, some slowly rotting in the tropical heat.

"This country," Bruno Manser once said when interviewed deep in the forest of the Penan, "is in a way one of the last paradises. In another way it is hell. The basis of existence of one of the last nomadic peoples is being destroyed." He was referring to the frenzy of logging that has in the last two decades gripped the east Malaysian state of Sarawak, a rate of deforestation twice that of the Amazon and by far the highest in the world. In 1983 Malaysia accounted for 58 per cent of the total global export of tropical logs. By 1985, 1.2 hectares of forest were being cut every minute of every day. With the primary forests of peninsular Malaysia becoming rapidly depleted, the industry turned to Sarawak. In 1985, over 240 000 hectares were logged, providing a full 39 per cent of the national production. Another 5.2 million hectares—60 per cent of Sarawak's forested land—was held in logging concessions which encompassed at least three-quarters of the traditional homeland of the nomadic Penan. Owners of logging concessions included each of the eight daughters of the former chief minister. In a remarkable inversion of the truth, the minister of the environment, also a prominent con-cessionaire, had stated that "logging is good for the forest," a remark symptomatic of the shadow world into which Bruno Manser first arrived in the spring of 1984. Nothing in his experience could have prepared him for the drama about to unfold all around him.

He was born in Basel, Switzerland, in 1954, but for the last twelve years before travelling to Sarawak, Bruno Manser had lived in the high mountains of eastern Switzerland, working seasonally as a shepherd and fisherman. Living alone, he grew his own food, sewed his own clothing and shoes, and made cheese which he sold in local markets. Besides painting, his main passion was spelunking, and by his own estimate he spent a third of his time underground exploring the spectacular caves that lie beneath the Alps. His innocent dream, however, was to travel to the tropical rain forest to live among an indigenous people untouched by the modern world.

"As a child," he told me when we first met in Hawaii a month after he had escaped from Malaysia, "I collected leaves and feathers, and at night lay in my room imagining that it had become a jungle. I wanted to live with a people of nature, to share their traditions, to discover their origins, to become aware of their religion and life, to know these things." In a library, he came upon a single black-and-white photograph of a Penan hunter with a caption that read simply: "A hunter gatherer in the forests of Borneo." No other material was available. Intrigued by the dearth of information, he dug further. His decision was made when he came upon an obscure report that described the traditional homeland of the Penan as a magical landscape of forest and soaring mountains, crystalline rivers and the world's most extensive network of caves and underground passages.

He travelled to West Malaysia and became conversant in Malay, then joined a British caving expedition headed for the mountains of Gunung Mulu, the heart of Penan territory in Sarawak. His illusions of paradise were first shaken at Kuala Baram, the port on the Baram River where he boarded one of the sleek express boats for the journey upriver to Marudi, the jumping-off point for all journeys to the interior. He sat shoulder to shoulder with an elderly Kelabit woman in a row of seats that looked as if they might have been lifted from a modern jet. Garlands of plastic leaves and flowers intertwined with Christmas tree lights ran the length of the enclosed cabin. The noise of the engine was deafening. With the air conditioner at full throttle, condensation covered the porthole windows, and the only view was forward toward the video monitor which played constantly at top volume. Travelling to and from the logging camps, Dayak workers, two generations removed from their head-hunting forefathers, huddled against the cold, eyes glued to the videotapes of the World Wrestling Federation that had made Hulk Hogan a folk hero throughout the hinterland of Sarawak.

On his way upriver, in the longhouse settlements on the Baram, Manser had his first contacts with the Kayan and Kelabit, swidden agriculturalists whose ancestors had sown rice in the forests of Borneo long before the rivers were born. From them, he learned to seek permission of the crocodiles before crossing a river, to spread blood on the trunk of a fallen tree to appease its soul. Their elders told stories of the human heads that still hung from the rafters of their longhouses, trophies taken by youths on the cusp of manhood to prove their worth to prospective brides. Pointing to the skulls, one elder had said, "Old and thin. I am like the son of the dead."

Sometimes the people danced, Kayan women with beautiful earlobes hanging to their shoulders and intricate tattoos that covered their feet and hands, men with shields and iron blades. It was dance as metaphor, gentle sweeping movements like wind through a rice field, suddenly punctuated with violent gestures: the flash of a blade, a sudden twist or a foot striking the ground. The calm life of the river and the image of a people alert to the ever-present danger of raiding parties in search of heads. Invariably, the rice wine flowed, and when Manser, after his fourth or fifth glass, politely declined, the women insisted. Cradling his head in their hands, they poured the wine into his mouth. "This is not poison," they said. "It is our love."

In Marudi, where Bruno sought information about the Penan, he discovered that most townspeople had never met the nomads. Nevertheless, many of the people he spoke with considered the Penan a national embarrassment, a dirty people, they claimed, "living like pigs in the filth of the jungle." Others said that they were beautiful, with skin like silk. "After living with them," Bruno observed, "I can tell you that if you put these two images together, you will discover the truth." One government official offered concrete advice, encouraging Manser to travel to the Ubong region where there was a chance he might encounter nomadic Penan. He promised that it would be a rare experience.

Manser continued upriver, passing from the Baram to the Tutoh and on to the Melinau River, the ancient trade route that connects the Tutoh and the Limbang watersheds. Here, in the immense and remote highlands that give rise to the affluents of the Baram, he encountered another world. In the air was a fluid heaviness, a weight of centuries, of years without seasons and life without rebirth. Yet thousands of years ago the ancestors of the Penan had entered this forest, and from adaptation a culture had emerged whose complexity rivalled even that of the dense vegetation from which it was born. To stay alive, the Penan had invented a way of life; lacking the technology to transform the forest, they had chosen instead to understand it.

The British expedition remained at the caves for two weeks; once they were gone, Bruno made plans to continue into the forest. From two semisettled Penan who had acted as porters for the British, he learned of a group of several nomadic families living in the foothills to the south. "I had a map and a compass, a fishnet and a few kilos of rice," Bruno recalls. So with food for a fortnight and a cumbersome pack that weighed over 25 kilograms, he set off for the Ubong River.

In the forest, his compass and map proved useless, and to remain oriented, he followed the mountain ridgelines, struggling through impossibly dense vegetation. For nine days he chopped his way through the elfin cloud forest, cutting for two to three hours, returning in fifteen minutes for his pack and then beginning again. For days there was no rain and no water to cook his rice. "In the evenings, I just lay in my blanket, and in the morning took my bush knife and began again." Manser went without food for four days, without water for two, until desperate, he discovered that he could drink from the pitcher plants, provided they were free of rotting insects. On his ninth day on the ridge, he climbed a tree and saw across the valley the white plume of a cooking fire.

It was nearly dark by the time he saw the footprints in the mud by the river. "I knew they would be afraid, so I made camp. The next morning I let the sun come up. Then I heard two voices, a man and a woman. For two minutes nothing happened. I held my hand up in greeting. The woman fled. But the man came to me. He had been downriver and spoke a few words of Malay. We touched hands and he drew his fingers back across his breast. He never looked me in the eye." Manser followed the Penan man up the slope to the encampment, where for the next months the clumsy outsider would play the role of a child.

"There was a boy in that first Penan group," Bruno tells me in Hawaii as we sit beneath the spreading branches of a *flamboyant* tree, "who came back with seven fish. I remember watching the headman give three to each family, and then carefully slice the remaining fish in two. That is Penan. You will never find one with a full stomach, and another who is hungry. I remember once an old man died. His son left him in his hut and placed his possessions at his side, including all of his *tahau*,

61

a highly prized and rare medicine. He said, 'If I can't share it with my father, why keep it?' "

It is difficult to know what impact six years in the forest has had on Manser. He speaks now as one imagines he always has—with modesty, purity of emotion and motivation, and a perspective that suggests that his reference points are not of this world. "Death for the Penan is a form of exile," he mentions. "The dead can no longer take part in the hunt, they cannot share their songs by the fire. So the soul turns bitter, darkens and falls from the heavens. That is why the leeches come with the rains—they are the dead's revenge on the living." A bird calls and Bruno looks up: "When the hornbill screams at night, you know that they are taking the dead to paradise."

Later that night, at a conference on wilderness preservation at which he is the obvious attraction, Bruno somewhat reluctantly joins a panel of speakers, who are surprised to find pieces of half-eaten fruit passed to them during the proceedings. When it is his turn to speak, he comes forward slowly, turning away from the spotlight as a Penan might turn from the sun. Embracing the podium, he seems even shorter than he is, and he speaks less of the Penan than of the underlying beliefs that have driven him throughout his life. "We have lost the ability to live in the moment. Yet eternity happens in the moment. It is so simple. Fate—you open the gates and it comes to meet you. I was drawn to the Penan for the simple reason that I feel well in nature. It is nothing romantic. When you live in the jungle you realize that daily life doesn't permit romanticism. One walks, the legs hurt, and the leeches and the rain, and then you see something beautiful—that is your wage. Then you remember that we are all of one heart."

The lights in the auditorium fade, and on a large screen behind the podium, stunning images appear, scenes from *Tong Tana*, a hauntingly beautiful Swedish documentary about Bruno Manser and the fate of the Penan. A foot steps into a pool of water, leaving in its wake a whirl of silt. Hunters move silently in the forest. The sound of leaves scraping space and, overhead, birds complaining against the gathering darkness. Trees come to life in their death, groaning as their trunks pivot, severed by chainsaws. Everything is alive, imbued with double meaning and an ambiguity of the spirit.

In the film Manser is transformed, his muscular body lean and glorious in a loincloth, his hair long and lost in the fur of a monkey that clings to his neck. After so much time away and so many months on the run, he responds only to the steady rhythm of the forest. Yet the impossibility of his situation, a fugitive straddling the cusp of cultures, reveals a complexity of character that is lost on the podium. "It is many years," he says simply, "since I owned anything that could remind me of the past. I spend my time taking notes about everything daily life brings with it." His journals, hundreds of lavishly illustrated pages written in beautiful script, are his one link to his previous life. In every other regard he has identified himself completely with the Penan, yielding even his thoughts and dreams to their language, subsuming his own dilemma in the enormity of their plight. A writer once suggested to Manser that perhaps in a previous lifetime he had been a Penan. Bruno replied, "Perhaps in a previous life I was a Swiss."

The world of the Penan described by Manser is a land of promise and tragedy. Numbering some 7,600, of whom perhaps a thousand remain deep in the forest, following their ancient way of life, the Penan are one of the few truly nomadic rain forest societies of the Earth. Related in spirit to the Mbuti pygmies of the Congo and the wandering Maku of the Northwest Amazon, the Penan never practised agriculture and depended instead on wild populations of sago palm for their basic carbohydrate supply. The prime minister of Malaysia, Datuk Mahathir Mohamad, has referred to them as wild creatures, expressing his government's desire that they "give up their unhealthy living conditions and backwardness. We don't want them running around like animals." Abdul Raham Yakub, a former chief minister of Sarawak, has said, "I would rather see them eating McDonald's hamburgers than the unmentionables they eat in the jungle." In truth, far from being "wild creatures in a trackless wilderness," the Penan dwell in a forest that is a homeland, an intricate and living network of sacred places linking past, present and future generations.

The Penan draw their life from the land, hunting mouse deer and gibbons, sambar deer, monkeys, civets, squirrels and, most important of all, *babui*, the bearded wild pig endemic to Borneo. Plants provide roots that cleanse, leaves that cure, edible fruits and seeds, and preparations that empower hunting dogs and dispel the forces of darkness. There are trees that yield glue to trap birds, toxic latex for poison darts, rare resins and gums for trade, twine for baskets, leaves for shelter and sandpaper, wood to make blowpipes, boats, tools and musical instruments. For the Penan, all of these plants are sacred, possessed by souls and imbued like the animals with magical powers.

"Each morning at dawn," Bruno remembers, "the gibbons howl and their voices carry for great distances, riding the thermal boundary created by the cool of the forest and the warm air above as the sun strikes the canopy. Penan never eat the eyes of the gibbons. They are afraid of losing themselves in the horizon. They lack an inner horizon —they don't separate dreams from reality. If someone dreams that a tree limb falls on camp, they will move with the dawn."

Every forest sound is an element of a language of the spirit. Trees bloom when they hear the lovely song of the bare-throated *krankaputt*. Bird calls heard from a certain direction bear good tidings, the same sounds heard from a different direction may be a harbinger of ill. Entire hunting parties may be turned back by the call of a banded kingfisher, the cry of a bat hawk. Other birds, like the spider hunter, summon the hunter to the kill. Before embarking on a long journey, the Penan must see a white-headed hawk flying from right to left, they must hear the call of the crested rain bird and the doglike sound of the barking deer.

Born of the forest and dependent on it for every aspect of their material lives, the Penan long ago embarked on a journey that knew no end. Fearful of the heat of the sun, ignorant of the seas, insulated from the heavens by the branches of the canopy, their entire cognitive and spiritual world became based on the forest. Distance and time became measured not in hours or kilometres but in the quality of the experience itself. With good hunting, a journey is short, though it might be measured by a European in weeks. A long arduous trek is one that exposes the Penan to the sun. The length of a journey is determined in the moment, by the discovery of wild fruits, a stand of sago, the chance to kill a wild pig. The passage of time is measured by the activities of insects, the sweat bees that emerge two hours before dusk, the black cicadas that electrify the forest at precisely six in the evening. If there is a pattern to the Penan migration, it is determined by the sacred growth cycle of the sago palm. It is a journey that may take twenty years to complete, an itinerary first described by the ancestors at a time when the Earth was young.

Bruno Manser did not travel to Sarawak as an environmental activist. The role was thrust upon him by circumstance and history. For over a hundred years Sarawak was ruled by a remarkable family dynasty, the descendants of James Brooke, an English adventurer who, supported by the ships of the Royal Navy, had established a trading monopoly in 1841. Known as the White Rajahs of Sarawak, the male scions of the Brooke family ruled until 1946 when, in the twilight of the British Empire, control of Sarawak passed to the English, who remained until independence in 1963. For the Penan, the colonial era is a living memory that has merged with legend. To them, it represents a period of their past when they were left alone, when their forests stood immense, inviolable, a mantle of green stretching across their entire world. Ask a Penan today what he wants, and nine times out of ten he will say the return of the English. Given this legacy, it was natural for the Penan to turn to the Europeans living among them for help in protecting their lands.

"By the end of 1984 I was touched by the logging. The people asked me to help." Manser remembers the first time the helicopter arrived with the government officials. The Penan expected to talk of the land. They stood stunned as an anthropologist asked to measure the size of their skulls. "The officials came to hunt. They asked the names of rivers and other prominent landmarks and added them to their maps. They told the Penan that the land belonged to the state and that it would be logged."

Resistance began, but slowly. It took four attempts in the fall of 1985 to gather representatives of the nomadic bands for a meeting. With Manser acting as secretary, the Penan sent a manifesto to the government, seeking protection for 1300 square kilometres of their traditional land. There was no reply. "I was so naive," recalls Manser, "it was such a small area of land. You could walk across it in three or four days. I really expected the government to set it aside."

After attempts to contact the international press failed, Manser and a frustrated group of Penan blocked a bulldozer constructing a bridge leading into their forests. The driver left, but the following morning there were thirty bulldozers at the roadhead, backed by police and company officials. Isolated and under siege, the Penan drew back. For another year the forest trembled, and Bruno became a marked man.

He retreated into the forest. By now he had become an adopted son of the Penan. Each day he discovered more about their lives. He learned to hunt, by spear or blowpipe. They showed him *tajem*, the source of their dart poison, and the dozen or more plants added to empower it. They taught him to recognize a hundred fruiting trees, the sources of fish toxins and dozens of medicinal plants. He gave up Western dress, grew his hair long and wrapped his limbs in a *chawat* that permitted the silent stalking of game. In the forest he went barefoot. He made fires as they did, with flint and steel and the fibrous covering of seeds. He came to recognize the six palms that yield sago, and he became strong by pounding their trunks to extract the starchy pith. They showed him how to weave, teaching him to blacken rattan with the sap of a plant and the mud from the watering hole of the wild pig. On his wrists they placed *jongs*, bracelets etched with symbols that ensured that the dreams of the Penan would fuse with his own.

Perhaps most incredibly, he found himself drawn into a world where there was no separation between the material and the immaterial, the natural and the supernatural. He discovered the meaning of omens, the abodes of the spirits, the nature of the dead, the significance of taboos. He saw children born, with men acting as midwives, the women braced against trees, an infant dropping to the ground to be lifted only by the mother, the cord cut with a slice of bamboo. He saw people die, their bodies rolled in sleeping mats and carried to a place that they had revered in life. In six years he never saw Penan quarrel. Only once did he see a hungry child neglect to share food. The prey was a pygmy squirrel, and thenceforth that child bore its name.

He laughed to recall the clumsy way he had first stumbled upon the Penan. Now he travelled light, carrying only a blowpipe with a spear lashed to its tip, a container of poisoned darts and a *parang*, or bush knife. When he was thirsty he drank from forest vines. If he climbed a tree, it was only to see the stars. He could follow the tracks of babui and deer. He could read the sign-sticks—branches or saplings decorated with symbols that maintained an open dialogue between the widely separated groups of Penan. The sign-sticks told him where and when a party had split up, the direction each group had travelled, the anticipated length of the journey, the difficulty of the terrain, and whether or not food was available. One stick, for example, that he observed in the Melinau River drainage, had the following configuration and message. A large leaf at the top showed that the stick had been left by the headman. Three small uprooted seedlings indicated that the site had once been occupied by three families. A folded leaf told mat the group was hungry, in search of game. Knotted rattan gave the number of days anticipated in the journey, and sticks and shavings at the base identified the group and revealed the direction of their travel. Two small pieces of wood equal in length and placed transversely on the sign-stick indicated that there was something for ali Penan to share, that all people of the forest were of one heart. In his years among the Penan, Bruno never saw a sign-stick that did not bear this simple message.

For all the joy and all the beauty, life in the forest was often difficult and sometimes dangerous. Twice, Manser succumbed to malaria; often, he was ill from parasites that riddled his body. On one occasion he was struck in the leg by a deadly viper. The agony came quickly. He tried to persuade his only companion, a young Penan boy, to slice into the wound to extract the venom. The boy was afraid. So Bruno took a knife to his own calf, cutting deeply into the flesh to remove the poison. The severed muscle witbdrew beneath his skin, and he was forced to reach up into his leg with a fishhook to pull it back into place before he could bind the wound with leaves and rattan. For three weeks he lay on the edge of death, quivering in delirium and awash in fever and pain.

During all these months, the logging continued. In the spring of 1987 the resentment of the Penan and all the Dayak peoples reached a flashpoint in the Baram. When yet another appeal to the government was ignored, the indigenous people again took direct action. On March 31, 1987, armed with their blowpipes, the Penan erected a barricade across a logging road in the Tutoh River basin. Within a week, a hundred Kayan at Uma Bawang blockaded a road that pierced their territory. In each instance, the actual barriers were flimsy, a few forest saplings bound with rattan. Their strength lay in the people that stood behind them. These human barricades of men, women and children, the old and the young, began as a quixotic gesture, a mere embarrassment to the government, but soon grew into a potent symbol of courage and resolve. Within eight weeks of the initial blockade, operations in sixteen logging camps had been brought to a halt, at a cost to the timber industry of several million dollars. The movement spread. By October 1987, Penan, Kayan and Kelabit communities had shut down roads at twenty-three different sites in the Baram and Limbang Districts. In all, some 2,500 Penan from twenty-six settlements took their place on the barricades.

The dramatic action stunned the Malaysian government, which predictably laid the responsibility on Bruno Manser. They were partially correct. "I can say," Manser acknowledges, "that the blockades were initiated by my person. It is not in the Penan tradition to make blockades. Yet before I arrived in Sarawak, there had been blockades by other indigenous groups." What had changed were the scale of the protest and the fact that Manser's involvement guaranteed coverage by the international media.

Stories circulated in the Malaysian press, describing Manser as a rajah to the Penan, a white Tarzan who was carried through the forest on a throne of bamboo. The government described him as a subversive Zionist and communist, a potent condemnation in an Islamic nation that still remembers a bloody leftist insurgency in the 1950s. In labelling Manser a threat to national security, the government granted itself free rein to bring him down. Manser's actual role in the blockades was far more ambiguous. An Australian environmentalist who spent time in the forest with Bruno and the Penan explains, "He was part of the family. There are no specialists among the Penan, yet everyone has their talents. Someone is good at calling the barking deer, someone is the healer, another the best hunter. Bruno was the person who could get the message out. That was his talent."

Though his only legal transgression involved the expiration of his visa, the government tried any means to ferret Manser out of the Penan homeland. A reward was issued for his capture and paid informers moved into the forest. Hired vigilantes threatened to unleash demonic men with tails to violate the women. Penan men were beaten, one fatally. Security forces established police checkpoints and dispatched military commandos to sweep areas where Manser had reputedly been seen.

From the spring of 1987 until early 1990 when he finally escaped, in disguise and with a false passport, Bruno Manser was actively hunted by military and security forces, his whereabouts known only to the Penan, who encircled him with a protective cordon. A Canadian photographer well known to the Penan recalls an elder taking him aside. "The old man placed a circle of small white stones on the ground. He put one in the middle and then laid sticks pointing inwards around the circumference of the circle. The sticks were the police, he said, the circle of stones the protective ring of Penan that moved through the forest with Bruno at its centre."

Within the ring, Manser was constantly on the move, passing from group to nomadic group, often spending long periods alone on isolated mountain slopes, in the sanctuary of caves or silent in the forest. After three years with the Penan, he could feed himself, gathering fruits, fishing by net and hunting by blowpipe. Yet, alone, he missed the camaraderie of the encampments, the dancing in the evening and the love poems spoken by the fire. He missed the warmth of human touch. But already he had chosen not to have a family, though he could have supported one. Now his decision was reinforced by necessity. He remained alone, and thus belonged to an entire people who called him Lakei Penan, Penan man.

Despite the protection, Manser had two narrow escapes. The first occurred by chance, early in the game, when a police guard at a routine checkpoint spotted him. He ran and was surprised to hear bullets passing over his head. Some months later, he was betrayed by a Malaysian reporter who had been invited to cover a clandestine meeting of all the Penan headmen. The reporter arrived and left by helicopter. Later that day it returned, only with a small band of men armed with M-16s who had been patrolling the region for a week. Manser escaped by diving into the rapids of the Magoh River. Once again shots were fired. Manser maintains that the Malaysians chose not to kill him. The Penan were less certain. To their chagrin, he continued to take what appeared to them to be unnecessary risks, often turning up at the blockades, hiding in the shadows of the forest within a stone's throw of his pursuers. When the pressure mounted, he simply fled into the mountains, seeking refuge in the caves.

"During those difficult days he must have been an inspiration to the Penan," suggests a Canadian journalist. "Once I was with a small group as they listened to a taped message from Bruno that was circulating among the settled villages. Bruno was singing in Penan these songs he had made up about the government. They must have been hilarious, for the people were convulsed with laughter. One of them proudly explained to me, 'He understands our language. He makes very good jokes.' I think that was one of Bruno's contributions. In the midst of the struggle, he kept an element of humour in the whole thing. He kept the spirits up.

"It is incredible that he was never betrayed by any Penan. I think it was understood among them that if a Penan did that, he or she would no longer be Penan, there would no longer be a people or a homeland."

Meanwhile, with Manser on the run, the blockades went on. The government responded by passing legislation specifically prohibiting the obstruction of traffic on a logging road and permitting forestry officials to enlist the assistance of vigilantes, officially described as agents of the companies, in dismantling the blockades. Despite hunger, heat exhaustion, harassment by the logging interests and repeated arrests, the protests continued. Dozens of Penan were imprisoned. From the fall of 1987 into 1989, sporadic blockades went up throughout Sarawak. Then, on September 10, 1989, in a massive show of opposition, indigenous peoples in nineteen communities in the Upper Limbang and Baram erected twelve new roadblocks. Five days later, the action spread south into the Belaga. In October, eleven Iban long-houses blockaded roads in the Bintulu District. By the end of 1989, an estimated four thousand Dayaks had joined the protest, temporarily shutting down logging in nearly half of Sarawak. The blockades have continued. To this day in Sarawak there are Penan men and women living away from the shelter of the forest, in thatch huts baked by the searing sun, placing their bodies and their children in the path of machinery.

Language is the reflection of the soul of a people. In Penan there are forty words for sago, and none for good-bye or thank you. In a forest of such abundance, in a culture in which sharing is an involuntary reflex, in a life of endless wandering, certain words have no relevance. Certain concepts have no meaning. For the Penan, land is a living entity, imbued with spiritual meaning and power, and the notion of ownership of land, of fragile documents granting a human the right to violate the Earth, is an impossible idea.

James Wong, Sarawak minister of the environment and tourism, believes that the government owns the land, and in a memorable comment he touched upon the dark undercurrent of the confrontation. "We don't want them," he said of the Penan, "running around like animals. Shouldn't they be taught to be hygienic like us and eat clean food?" One struggles to reconcile such a statement with an image of the Penan bathing in their clear streams, or in the forest manipulating their plants with a dexterity equal to that of a laboratory chemist.

I remember one morning in Sarawak in 1989, when some colleagues and I shared some of our "clean" food with Asik Nyelik, a nomadic Penan from Sungai Ubong, the same people that Bruno Manser met when he entered the forest. Asik had slept poorly in a bed, and that morning at breakfast, looking rather tired, he sat uncomfortably in a chair. He drank from a glass of water as would a deer, dipping his mouth to the surface. Then came a depressing offering of cold canned beans, a sorry-looking fried egg and a slice of tinned sausage. Asik looked politely around the table, then at his plate, then again at the people eating this food. He rotated his plate, hunting perhaps for an angle from which the food might appear palatable. Backing away from the table with a look of sincere pity, he slipped out of the building and into the forest. An hour later smoke rose from the edge of the clearing, and Asik was found hunched over a fire, slowly roasting a mouse deer that he had killed with a blade. Mercifully, he invited all of us to join him for breakfast.

Several nights later there was a full moon. It reminded Asik of a story he had heard about some people who had travelled there and returned with dust and rocks. He asked me if the story was true. Told that it was, he remained silent for a moment. Then he said, "Why did they bother?"

A week later Asik confronted a government official. "All we Penan know," he said, "is that we human beings cannot create land, only God can. If our land in Sungai Ubong belongs to somebody else, we want to ask them 'When did you create the land, or plant the fruit trees there, and where are the burial grounds of your ancestors?' We say the land belongs to the countless who are dead, the few who are living and the multitudes who have yet to be born.

"Our tears are as rain from the sky when we think of our children and grandchildren. The sickness in our lands comes not from God but from other human beings—the government. We stand for what we know to be right, and they call us outlaws. We are like fish out of water. We are children left alone in an empty hut without father or mother."

By early 1990 the logging industry in Sarawak, supported by all the power of the Malaysian government, had recovered completely. Three months later, his usefulness at an end, Bruno Manser left the forest that had been his home for six years to carry the Penan struggle abroad. To this day he spends every waking moment fighting for their cause. He is the last dreamer.

"In the time that I was with them," he explained to me, "I watched as one-third of their homeland was destroyed. Roads are being carved into what remains. Soon all the road junctions will be forged, the network complete and the fate of the forests sealed. The land of my own family, the Penan I first met in the Ubong in 1984, a territory of a mere seventy square miles, now is overrun with forty bulldozers. Together they haul sixteen hundred trees from the forest each day. Nearly as many are cut but discarded."

71

Throughout Sarawak, the sago and rattan, the palms, lianas and fruit trees lie crushed on the forest floor. The hornbill has fled with the pheasants, and as the trees fall in the forest, a unique way of life, morally inspired, inherently right and effortlessly pursued for centuries, is collapsing in a single generation.

THE
CLOUDED LEOPARD

One morning in Tibet I awoke before dawn, splashed my face with icy water, and left my companions to wander out into the velvet light and climb the flank of the Shining Crystal Monastery at Shegar. At the foot of the mountain, a dirt track ran along the river and then wound through a warren of houses, small compounds of white walls and ledges decorated with stacks of gnarled firewood, windows adorned with pleated awnings of blue, red and yellow, muted in the early morning light. In courtyards, stiff and solemn yaks stood silently, and from a hidden temple I heard the murmur of a monk chanting. Butter lamps and candles lit my way until the sun rose, touching first the needle crest of the summit, crowned with a fortress, broken down and long abandoned. As I climbed toward the entrance of the monastery, the shadows moved lower on the mountain, revealing walls and rubble, piles of spent rock, silhouettes on the earth of structures unknown and unimagined. Then the shadows drew in, quivered at the last moment, and gave way to a flood of sunlight that washed impartially over what remained of the ancient monastery.

By the time I reached the wooden gates, red and bolted with iron, the sun was bright and the dawn lost. Finding the way barred, I tried climbing over the wall and followed a steep chimney of rock that took me just to the point where fear set in, and I didn't know which would be worse, to pursue the line to the top or risk turning back. I retreated to the bottom and sat humiliated on a stone. Then, quite unexpectedly, the latch turned and the gate swung open to reveal the soft and kindly face of a young monk.

He led me to a path of stones, smooth from centuries of use. To the right, the restored walls led to the centre of the complex, a temple that perhaps had survived or perhaps had been rebuilt; in Tibet it can be difficult to tell. On its gilded roof stood the Dharma Chakra, the Wheel of Religion, supported by sacred deer represented in copper and gold, the symbol of the Buddhist path, life constantly in motion.

But to the left, dirt paths ran through ruins, green weeds and cut stones, a labyrinth of trails that spread up and across the mountain. With a slight bow, I thanked the monk, and climbed away from the silence of the monastery. Glancing back, I saw him standing alone, greeting the sun on a terraced balcony overlooking the distant and fertile fields of the valley.

Two generations ago there were four hundred monks living here. What began in the thirteenth century as a scattering of meditation huts hanging like swallows' nests from the rocky crags evolved by the seventeenth century, under the Fifth Dalai Lama, to a full-scale monastery, a major religious centre with the finest library of woodcut books in Tibet. Until the British Expedition of 1921, the first reconnaissance of Everest, the monks and people of Shegar had never seen a European. The leader of that expedition, Lt. Col. C. K. Howard-Bury, wrote of a sublime ridge top, where turreted walls rose to "a curious gothic-like structure on the summit of the hill where incense is offered up daily." At the foot of the mountain, on the road that linked Shegar to Tingri, the British climbers met a prostrating pilgrim, a Mongolian eleven months out of Lhasa, moving toward Kathmandu one body length at a time. For the young Englishmen, fresh from the horrors of Flanders, it was a stunning affirmation of religious purpose. Fifty years later, during the Chinese Cultural Revolution, all of Shegar monastery was blown apart by children with sticks of dynamite. It was just one act in a wave of destruction that left more than a million Tibetans dead and reduced some six thousand temples of wisdom and veneration to riprap and piles of dust.

The path through the wreckage rose more than 500 vertical metres, along the walls of the fortress that once shielded Tibet from the marauding armies of Nepal. Near the summit, the exposure became extreme, though the climb never left ruins. To build in such a place was to defy gravity. The summit itself was a pile of broken rocks, with remnants of walls wrapped in prayer flags. At the foot of the walls were small piles of ash, spent incense and dried blossoms. Overhead, a flock of choughs dipped and sparked, and when I looked north I saw a griffon, buff and brown, turning in the wind. The prayer flags were blue and white, the colours of the Sky God, embodiment of space and light. Looking south, I saw the white fang of a distant peak, alone above the horizon. This was Everest, known to Tibetans as Qomolangma, Goddess Mother of the World, the highest point on Earth, the destination and focus of our journey.

When I came down and passed by the monastery, I glimpsed the young monk playing in the bright light with a feral dog. I shouted a greeting, and he waved me into the small cell that was his home, perched on the edge of a bluff overlooking the ruins. We spoke in smiles and small gestures. I gave him a photograph of my children. He gave me a brass medallion hung by a blue thread to wear about my neck as I climbed into the mountains. As we drank tea, yak butter and salt brewed with the black leaves of India, there came a strange and simple silence. A yearning from each of us, he to know the world to which His Holiness the Fourteenth Dalai Lama had fled, I perhaps to understand a place where spirit and religion inspired so much of daily life. When we parted, it was with the sense that each of us might inform the other, that my journey into his mountains might reveal something of benefit, and that his goal might one day become mine, the unsentimental embrace of all existence.

Our purpose was not to climb Everest but rather to explore the hidden drainage of the Kama Chu, the river that begins in the ice at the base of the East Face. There, in what the British described as the most beautiful valley in the Himalayas, amidst meadows and rocky ledges overlooking the Kangshung glacier, live snow leopards and blue sheep. Beyond the river to the south soars a wall of ice mountains, Lhotse, sister to Everest, Chorno Lönzo and Pethangtse, each higher than anything in North America, and finally Makalu, by all accounts the most stunning peak on Earth, fifth in height but unmatched in beauty. In 40 kilometres, the Kama Chu falls 4300 metres, dropping down a spectacular series of waterfalls into the deepest ravine on Earth, the canyon of the Arun, a river older than the Himalayas.

Beneath the cliffs and ice fields of Makalu, a mere 25 kilometres from the base of Everest, thrive immense forests of juniper and fir. Farther downstream, in thickets of bamboo and rhododendrons, mountain ash and birch, we hoped to find the most elusive cat of all, the clouded leopard, a creature so rare and mysterious that early observers traced its lineage to the sabre-toothed tiger. Secretive and solitary, possibly nocturnal, it had never been photographed in the wild in Central Asia. Local legend describes it as a tree dweller, half human and capable of leaping twice its body length as it moves through the branches, hunting monkeys and pheasants, falling like a shadow to the ground to kill musk deer and red pandas.

Weighing no more than 27 kilograms, far less than a snow leopard, with a total length of perhaps 180 centimetres including the tail, the clouded leopard is relatively small, but its upper canines are especially prominent, larger in relationship to the skull size than those of any other cat, hence the comparison to the sabre-toothed tiger. Photographs of the animals in captivity reveal penetrating eyes, enormous paws and, for balance, an unusually long tail, thick to the tip. The chest is a blaze of white, the dense coat mottled with dark rosettes that float like clouds in the rich yellowish fur. Whereas the snow leopard generally lives above tree line close to the ice, the clouded leopard lives in the forests below 3700 metres. Once found throughout Asia from the foothills of the Himalayas to the islands of Borneo and Sumatra, its range has been much reduced, and the animal has become a true avatar of the wild.

To seek the clouded leopard in the valley that leads to the base of Qomolangma was a quixotic idea, the dream of two Americans, father and son, Daniel and Jesse Taylor-Ide. Fluent in Hindi, Daniel grew up in the foothills of the Himalayas, the son and grandson of medical missionaries. His grandfather, a cowboy in Dodge City before he got religion and went off to seminary and medical school, sailed with his wife for India in 1914. By the time Daniel's father, Carl, was born two years later, the Taylor family had found its destiny in the foothills of Mussoorie, a hill station where British officers and their wives came to escape the summer heat and revel in the twilight of the Raj. With Mussoorie as a base, the Taylors spent six months of every year on the move, children and gear piled high in an oxcart, a mobile med-ical clinic that bounced and rattled over the rutted jungle tracks of northern India. This went on for a quarter of a century. Carl Taylor grew up in the forest, free as a gypsy, wild as Mowgli. When it came time for him to study medicine, he chose Harvard, the first applicant on record to have learned anatomy at the side of his father, cutting open tigers.

After medical school and four years serving in Panama during the Second World War, Dr. Taylor returned to India in 1947 with his young family, which included Daniel who was then two. It was the year of partition, and the frontier between India and Pakistan erupted in violence. Backed by Muslim and Hindu alike, with the personal support of Nehru and Mountbatten, Taylor crisscrossed the zone of horror, providing emergency medical relief. In places he came upon rivers of blood, women and children dead by the thousands. Later, he escaped the carnage and travelled north to Nepal, becoming in 1949 a member of the first Western team to enter the ancient and isolated kingdom. With legendary ornithologist Robert Fleming, he hunted birds at 5500 metres on Annapurna and Dhaulagari, the first foreigners to set foot on these great peaks. After a disastrous fall on Dhaulagari, he saved his life by executing a self-arrest in the snow with the barrel of his gun.

Raised by such a father, Daniel had no ordinary childhood. "As important as learning good table manners in our family," he once wrote, "was learning to walk quietly. Hunting and climbing were in our blood." Believing that sabbaticals were as valuable for children as for tenured professors, Dr. Taylor lifted his children out of school once every five years and led them into the world. In 1955, when Daniel was ten, he accompanied his father for a year, searching for medicinal plants. Other adventures followed. When the family drove from England to India in 1961, they rolled their vehicle at the foot of Mount Ararat on the Turkish-Iranian frontier. Hours later they were ambushed by bandits in Afghanistan.

Through all these years, Daniel was climbing. In the summer of 1965 he made five first ascents in northern India. On his way out of the mountains, he met a road crew of Tibetan refugees. Swapping clothes with one of them, he spent a fortnight on the roadside, living as they did, crushing rock with small hammers, sleeping in the open, drawing water from a ditch, eating what food was at hand. It was during this time that he picked up a mild but incurable fungal disease that kept him out of Vietnam.

Instead, after a season as a mountain guide in the Tetons of Wyoming, he went to Mount Logan, the highest peak in Canada, and helped the Canadian army build a research hut at the summit. When the job ended, he became the first person to ski down Logan.

Inevitably, Daniel was drawn back to the Himalayas, and in 1988 he took a job as a consultant to the Tibetan exile community in Mussoorie. Trained at Harvard in education and development, Daniel expected to assist in the design of a school system for refugee children.

His Holiness the Fourteenth Dalai Lama preferred that he write a plan for preserving the religion and identity of a people who might be in exile for a thousand years. Through this pivotal experience, he came to realize and understand the depth of the Dalai Lama's commitment to his culture and homeland.

From India, Daniel moved to Kathmandu, taking a job in family planning for the U.S. Agency for International Development. At twenty-four, he had a budget of $1 million and free rein in a city that had become the Camelot of the counterculture, a caravanserai of the spirit, on a route that stretched south to Goa and west to Europe and America. Living in Nepal from 1969 through 1971, he bought a motorcycle and restored a 1928 Phantom II Rolls-Royce that had been carried overland to Kathmandu in pieces and last used in 1961 for the visit of Queen Elizabeth. He also met and fell in love with the daughter of his boss. Her name was Jennifer Ide, and in 1980 she bore him a son, Jesse Taylor-Ide. By then they were back in the States, living on a mountaintop in West Virginia.

Jesse, like his father, was born in America but nursed in the Himalayas. At the age of six months he was taken by his parents in a canoe through the jungles of Nepal as they sought and found the mythical Octagon Well, the sacred Hindu site where Rama and Sitamet met and loved. At two he was carried on his father's back for two months through the jungles of the Barun Valley, as a team of adventurers and scholars sought proof of the existence of the *yeti*, the hairy manlike beast known to the West as the abominable snowman. At five he first saw the Potala Palace in Lhasa, home of the Dalai Lama, and climbed up the narrow passageways that opened into dark chambers where placid Buddhas were illuminated by tiny candles. In rooms full of treasure, he watched as old wizened pilgrims placed coins into heaps of yak butter. When he was nine he slept in the meadows of the Kyrong, a member of the first foreign party to enter the valley since Heinrich Harrer, author of *Seven Years in Tibet*. That same season Jesse walked around Kailas, the mountain sacred to Hindu and Buddhist alike, the source of the Indus and Brahmaputra. At fifteen he first entered the Kama Valley, and with his father made the second ascent of Kartze, a peak of 6550 metres, climbed first by George Mallory in 1921 as he sought a route to the summit of Everest. Unlike Mallory, Jesse hauled a snowboard to the top and slipped off the mountain to complete the second-highest run ever made.

Now seventeen, he is fresh from two months living in the jungle on the southern, Indian, side of the Himalayas, in the Talle valley of Arunachal Pradesh, amongst the Aputani, a tribal people known as the rat hunters. There, amidst dense thickets of bamboo, in a montane forest where the rain never ends, he conducted a wildlife survey, establishing twenty-three photographic traps, with infrared monitors wired to remote flash cameras, placed along game trails, at stream crossings and in the canopy. The traps were of two sorts. In one case the camera is triggered when an animal breaks the plane of a narrow laser shot across a path. The second type radiates a wider field of sensitive light that, once entered, sets off the camera.

After positioning the cameras, Jesse went rat hunting. At the height of the season, he discovered, with bamboo in flower, a pair of Aputani hunters could kill a thousand rodents in a day.

"They're just like hot dogs," Jesse told me when we first met in Lhasa. "The first night I was with them, this hunter pulls a bamboo skewer out of the fire, snaps off the legs and tail, and hands them to me to eat. It was good, like squirrel. Then he scraped off the burnt hair and stuck it back in the fire to cook. Leopards live on rats too, but they always leave the head. The Aputani leave nothing."

Despite problems—lasers triggered by torrential rains, cameras knocked about the canopy by curious monkeys—Jesse is confident, on the basis of tracks found in the mud, that he has secured photographs of civets, sun-bears, red pandas and wild dogs. Pugmarks that could have been clouded leopard were blurred by the rain. Whether he managed to photograph the elusive animal will not be known for a few weeks, as the film is being developed in Delhi. Still, the effort was successful, though he was forced to flee the forest after succumbing to a fever that nearly killed him. Now that the trial run is over, he faces the more challenging task of working the north side of the mountains. There has been no attempt to survey me wildlife of the Kama Chu since the British Everest Expedition in 1921, whose primary goal had been to scout a route up the mountain. Seventy-five years later, Everest, still dangerous, is well known. In the disastrous spring of 1996, when twelve climbers died, some thirty expeditions attempted to reach the summit, all from the Nepal side. What remains to be discovered is the wonder of the creatures and the people who think of these Tibetan valleys as home.

• • •

"Isolation was in our blood," the Dalai Lama once wrote. Distilling several thousand years of history into a single phrase, His Holiness perfectly captured the Tibet of Western imagination, a serene and lofty kingdom hidden behind a veil of myth and mountains, a peaceful people disengaged from time, living alone on the roof of the world. Such an image is easy to embrace in the dawn light on the summit of the Pang La, a 5200-metre pass on the dirt road that runs south from Shegar 130 kilometres toward Kharta and the northern approaches to Everest. In bitter cold, amidst a small forest of rock cairns, we watched the sun rise over the Himalayan range, a solid wall of mountains, including four of the five highest on Earth, each soaring above 8200 metres. Running from Kanchenjunga in the east through Makalu, Lhotse, Everest, Nuptse and Cho Oyu was the planet's greatest geological panorama, the slow drama of two worlds in collision. Forty million years ago the Indian subcontinent drifted away from Africa and slipped beneath Asia, crushing the face of a continent and rolling back the Earth's crust like a carpet to form mountains that to this day grow skyward at a rate of 12 millimetres per year. Such was the force of impact that an area of land half the size of the United States was lifted from sea level to 4800 metres, thus forming the Tibetan plateau. As the mountains rose, the Arun River, flowing south since the dawn of time, cut a deeper and deeper canyon, through sediments laden with fossil seashells and valleys that reached to the sky.

Coming out of the Pang La, descending rapidly through a series of switchbacks, the road passes through small settlements into valleys and canyons lined with marbled stones and contorted cliffs. Near the village of Phagdruchi, the road forks, with one branch heading for Rongbuk and the base camp of Everest, the other heading for Kharta and the passes leading to the Kama Chu. Following this route, dropping to the drainage of the Arun, we drove along a narrow dirt track through a landscape dominated by ruins, all that remains of the dozens of ancient fortifications that once guarded the approaches to Nepal. Here was the image of another Tibet, less a land of isolation, hermetically sealed from the winds of time, than a crossroads of trade and empire sitting atop the heart of Asia.

Westerners, of course, knew little of old Tibet. Until 1979 fewer than two thousand had entered the nation, and most of these were members of the British invasion force of 1904, under the command of Sir Francis Younghusband. But if Europeans had trouble reaching Lhasa, others did not. In the eighteenth century the streets of the Tibetan capital were crowded with Tartars, Muscovites, Chinese, Kashmiris and Nepalese, merchants and traders who came from all parts of Central Asia. Monasteries drew monks and pilgrims from as far away as the Black Sea. Elements of Tibetan dress are found in the court costumes of Persia.

Nor were Tibetans always peaceful. Their armies fought the Ladhakis in 1681, took on the Mongols in 1720, rallied against Nepalese invaders in 1788-92 and again in 1854. Younghusband had to fight his way to Lhasa in 1904, killing more than a thousand Tibetan soldiers in pitched battles. Indeed, the ebb and flow of warfare has swept over Tibet for centuries. The image of the land as an earthly paradise, the culture a cosmic meritocracy, is an illusion.

Like any complex society, Tibet had great inequalities. Power was concentrated in the hands of an aristocratic elite, dominated by the great Gelugpa monasteries. The selection of the Dalai Lama was an awesome event, inspired by oracles and infused with magical and cosmological significance, all derived from the Buddhist belief that a bodhisattva chooses the moment and place of reincarnation. But the process was not removed from politics. The entire ritual complex, the dispatching of search parties, the interpretation of signs, the very notion that the memory and spiritual authority of an elder could be reborn in the soul of child, was, at least in part, a seventeenth-century invention. In subsequent years several young boys, ordained by divination and anointed as gods, failed to reach maturity, their lives severed by intrigue and deception. At least one Dalai Lama was poisoned. Another died in bed, after an enemy sawed away the posts supporting the roof of the room. A third dispensed with Buddhist vows altogether to revel in love and sensual trysts on an island in a lake at the foot of the Potala Palace.

The fact that Tibetans are mortal, a people of politics and power as well as the spirit, in no way belittles their legacy. To the contrary, a realistic knowledge of their history and traditions reinforces the legitimacy of their sovereignty. The roots of the current conflict between China and Tibet go back to the thirteenth century and the Mongol conquest of Asia. Tibetans submitted to Genghis Khan in 1207 and within forty years were providing religious instruction to the invaders. In 1279 the Mongols under Kubla Khan conquered China, founding the Yuan dynasty and bringing the ancient land into an empire that already included Tibet. The Chinese today trace their claims to this moment, when both nations succumbed to the Mongols. The Tibetans, by contrast, remember that distant era as the time when two sovereign nations fell in succession to a single enemy. When the Yuan dynasty collapsed, Tibet reclaimed its independence.

The country that emerged over the centuries was not a perfect society, but its failures and complexities were its own. Looking south and east, fending off invasions, struggling with civil strife and intrigue from within, Tibetans engaged the sordid realities of nationhood. When the Nepalese invaded in 1788, reaching Shigatse and looting the sacred monastery of Tashihunpo, Tibet forged an alliance with China. The Qing emperor dispatched an army that vanquished the Nepalese and then, in the wake of victory, refused to leave. The Chinese maintained a modest presence in Lhasa until Qing influence faded in the late nineteenth century. By then China faced its own enemies, European powers descending on Asia from the eastern sea. In the early years of this century, Chinese authority in Tibet was symbolic, marginal at best. Whatever claim they had ended in 1911 with the overthrow of the Qing dynasty. From 1913 until the invasion of the Red Army in 1949, Tibet was again an independent nation, albeit a complex land on the cusp of change. The very idea of China today claiming Tibet, a land and people unique by any ethnographic or historical definition, is as anachronistic as England laying claim to America simply because it was once a British colony.

Our road ended at a wooden footbridge over the Kharta Chu, a rushing mountain stream draining a broad treeless valley strewn with boulders. Across the way, on a rise overlooking the river, was the small village of Yueba, a cluster of stone houses emerging from the earth. The land was beautiful, the brown and russet of fields, the pale yellow of barley stalks, a distant copse of juniper around a small monastery on the flank of a mountain dusted with snow. Within minutes of our arrival at the trailhead, villagers appeared, herdsmen in sheepskin coats and homespun woollen trousers, old men and women thumbing dark beads and spinning silver and copper prayer wheels, mothers and young children with faces blackened by yak butter and charcoal.

Under their watchful eyes, we set up camp and awaited the rest of our party. There were eleven of us, including local officials, travelling in three land cruisers. The bulk of the supplies and gear followed in a larger truck, along with three Sherpas hired as cooks in Kathmandu. Our translator was a government employee named Lhakpa, a Tibetan from Shegar who had been raised in Dharamsala. Tall and handsome, with a gentle manner and easy smile, he seemed ill cast in his role as a forest warden. His green uniform hung loosely on his long limbs. The military cap, a size too large, tilted at an angle that appeared either rakish or clumsy depending on the moment. Like the local farmers and herders, he wore canvas sneakers made in China, miserable footwear for a march through ice and snow.

While Daniel and Lhakpa met with the villagers and settled on a price for hiring yaks to continue our journey, the rest of us stayed in camp, taking care of the last-minute preparations that invariably mark the eve of an expedition. Talk for the most part was about the strange turn of the weather. November in the Himalayas is normally a month of clear skies, warm days and cold nights, ideal for trekking. This year the winter had come early, and snow already blanketed the three high passes leading from the Kharta valley south into the Kama Chu. When the British first scouted Everest from the east in 1921, they moved through this very camp, up the Kharta River and over the distant Langma La, a 5500-metre pass that leads to the Kangshung, or East Face, of the mountain.

Our plan was to climb the Samchung La, the first of the passes, and then traverse the splendid valley of the fourteen lakes to drop into the Kama further downstream. En route we would set cameras, above and below tree line, and in the dense forests of the lower river. Then, proceeding up valley toward the East Face, we would establish more traps on the rocky ledges and in the meadows frequented by snow leopards and blue sheep. After ten days, Daniel and I, with the rest of our party, would return to Kharta over the Langma La. Jesse, accompanied by a guide, would retrace our journey, retrieving the cameras, and meet us in Kharta.

It was a fine plan that dissolved in the reality of the season. The yak herders, once hired, informed Daniel that two of the passes, the Langma La and Samchung La, were too deep in snow to permit safe passage. That left the Shao La, the route the British had taken in August of 1921 when they retreated from Everest, having abandoned the East Face. Howard-Bury had led the way, climbing in thick rain, through juniper growing at the edge of snow fields, past beautiful lakes and covens of Himalayan snowcocks feeding in open grass beneath the ice. With luck, Daniel was told, we might traverse the Shao La, follow the Kama Chu to the base of Qomolangma, and return before the snows became too deep to cross back over the pass.

With few options, we embarked in the morning, our ranks swollen by a dozen yak herders, each pushing two animals, laden with supplies, up the narrow track that rose along the south bank of the Kharta Chu. Jesse went ahead and I enjoyed walking with him. The previous day we had slipped away from camp and scrambled up a steep ridge. There on the summit, in a ruined fortress, he had told me an interesting story about his father. In India, near the family home at Mussoorie, Daniel's grandfather, a devout Christian, had met a Hindu *sadhu*, a wandering holy man. A mutual fascination with spiritual mysteries forged an unlikely friendship. "There are senses beyond science," Grandpa Taylor had told young Daniel, "beyond the five that we acknowledge. These we can develop. Prayer is one, but there are others. A hunter senses impending danger. All of these senses lead to knowledge."

Encouraged by his family, Daniel as a child sought out the sadhu, and whenever possible sat beside him, unperturbed by his naked body, the filthy loincloth and trident, the shaggy hair, ashes and beard to the waist. In time the sadhu took the boy under his wing, sharing certain mysteries, techniques of meditation and insight. Daniel never forgot these lessons, even as he turned his attention to new adventures, like seeking the identity of the strange creature known as *metoh kangmi*, the abominable snowman, the yeti of Tibetan lore. In a school library, Daniel first saw photographs of the creature s footprints, brought back from Everest in 1951 by the great mountaineer Eric Shipton. A year later a famous Swiss zoologist floated the theory that the yeti was a remnant creature, a distant relative on the tree of man.

Daniel, captivated, embarked on a quest that would consume much of his life. From the early literature, he learned that his great heroes, the British climbers of 1921, George Mallory and Guy Bullock, Lt. Col. Howard-Bury and Major Wheeler, had actually encountered the yeti, a shadowy figure, a dark spot on the ice, as they crossed over the Shao La, the very pass we would take into the Kama Chu. Throughout the 1950s virtually every mountaineering expedition brought back some trace of the creature, a pugmark in the snow, a rumoured sighting in a distant village. Daniel structured his life around his pursuit of the yeti, taking any position or job that would afford him a chance to pursue the mystery and travel the back country of the Himalayas. In the process he learned Russian, Urdu and Nepali, charted routes through unsurveyed valleys, and became the first to survive a descent by raft of the Sun Kosi, the Golden River of Nepal.

After more than twenty years, Daniel made a discovery that transformed his childhood quest into a deeper exploration. In the valley of the Barun, on the south side of the Himalayas in Nepal, he found what appeared to be a new species of bear, closely related to, but distinct from, the common Asiatic black bear. Collecting skulls from villagers, recording descriptions related by wandering hunters, he pieced together over a dozen expeditions a tale of immense potential, the existence of a rare endemic species, arboreal and shy, living in the most remote corridors of the Himalayas. Even more astonishing was the possibility, supported by anecdote and intuition, that this new creature was, in fact, the yeti of legend.

More time passed, with Daniel forwarding skulls and stories to the zoologists at the Smithsonian, scholars who welcomed the diversion but had no idea what to make of the data. Finally, one evening in Kathmandu, Daniel shared the story with his former Harvard roommate, His Royal Highness, King Birenda. The king, like most Nepalese, had little interest in the yeti, but the idea of a new species of bear caught his fancy. If such a creature existed, the king asked, what could be done to protect it in a nation that within a generation had seen its forests cut away, its rivers darkened with erosion? For Daniel, this conversation was seminal. Why chase the yeti, or even the curious bear? What mattered was the preservation of habitat, so that all creatures, real or imagined, would have a chance to live. After two decades, he let the yeti go. Years later, when the Makalu-Barun National Park was finally created, Daniel was knighted by King Birenda for his efforts on behalf of conservation in Nepal.

A park protecting a single drainage was just a beginning. According to Jesse, his father still practises the techniques taught to him by the wandering sadhu. One morning in 1985, in the midst of a blizzard at their mountaintop home in West Virginia, Daniel emerged from a night of reflection and meditation with an idea for an entirely new kind of protected area, an international nature preserve, centred on Qomolangma. The ultimate goal was the preservation of the entire Himalayas.

A month later he was in Kathmandu, scheduled to deliver a speech. At the opening banquet, attended by King Birenda, he met the official in charge of the Chinese geological survey of the borderlands. When Daniel gently encouraged him to experience Qomolangma, the bureaucrat offered to go if passage could be arranged by air, an impossible task, or so it seemed. Daniel excused himself, strolled over to the king, and borrowed the royal helicopter, on the condition that he would pay for the gas.

Airborne at dawn, the Chinese geologist sat stunned by the wonder of the vista, not just the mountains but the lush valleys that reached into Tibet. Joining forces with Daniel, he carried the story to Beijing, and a month later negotiations began in earnest for the creation of a nature preserve, not administered by distant bureaucrats but protected by the people who dwelt within its boundaries. It was a bold idea, so novel that at every meeting Daniel was able to increase the size of the proposed park, until ultimately it embraced 2.4 million hectares, an area larger than Massachusetts, straddling the heart of the Himalayas. As Jesse wound up his story, I looked east to distant mountains, white with snow. The entire horizon was within the cordon of the Qomolangma Nature Preserve. His father's dream had become reality.

During the day, we climbed some 600 metres, leaving the fields and villages behind, and made camp on the snow at the foot of the Shao La. As soon as the sun went down, the temperature dropped well below freezing. The bright stars were promising, but the signs of winter ominous. Even at this elevation, the barberry and rhododendrons lay beneath deep drifts that swept over the frozen streams. From a ridge above camp, in snow to the knee, I watched the herders drive the yaks up the slope to graze; already they had expressed concern about the availability of feed. Later I followed them back to their fire where they joked and laughed, huddled together, sharing dried yak meat, *tsampa* flour ground from barley, and *rakshi*, raw spirits distilled from grain. Though by morning ice would cling to their clothes, they made no effort to put up tents, preferring to sleep beneath sheepskins in the open air, curled alongside the fire.

It snowed during the night, but the sun broke through soon after dawn, and the air was warm by the time we set out ahead of the yaks, heading for the pass. The trail rose gradually at first, and then climbed steeply to a high treeless valley, enveloped in cloud. Skirting the edge of a beautiful lake, past stone corrals and walled shelters piled across the mouths of caves, the route approached the base of the pass, a 300-metre climb on a trail through deep snow. From the valley bottom, I glimpsed three tiny figures on the summit, darting in and out of view. An hour later, they walked silently past me on the trail, young women in wool skirts and bright aprons, bent low beneath illicit loads of lumber, their eyes shielded from the sun by long braids entwined with turquoise. The wood was silver fir, the only Himalayan tree that splits easily into boards and beams with wedges and hammers made from rhododendron limbs. Harvested in spring in the depths of the Kama Chu, the timber is stacked to dry until the last possible moment in the fall, when, fighting the season, the woodcutters haul 45-kilogram loads over the pass to Kharta. Used mostly for window and door frames, with as much as 90 per cent of the source tree wasted on the forest floor, the wood eventually makes its way to Shegar and beyond. There is a construction boom underway in Tibet, as tens of thousands of ethnic Chinese flood the country. In Lhasa, the once quiet lanes that link the sacred sites are now awash in noodle shops and karaoke bars. Less than half of the population is Tibetan, and the Chinese own more than 80 per cent of businesses. The Tibetan capital has become a Chinese outpost.

Cloud cover obscured the top of the pass, and the wind blew fiercely from the south. Everything was sheathed in ice, the red and yellow prayer flags marking the summit, the small piles of the mani stones inscribed with invocations at the foot of the rock cairn, the trail itself as it fell away through deep snowdrifts toward the Kama Chu. Seeking shelter in the lee of a rocky ledge, I stumbled upon other woodcutters, asleep in the snow, apparently unfazed by the cold. Their only protection was a thin patchwork of Chinese army jackets, tattered pants and sodden sneakers without socks. Startled, they leapt to their feet, hoisted their loads and scrambled down the slope, just in time to catch sight of Jesse sweeping down the draw on his snowboard.

While our yaks slowly and steadily lumbered their way toward the pass, Daniel and I waited in the rocks, somewhat stunned by the severity of the season. Already, two passes into the Kama were sealed. The Shao La, at 5000 metres, was the middle of the three. But with so much snow falling and the visibility reduced by violent gusts, the possibility of becoming trapped for the winter in the Kama Chu skirted our thoughts.

"Tibetans," Daniel said, his voice barely audible above the wind, "consider a pass to be place of energy, marking the transition between worlds. Prayer flags bring luck, as do the small bits of paper, inscribed with blessings, that travellers toss into the air as they cross a divide. But snow is the work of demons, a blizzard the test of a pilgrims sincerity. This snow will not melt. It will only get deeper."

As we marched out of the pass, beginning a long gradual descent, the yak herders started to chant, one by one, without thought, as they moved the animals forward. Away from the summit, the wind died, and all that could heard was the sound of their voices, the tinkling of yak bells, and the slow scuffle of boots on a rocky trail that ran to the valley below. A shaft of light cut through the clouds, which slowly opened to reveal black cliffs the height of mountains. To the south emerged a row of peaks, as impressive as any in the Americas. Then, as the clouds lifted higher, the unearthly sight of the Himalayas was revealed, Makalu and Chomo Lönzo, a range so grand as to reduce the icy crags in the foreground to mere foothills. Exhilarated by the sight, I noticed one of the herders, a man named Tandu, standing to one side, staring back at the pass. Perhaps it was cruel coincidence, or possibly he sensed something. But two weeks later, when we returned to Kharta, we would learn that even as we had walked out of the Shao La, an avalanche had swept off the slope not 300 metres from the pass, leaving a solitary woodcutter to die, buried to the neck in snow.

It was late by the time we reached the bottom of the pass, and the last few kilometres to camp were a race against the failing light. Even in the darkness, one could discern the absence of snow amidst the fragrance of rhododendron and wild rose. Exhausted, we pitched tents in a damp meadow just beyond the floodplain of the stream we had followed since first dropping into the valley. Hot lemon tea and a dinner of rice and curry lifted morale, and in the cold night air I wandered beyond the camp, climbing in and about a nest of massive boulders. A forest of juniper spread up one side of the valley to rock bluffs, silver in the moonlight. Though I was aware of the distance we had come and felt the looming presence of Everest, it was the subtle beauty of the plants that was most impressive: mountain ash and birch, willows, spiraea and poppies, a score of familiar genera and species growing at such a height. The British, upon first entering the Kama Chu, had been similarly impressed. George Mallory described it this way:

When all is said about Chomolungma, the Goddess Mother of the World, I come back to the valley, the valley bed itself, the broad pastures, where our tents lay, where cattle grazed and where butter was made, the little stream we followed up to the valley head, wandering along its well-turfed banks under the high moraine, the few rare plants, saxifrages, gentians and primulas, so well watered there, and a soft, familiar blueness to the air which even here may charm us. Though I bow to the goddesses I cannot forget at their feet a gentler spirit than theirs, a little shy perhaps, but constant in the changing winds and variable moods of mountains.

The British, of course, had seen the Kama Chu in August. Now it was November. Walking back to camp, I noticed that the yak herders had put up their tents, black shadows against the stones.

The snow began to fall soon after midnight and did not stop for three days. By morning the yaks stood belly deep in fresh powder, and the valley and forest had been transformed. Leaving the others in camp, Jesse, Daniel and I set off just before noon, during a slight break in the storm, and walked to the edge of the hanging valley, where the route divided: one trail stayed high, climbing steeply to the east toward Everest, and the other dropped through juniper and birch to the canyon of the Kama Chu. Within an hour we reached the river, just below the point where the channel broadened to a wide glacial bar, which we followed for some time, scouting for signs of game, pugmarks that might reveal the presence of cats. A wooden footbridge drew Jesses attention. Leopards avoid water, and this was the only dry crossing within kilometres. On the far side of the bridge he found a faint track, perhaps that of a snow leopard pushed below its normal range by the early onset of winter. But the scat discovered a moment later suggested otherwise. Snow leopard feces smells sweet. This had a pungent odour, not unlike that of the common house cat. It was, according to Daniel, the stool of a clouded leopard.

"How can you be sure?" I asked.

"I can't," he replied with a broad grin. "But then nothing is certain with this cat. Every bit of data is anecdotal. I don't know a damn thing about the creature, but no one else does either. That's what makes it so great."

As Daniel struggled to rig a camera beneath the bridge, Jesse and I set the laser monitor between two stones, camouflaged the connecting wires with wood and bark, then checked the angle to make sure that anything crossing would trigger the shutter.

"With these woodcutters passing through," remarked Jesse, "we'll probably just get thirty shots of somebody's legs."

"With all this snow you may be lucky to get that," said his father.

For the rest of the afternoon we followed the valley downstream and set a series of photo traps along the trail, wherever we encountered signs of leopard prey: tracks or scat of red pandas, musk deer or pheasant. Daniel, in particular, worked with a wild intensity, as if effort alone might conjure the cat. Then, after a long day, and with the storm building upon the face of Makalu, we retraced our steps upriver and climbed back through the forest to camp, arriving just as the blizzard began in earnest. Snow fell throughout the night.

A day in camp, relieved only by a short outing to establish a camera on the high trail to Everest, followed by another night and day of heavy snow, left all of us wondering whether we might be forced to retreat. By the third morning, when we woke to grey skies still swirling with snow, the yak herders themselves seemed fearful. Their animals had not eaten in three days, and the storm showed no signs of letting up. With winter coming on, not one of them was keen to climb thousands of metres higher to the East Face of Qomolangma. While Daniel, Lhakpa and others sat in the cooktent, talking tilings over, I noticed Tandu, the quiet leader among the Tibetans, placing a large flat stone on the snow. Kindling a fire with dried juniper, he burned incense and green boughs, then added offerings of tsampa, yak butter and tea, all the while singing a deep melodious chant that drew everyone out of the tents into a wide circle around the flames. The ritual *puja,* a ceremonial prayer, in this case for good weather, had two immediate and gratifying effects. First, it brought our group together, dispelling in a moment any thoughts of retreating over the pass. Secondly, the sky cleared. Within an hour the clouds lifted, and the sun emerged. A day later, having fed the yaks with bamboo gathered low in the valley of the Kama Chu, we began our climb toward the East Face of Everest.

The following days took us past the dazzling cliffs of Makalu and Chomo Lönzo, rising 3000 metres above the river, as we climbed through juniper forests and beyond the tree line to snow fields that stretched for kilometres across the flanks of impossibly vast mountains. By day the sun was hot and luminous. At night the temperatures fell far below freezing, and the only sounds were those of yak bells, ringing in perfect clarity. Mornings began with the thunder of avalanches tumbling like clouds down the sheer face of the mountains. For three days our route followed the tracks of a snow leopard, while overhead bearded vultures soared, and ravens and black-eared kites darted in the wind.

Everest first came into view as we crested a ridge and happened upon a number of rock cairns, Buddhist tombs deliberately placed within sight of the sacred mountain. At first its peak seemed almost lost, overshadowed by Lhotse and Chorno Lönzo, and the two glaciers, Kangshung and Kangdoshung, that flow into the valley. But the closer we came, the more astonishing the mountain appeared. By the time we reached our highest camp, in the snow overlooking the Kangshung, just below a series of ledges frequented by blue sheep, the mountain dominated every thought. To be this close, just shy of Pethang Ringmo, the gentle meadows celebrated by the British climbers of 1921, was to feel something of their spirit. George Mallory first saw Everest from the north as he climbed the Rongbuk glacier, having paid homage to the lama of the legendary Rongbuk monastery, a simple monk who found the passions of the English somewhat difficult to understand. "I was filled with great compassion," the lama later reflected, "that they underwent such suffering in unnecessary work."

But for Mallory and his comrades, all inured to death, the mountain was an exalted radiance, immanent, vast, incalculable. He described his first sighting:

We had mounted perhaps a thousand feet when we stopped to wait for what we had come to see. As the clouds rolled asunder before the heights, gradually, very gradually, we saw the great mountainsides and glaciers and ridges, now one fragment, now another, through the floating rifts, until, far higher in the sky than imagination dared to suggest, a prodigious white fang—an excrescence from the jaw of the world—the summit of Everest, appeared.

Though the lama was puzzled as to why one would tread upon sacred ground and disturb the spirit of the mountain, the British, in fact, approached the peak with a reverence that even Tibetans might find difficult to match. To placate the monks, Mallory and Howard-Bury described their expedition as a group of mountain worshippers embarked on pilgrimage. Cryptic as they intended the message to be, it in fact perfectly encapsulated who they were, climbers willing to sacrifice all to reach the summit of the unknown. The word *sacrifice*, of course, means "to make sacred," and when Mallory in his famous retort explained that the reason for climbing Everest was nothing more than the fact that it was there, he distilled the perfect notion of emptiness and pure purpose.

In the spacious silence of Pethang Ringmo, we looked up at the mountain's entire profile, including the northern approach, where perhaps Mallory's body lies. With binoculars, I could just make out the first and second steps, the rock ledges where on June 8,1924, Mallory and his companion, Sandy Irvine, were last seen going strong for the top.

Like the rest of their expedition, they were pathetically underdressed, wearing simple wool vests, flannel shirts, Shackleton smocks, gabardine knickers, soft elastic cashmere puttees and fur-lined leather motorcycle helmets. They knew nothing of the death zone, the altitude above which oxygen deprivation reduces any climb to a pure and horrendous act of will. They had no idea that the peak of the mountain lay in the jet stream, where winds of 250 kilometres per hour drive ice crystals in dark plumes off the summit. They had oxygen to breathe, but disdained its use and had no faith in the primitive apparatus, which kept breaking down in the cold. At 8200 metres, they read Shakespeare in the snow, in flimsy tents designed for the mud of Flanders.

As the mist rolled in, enveloping their memory in myth, there was one witness, a brilliant climber in support, Noel Odell, who never doubted that they had reached the top. Nor did he question the sublime purpose that had taken them all, 650 kilometres on foot from India and across Tibet just to reach the base of the mountain. Odell wrote of Mallory:

> My final glimpse of one, whose personality was of that charming character that endeared him to all and whose natural gifts seemed to indicate such possibilities of both mind and body, was that he was "going strong," sharing with that other fine character who accompanied him such a vision of sublimity that it has been the lot of few mortals to behold; nay, few while beholding have become merged into such a scene of transcendence.

From the base of Everest, thinking about these men, I stared skyward at a mountain that has killed one climber for every four that have reached the summit. It was an awesome sight. Though I was standing on ground higher than any in North America, the mountain rose 3200 metres above, fluted ribs and ridges, gleaming balconies and seracs of blue-green ice, shimmering formations ready to collapse in an instant. "We must remember," Mallory once wrote, "that the highest of mountains is capable of severity, a severity so awful and fatal that the wiser sort of men do well to think and tremble even on the threshold of their high endeavor."

Once it became known that Mallory and Irvine had died in their summit attempt, the other British climbers, waiting in their advance camp, retreated from the valley. "We were a sad little party," wrote Teddy Norton, leader of the 1924 expedition, who himself had reached 8573 metres without oxygen, "but from the first we accepted the loss of our comrades in the rational spirit which all of our generation had learnt in the Great War, and there was never a tendency to a morbid harping on the irrevocable. But the tragedy was very near."

"There was something Homeric about those men," Daniel said one evening as he and I walked along the ridge above our camp, downwind from a band of blue sheep grazing on the windswept terraces. "After that war, when so many had died, life became less precious than the moments of life. I think that explains Mallory's willingness to climb on, accepting a degree of risk that might have been unimaginable before the war. They were not cavalier, but death was no big deal. They had seen so much that it had no hold on them. What mattered was how one lived. It always seemed fated to me that they would meet their end in the Himalayas, and not just because of that one mountain."

"What do you mean?" I asked.

"Well, I think that's why we all come here, why the landscape and the religion hold such an attraction for people from the West. I started with the yeti. I was desperate to find it, to prove that it existed. But then gradually the creature ceased to be a physical mystery and became instead a symbol of the unknown, an image that allowed me to tie together things that were known and things I merely sensed. That's why I turned to conservation. We all need a place on Earth to hide the wild parts of ourselves. With land preserved, each generation can search again for the yeti and discover the science of life, which is ecology, and participate in the art of science violated, which is magic. In the end what we discover is a greater sense of who we are, and a knowledge that what we are is just what is."

Despite our efforts, the clouded leopard eluded us. After several days at the foot of Everest, we retraced our steps only to find our cameras buried deep in snow. Two months later, however, word came from Delhi that in the forests of India, Jesse had indeed caught the elusive creature on film, the first photograph of the clouded leopard ever recorded in Central Asia.

THE
WHITE DARKNESS

Haiti is saturated with cliché—the poverty, the tortured landscape, the spate of abominable political leaders, consistent it seems only in their personal greed and disregard for their people. But find a quiet place somewhere—perhaps beneath the spreading branches of a sacred *mapou* tree, or on a hotel verandah at dawn, when from sheer exhaustion or moved by the splendour of the city basking in such soft light, you can forget all that you have heard about this turbulent country. Breathe deeply and listen to the rhythm of the land, and you will hear voices speaking of another Haiti, one whose beauty and magic make it unique in all the Americas.

The challenge of travel is to find a way to isolate and understand the germ of a people, to measure and absorb the spirit of place. In Haiti one begins in Port-au-Prince. The capital lies prostrate across a low, hot, tropical plain at the head of a bay flanked on both sides by soaring mountains. Behind these mountains rise others, creating an illusion of space that absorbs Haiti's multitudes and softens the country's harshest statistic: a land mass of only 26 000 square kilometres inhabited by over 7 million people, making it one of the most densely populated nations on Earth. Port-au-Prince is a sprawling muddle of a city, on first encounter a carnival of civic chaos. A waterfront shantytown damp with laundry. Half-finished public monuments. Streets lined with *flamboyant* trees and redolent with the stench of fish and sweat, excrement and ash. Dazzling government buildings and a presidential palace so white that it doesn't seem real. There are the cries of the marketplace, the din of untuned engines, the reek of diesel fumes. It presents all the squalor and all the graces of any Caribbean capital.

Yet as you drive through the city for the first time, down by the docks perhaps, where the shanties face the gleaming cruise ships and men with legs like anvils haul carts loaded with bloody hides, notice something else. The people on the street don't walk, they flow, exuding pride. Physically, they are beautiful. They seem gay, jaunty, carefree. Washed clean by the afternoon rain, the entire city has a rakish charm. But there is more. In a land of material scarcity, the people adorn their lives with their imaginations—discarded Coke cans become suitcases or trumpets, rubber tires are turned into shoes, buses transformed into kaleidoscopic *tap-taps*, moving exhibits of vibrant, naive art. And it isn't just how things appear, it is something in the air, something electric—a raw elemental energy not to be found elsewhere in the Americas. What you have found is the lens of Africa focussed upon the New World.

When Columbus first arrived on the shores of what became Hispaniola, he found a tropical paradise. Nowhere in his travels had he seen a land of such abundance, where the rivers ran so clear and the trees reached into the heavens. The native Arawakan Indians he described as generous and good. In rapture, he sent word to his Queen Isabella, beseeching her to take the island under her dominion. The Spaniards introduced all the elements of fifteenth-century European civilization, and within fifteen years a combination of disease and wanton cruelty had reduced the native population from 500,000 to 60,000. For over a hundred years the weight of death hung over the island, and the western half that eventually became the French colony of Saint Domingue and later Haiti, with its rugged mountainous terrain and dearth of navigable rivers, remained virtually deserted.

By the end of the eighteenth century, however, slavery and sugar — 74 million kilograms of it each year—had transformed Saint Domingue into the envy of all Europe. A mere 36,000 whites and an equal number of free mulattos dominated a slave force of almost half a million and generated two-thirds of France's overseas trade—a productivity that easily surpassed the total annual output of all the declining Spanish Indies combined. Each year vast stores of indigo and hides, cotton, coffee, cacao and sugar filled the holds of over four thousand ships. In France, no fewer than 5 million of the 27 million citizens of the *ancien régime* depended economically on the trade. This tremendous concentration of wealth readily cast Saint Domingue as the jewel of the French Empire and the most coveted colony of the age.

All of this came to a cataclysmic end in 1791, with the beginnings of the only successful slave revolt in history and perhaps the greatest revolution the Americas have ever seen. It began at a nocturnal Vodoun ceremony on a secluded knoll at Bois Caiman near Morne-Rouge. There, on August 14, beneath the spindly branches of a frail acacia, with the wind twisting the ground and jagged lightning crashing on all sides, an old woman stood transfixed by the night, quivering in the spasm of spirit possession. The voice of Ogoun, the god of fire and war, called for the cutlass and with a single blow severed the head and spilt the blood of the black pig of Africa. The cry of freedom rode the sounds of the conch trumpets across the northern plain. By dawn the plantations were afire, and the glow of an entire land aflame reddened clouds as far away as the Bahamas.

In time, the slaves that rose up to throw off the shackles of bondage were called upon to defeat the greatest powers of Europe. First the French, then the Spanish, then the English, and once again the French invaded the island. In 1801, Napoleon at the height of his power dispatched, under command of his brother-in-law Leclerc, the largest expeditionary force ever to sail from Europe. Its mission was twofold: it was to sail up the Mississippi, hem in the expanding United States and re-establish French hegemony in North America. En route, and rather incidentally, Leclerc was expected to pass by the former colony of Saint Domingue and crush the slave revolt. Leclerc and his thirty thousand troops never saw the Mississippi. They were annihilated in Haiti.

The revolutionary slaves who settled the tortuous recesses of the mountainous island came from many parts of Africa. Among them were artisans and musicians, herbalists, carvers, metalworkers, boat builders, farmers, drum makers, sorcerers and warriors. There were men of royal blood, and others who had been born into slavery in Africa. In common was their experience of a heinous economic system that had ripped them away from their material world, but crucially they also shared an oral tradition that was unassailable—a rich repository of religious belief, political organization, knowledge of agriculture and medicine, music and dance that they carried with them into every remote valley. The evolution of these various traditions—their fusions and transformations—was deeply affected by the blanket of isolation that fell upon the country in the early years of the nineteenth century.

The nation that emerged from the revolutionary era was a pariah in the eyes of the international community. For over a hundred years

Haiti ranked as the only independent black republic, and in an imperialist age its very existence was a threat to the established order. The Haitian government supported any revolutionary struggle that promised to eliminate slavery. In a more symbolic gesture, the government purchased shipments of slaves en route to the United States, only to grant them their freedom. Moreover, Haiti defied international commercial interests by prohibiting any foreigner from owning property or land in the country. Even the power of the Roman Catholic Church was denied, and during the formative years of the nation, the church had practically no presence in the countryside.

Within Haiti, another form of isolation occurred. The breakdown of the colonial infrastructure of roads and bridges heightened an emerging disparity between the two halves of the Haitian reality, the rural peasants and the urban elite. The former were ex-slaves; the latter, in part, descendants of free mulattos who, during the colonial era, had enjoyed both great wealth and all the rights of French citizens, including the ignoble right to own slaves. After independence, the obvious differences between these two groups crystallized into a profound separation that went far deeper than class lines. They became more like two different worlds, coexisting within a single country.

The urban elite—perhaps 5 per cent of the population—looked to Europe for inspiration. They spoke French, were Roman Catholic and lived by rules invented in Paris. In the hinterland, however, the exslaves created an utterly different society based on their own ancestral traditions. Typically, the rural peasants thought of themselves as *ti guinin*—Children of Guinée, of Africa, their ancient homeland, a place that had slowly drifted from history into the realm of myth. Over time, what had been the collective memory of an entire disenfranchised people became the ethos of new generations and the foundation of a distinct and persistent culture.

Today, evidence of the African heritage is everywhere in rural Haiti. In the fields, long lines of men wield hoes to the rhythm of small drums; just beyond them sit steaming pots of millet and yams ready for the harvest feast. Near the centre of a roadside settlement, or *lakou*, a wizened old man holds court. Markets sprout up at every crossroads, and like magnets they pull the women out of the hills; one sees their narrow traffic on the trails, the billowy walk of girls beneath baskets of rice, the silhouette of a stubborn matron dragging a half-dozen donkeys laden with eggplant. There are sounds as well. The echo of distant songs, the din of the market and the cadence of the Creole language itself, each word truncated to fit the meter of West African speech. Every one of these disparate images, of course, translates into a theme: the value of collective labour, communal land holdings, the authority of the patriarch, the dominant role of women in the market economy. And these themes, in turn, are clues to a complex social world.

Yet images alone cannot begin to express the cohesion of the peasant society; this, like a psychic education, must come in symbols, in invisible tones sensed and felt as much as observed. In this country of survivors and spirits, the living and the dead, the Vodoun religion provides the essential bond. *Vodoun* is a Fon word from Dahomey that simply means "spirit" or "god." It is not a black magic cult; it is a system of profound religious beliefs concerning the relationships among man, nature and the supernatural forces of the universe. Like all religions, it fuses the unknown to the known, creates order out of chaos, renders the mysterious intelligible.

Vodoun not only embodies a set of spiritual concepts, it prescribes a way of life, a philosophy and code of ethics that regulate social behaviour. As surely as one speaks of a Christian or an Islamic society, so one can refer to a Vodoun society, and within that world find completeness: a distinct language, a complex system of traditional medicine, art and music inspired by African antecedents, education based on the oral transmission of songs and folklore, a system of justice derived from indigenous principles of conduct and morality. The religion cannot be abstracted from the day-to-day lives of the believers. In Haiti, as in Africa, there is no separation between the sacred and the secular, between the holy and the profane, between the material and the spiritual. Every dance, every song, every action is but a particle of the whole, each gesture a prayer for the survival of the entire community.

Vodoun is not an animistic religion. The believers do not endow natural objects with souls; they serve the *loa*, which are the multiple expressions of God. There is Agwe, the spiritual sovereign of the sea, and there is Ogoun, the spirit of fire, war and the metallurgical elements. But there is also Erzulie, the goddess of love; Guede, the spirit of the dead; Legba, the spirit of communication between all spheres. Vodounists, in fact, honour hundreds of loa because they recognize all life, all material objects and even abstract processes as sacred expressions of God. Though God is the supreme force at the apex of the pantheon, he is distant, and it is with the loa that Haitians interact on a daily basis.

The spirits live beneath the great water, sharing their time between Haiti and the mythic homeland of Guinée. But they often choose to reside in places of great natural beauty. They rise from the bottom of the sea, inhabit the rich plains and clamber down the rocky trails from the summits of mountains. They dwell in the centre of stones, the dampness of caves, the depth of sunken wells. Believers are drawn to these places as we are drawn to cathedrals. We do not worship the buildings; we go there to be in the presence of God.

In summer in Haiti the spirits walk, the people follow, and for weeks the roads come alive with pilgrims. The most revered site is a waterfall named Saut d'Eau, where years ago Erzulie, the goddess of love, escaped the wrath of the Catholic priests by turning into a pigeon and disappearing into the iridescent mist. Saut d'Eau is doubly important to Vodounists, for it is also the home of Damballah-Wedo, the serpent god, the repository of all spiritual wisdom and the source of all the falling waters. Legend has it that when the first rains fell, a rainbow, Ayida Wedo, was reflected. Damballah fell in love with Ayida, and their love entwined them in a cosmic helix from which all creation was fertilized.

The waterfall carves a deep hidden basin from a limestone escarpment, and for three days in July the trail descending to the falls quivers with the mirage of pilgrims coming and going. There is no order to their arrival, but it is a constant stream—as many as fifteen thousand appear—and the basin nestled into the edge of the mountain swells like a festive carnival tent to absorb everyone. It is a joyous occasion; one sees it on the faces of the children, the young city dandies leaping over the rocks like cats, the ragged peasants laughing derisively at a fat, preposterous government official. But for the devout, it is also a moment of purification and healing, one chance each year to partake of the power of the water, to bathe and drink, and to bottle a small sample of the cold thin blood of the divine.

In the cool, limpid light of dawn the pilgrims gather around the periphery of the basin where the herbalists set up their dusty stations, displaying sooty boxes, hunks of root, loose bags of healing leaves, and tubs of water and herbs. *Houngan* and *mambo*—Vodoun priests and priestesses—speak of magic done with dew, and tie brightly coloured strings to barren young women, or around the bellies of plump matrons who, in time, dangle the strings from wax stuck to the surface of the mapou tree, consecrated for the blessings of the gods.

One need only touch the water to feel its grace, and for some it is enough to dip into the shallow silvery pools, leaving their offerings of corn and rice in small piles. But most go directly to the cascades, women and men, old and young, baring their breasts and scrambling up the wet slippery bedrock that rises in a series of steps toward the base of the falls. At the lip of the escarpment the river forks twice, sending not one but three waterfalls plunging more than 30 metres. What is not lost in mist strikes the rocks with tremendous force, dividing again into many smaller chutes, each one becoming a sanctuary. The people remove their clothes, cast them into the water and stand, arms outstretched, beseeching the spirits. Young men move directly beneath the head of the falls, which batters their numb bodies against the rocks. Their prayers are lost to the thunderous roar, the piercing shouts and the screams of flocks of children. Everything is in flux, with no edge and no separation—the sounds and sights, the passions, the lush soaring vegetation, primeval and rare. Merely to submit to the waters is to open oneself to Damballah, and at any one time at the base of the waterfall in the shadow of the rainbow, there are a hundred or more pilgrims possessed by the spirit, slithering across the wet rocks.

The ease with which Haitians walk in and out of their spirit world is a consequence of the remarkable dialogue that exists between human beings and the spirits. The loa are powerful, and if offended can do great harm, but they are also predictable, and if properly served will reward men and women with good fortune. But just as humans must honour the spirits, so the loa are dependent on people. They arrive in response to the invocation of the songs, riding the rhythm of the drums. Once possessed, the believer loses all consciousness and sense of self; he or she becomes the spirit, taking on its persona and powers.

One night on the coast just beyond the Carrefour road, I was invited to the temple of a prominent Vodoun priest. I watched quietly as a white-robed girl—one of the *hounsis*, or initiates of the temple—came out of the darkness into the shelter of the peristyle. She spun in two directions, placed a candle on the dirt floor and lit it. The mambo, bearing a clay jar, repeated her motion, then carefully traced a cabalistic design on the earth, using cornmeal taken from the jar. This was a *vévé*, the symbol of the loa being invoked. After a series of libations, the mambo with a flourish led a group of initiates into the peristyle and around the centrepost, the *poteau mitan*, in a counterclockwise direction, until they knelt as one before the Vodoun priest. Bearing a sacred rattle and speaking in a ritualistic language, the houngan recited an elaborate litany that evoked all the mysteries of an ancient tradition.

Then the drums started, first the penetrating staccato cry of the *cata*, the smallest, whipped by a pair of long, thin sticks. The rolling rhythm of the *seconde* followed, and then came the sound of thunder rising, as if the belly of the earth were about to burst. This was the *maman*, largest of the three. Each drum had its own rhythm, its own pitch, yet there was a stunning unity to their sound that swept over the senses. The mambo's voice sliced through the night, and against the haunting chords of her invocation, the drummers beat a continuous battery, a resonance so powerful and directed it had the very palm trees above swaying in sympathy.

The initiates responded, swinging about the peristyle as one body linked in a single pulse. Each hounsis remained anonymous, focussed inward toward the poteau mitan and the drums. Their dance was not a ritual of poised grace, of allegory; it was a frontal assault on the forces of nature. Physically, it was a dance of shoulders and arms, of feet flat on the ground repeating deceptively simple steps over and over. But it was also a dance of purpose and resolution, of solidarity and permanence.

For forty minutes the dance went on, and then it happened. The maman broke—fled from the fixed rhythm of the other two drums, then rushed back with a highly syncopated, broken counterpoint. The effect was one of excruciating emptiness, a moment of hopeless vulnerability. An initiate froze. The drum pounded relentlessly, deep solid blows that seemed to strike directly to the woman's spine. She cringed with each beat. Then, with one foot fixed to the earth like a root, she began to spin in a spasmodic pirouette, out of which she soon broke to hurtle about the peristyle, stumbling, falling, grasping, thrashing the air with her arms, momentarily regaining her centre only to be driven on by the incessant beat. And upon this wave of sound, the spirit arrived. The woman's violence ceased; slowly, she lifted her face to the sky. She had been mounted by the Divine Horseman; she had become the spirit. The loa, the spirit that the ceremony had been invoking, had arrived.

Never have I witnessed a phenomenon as raw or as powerful as the spectacle of Vodoun possession that followed. The initiate, a diminutive woman, tore about the peristyle, lifting large men off the ground to swing them about like children. She grabbed a glass and crunched it in her mouth, swallowing small bits and spitting the rest onto the ground. At one point the mambo brought her a live dove; this the hounsis sacrificed by breaking its wings, then tearing the neck apart with her teeth. Soon two other hounsis were possessed, and for an extraordinary thirty minutes the peristyle was utter pandemonium, with the mambo racing about, spraying libations of water and rum, directing the spirits with the sound of her rattle.

The rhythm changed and the spirits arrived again, only this time riding a fire burning at the base of the poteau mitan. A hounsis was mounted violently—her entire body shaking, her muscles flexed—and a single spasm wriggled up her spine. She knelt before the fire, calling out in some ancient tongue. Then she stood up and began to whirl, describing smaller and smaller circles that carried her like a top around the poteau mitan and dropped her, still spinning, onto the fire. She remained there for an impossibly long time, and then in a single bound that sent embers and ash throughout the peristyle, she leapt away. Landing squarely on both feet, she stared back at the fire and screeched like a raven. Then she embraced the coals. She grabbed a burning stick with each hand, slapped them together, and released one. The other she began to lick, with broad lascivious strokes of her tongue, and then she ate the fire, taking a red-hot coal the size of a small apple between her lips. Then, once more, she began to spin. She went around the poteau mitan three times, until finally she collapsed into the arms of the mambo. The burning ember was still in her mouth.

For the nonbeliever, there is something profoundly disturbing about spirit possession. Its power is raw, immediate and undeniably real, devastating in a way, to those of us who do not know our gods. To witness sane and in every regard respectable individuals experiencing direct rapport with the divine fills us with either fear—which finds its natural outlet in disbelief—or envy. Most psychologists who have attempted to understand possession from a scientific perspective have fallen into the former category, and perhaps because of this they have come up with some bewildering conclusions, derived from quite unwarranted assumptions. For one, because the mystical frame of reference of the Vodounists involves issues that cannot be approached by their calculus —the existence or nonexistence of spirits, for example—the beliefs of the individual experiencing possession are dismissed as externalities. To the believer, the dissociation of personality that characterizes possession is the hand of divine grace; to the psychologist, it is but a symptom of an "overwhelming psychic disturbance." One prominent Haitian physician, acknowledging that possession occurs under strict parameters of ritual, nevertheless concluded that it was the result of "widespread pathology in the countryside which far from being the result of individual or social experience was related to the genetic character of the Haitian people," a racial psychosis, as he put it elsewhere, of a people "living on nerves." Such inadequate explanations are typical of uninformed observers of the Vodoun faith.

Until the turn of this century, most references to Vodoun merely acknowledged its role as a catalyst in the only successful slave revolt in history. The entire notion of Vodoun as something evil and macabre emerged largely after 1915, when the U.S. Marine Corps occupied Haiti. For twenty years the island was inundated with missionaries and marines, mostly from the American south, who were both captivated and appalled by everything they saw, or thought they saw, in the infamous Black Republic. Americans at home shared the fascination. Books with titles such as *Voodoo Fire in Haiti, Black Baghdad, A Puritan in Voodooland, The White King of La Gonave, Cannibal Cousins* and *The Magic Island* in turn inspired a succession of Hollywood B-movies —*I Walked with a Zombie, The White Zombies, Zombies on Broadway* and *Zombies of the Stratosphere*. In any other era, these books and movies, full of pins and needles in dolls, children bred for the cauldron, and zombies crawling out of the grave to attack people, would have been immediately forgotten. However, appearing when they did, they conveyed an important message to the American public—any country in which such abominations took place could find its salvation only through military occupation. This false and absurd depiction of Vodoun accounts for the reputation the religion has as a nefarious black magic cult.

Vodoun, in truth, is a complex, metaphysical worldview distilled from profound religious ideas that have their roots in Africa. The essence of the faith is a sacred cycle of life, death and rebirth unique to the religion. For the acolyte, death is not feared for its finality but as a crucial and vulnerable moment in which the spiritual and physical components separate. One aspect of the soul, the *ti bon ange* (little good angel) goes beneath the Great Water. A year and a day after the death, in one of the most important of all Vodoun rites, the ti bon ange is ritualistically reclaimed and placed by the houngan in a *govi,* a small clay jar, which is stored in the temple's inner sanctuary. That soul, initially associated with a particular relative, in time becomes part of a vast pool of ancestral energy from which emerge the archetypes which are the loa, the 401 spirits of the Vodoun pantheon. To Haitians, this reclamation of the dead is not an isolated sentimental act; on the contrary, it is as fundamental and inescapable as birth itself. One emerges from the womb an animal, the spiritual birth at initiation makes one human, but it is the final re-emergence that marks one's birth as sacred essence.

It is possession, the return of the spirits to the body, that completes the sacred cycle: from human to ancestor, ancestor to cosmic principle, principle to personage, and personage returning to displace the identity of man or woman. Hence, while Vodounists serve their gods, they also give birth to them. The ultimate experience in Vodoun ritual, then, is the moment when the loa responds to the invocation of the drums and rises from the earth to inhabit the body. In many ways Vodoun is the most quintessentially democratic faith, for the believers not only have direct access to the spirits, they actually receive the gods into their bodies. That moment of spirit possession—what Maya Deren, dancer and author, described as "the white darkness"—is by no means a pathological event. On the contrary, it is the manifestation of divine grace, the epiphany of the Vodoun faith. As Haitians often say, "White people go to church and speak about God, we dance in the temple and become God."

To be sure, there are other less benign forces in Vodoun, the conjurers of dark magic, the manipulators of the hexing herbs. Yet to ask why there is sorcery in Vodoun is ultimately to ask why there is evil in the universe. The answer, if there is one, is the same as that given by Krishna to a disciple when he said, "To thicken the plot." Indeed, nearly every religion has a notion of darkness and light. In Christianity, there is the fallen archangel who is the devil, and the Christ child, the son of God. For Vodounists, sorcery is merely the manifestation of the dark side of the universe. Balancing those malevolent forces with the magical power of the positive is the very goal of the religion.

The god of war and fire dwells in the north, in the shadow of a mapou tree that marks the place where once each year a mud pond spreads over a dry roadbed near the centre of the village of Plaine du Nord. Like the waters of Saut d'Eau, the mud of the basin is said to be profoundly curative, and each year thousands of pilgrims arrive, some to fill their bottles, some to cleanse their babies, many to bathe. Unlike Saut d'Eau, the area around the basin is hemmed in by houses that funnel all the energy of the pilgrims into a small, intensely charged space. And in place of the serenity of Damballah, there is the raging energy of Ogoun.

Around the basin, a ring of candles burns for the spirit, and the pilgrims, dressed in bright cotton, lean precariously over the mud to leave offerings of rum and meat, rice and wine. There is a battery of drums to one side, and those mounted by the spirit enter the basin, disappear and emerge transformed. A young man, his body submerged with only his eyes showing, moves steadily like a reptile past the legs of naked women, their skin coated with slimy clay. Beside them, children dive like ducks for tossed coins. At the base of the mapou, Ogoun feeds leaves and rum to a sacrificial bull; others reach out to touch it and caress its flank, then the machete cuts into its throat, and the blood spreads over the surface of the mud.

On my last day in Haiti, I was watching all this when I felt something fluid—not water or sweat or rum—trickle down my arm. I turned to a man pressed close beside me and saw his arm riddled with needles and small blades, the blood running copiously over the scars of past years, staining some leaves bound to his elbow before dripping from his skin to mine. The man was smiling. He too was possessed, like the youth straddling the dying bull, or the dancers and the women wallowing in the mud. Men and women, descendants of those who had been dragged in chains from an African homeland, embraced by a new landscape which they, in turn, had impregnated with all the forces of light and darkness. "Haiti," a Vodoun priest once told me, "will teach you that good and evil are one. We never confuse them. Nor do we keep them apart."

THE
SHELTERING SKY

There is a silver thread that reaches from the base of the spine to the heavens where it becomes interwoven in the fabric of destiny. One's own will is meaningless. All is written. This is *mektoub,* or fate, a concept ultimately incomprehensible to those who have not experienced the searing blue dome of the Saharan sky, who have never known a landscape of rock, sand and wind where plants live by dew, and the sun turns cliffs to iron, bleaches doves to the colour of earth. In the void created by the absence of will, the spirits of light and darkness have room to move.

Paul Bowles, among the greatest writers of the latter half of this century, understands all of these things. Living in self-imposed exile in Tangier, he has for over fifty years embraced North Africa, moving incessantly through a "topography rich in prototypal dream scenes," intoxicated by the scents and sounds, the mystic possibilities of a land fresh with the promise of wisdom, ecstasy and death. His stark prose is infused with a spirit of place, ruthless in its lack of sentiment, detached and clinical as the midday desert sun. In "The Delicate Prey," one of his most haunting short stories, a Mougari man slices off the genitals of a young boy, only to bury them in an incision he cuts in the victim's belly. Discovered by the boy's kin, the murderer is taken into the desert and buried up to his neck. "When they had gone," the author writes, "the Mougari fell silent, to wait through the cold hours for the sun that would bring first warmth, then heat, thirst, fire, visions. The next night he did not know where he was, did not feel the cold. The wind blew dust along the ground into his mouth as he sang."

The Sheltering Sky, Bowles's first and best novel, is the story of a New York couple, Port and Kit Moresby, who in 1947 set out with a friend,

George Tunner, to escape their war-torn synthetic age, hoping that a sojourn in the Sahara will repair the rift that has come between them. Instead, as they drift deeper and deeper into the desert, they encounter only oblivion. Port is consumed by fever, Kit by betrayal and madness. In the end, the innocuous Tunner is the only survivor, but even he can never be the same. In a letter to his publisher, Bowles described the book as "an adventure story that takes place on two planes simultaneously: in the actual desert and in the inner desert of the spirit. The occasional oasis offers relief from the actual desert, but the shade is insufficient, the glare is always brighter as the journey continues. And the journey must continue—there is no oasis in which one can remain." In all of Bowles's writing is a pitiless clarity and an unrelenting exploration of the intuitive mind that might slip through the hands of the wrong filmmaker. For over thirty years the motion picture rights to *The Sheltering Sky* were held by Robert Aldridge, maker of *The Dirty Dozen.* Fortunately, the option was eventually acquired by British producer Jeremy Thomas, who brought the story to Bernardo Bertolucci. Together, they reassembled the creative team that had made *The Last Emperor,* including long-time Bertolucci cinematographer Vittorio Storaro, and cast John Malkovich and Debra Winger to play Port and Kit Moresby.

Paul Bowles and Bernardo Bertolucci met for the first time in 1986, in Bowles's three-room flat in the apartment building on the outskirts of Tangier where he has lived since 1956. Bowles remembers the encounter with obvious fondness. He had not seen any of Bertolucci's films. Indeed, he hadn't seen any film in twenty years. But Bertolucci impressed him as "a subtle man, a civilized man. We spoke for three days. He seemed very intelligent for a film director. I suppose because he's not an American."

After a few hours in the dark flat, with its memories of distant nights of conversation and joy, intrigue and confusion, Bertolucci knew that it was more than Bowles's age that made him appear so genteel and proper: "His appearance and behaviour are extraordinarily sweet and formal, even courtly, only because he is a man so intimately transgressive and wild. Through the windows of his eyes you can see it. His outward demeanour is only to balance something incredibly explosive that lies inside his spirit. Without that precise exterior, his interior would explode all over the place.

"He feels the world is so full of poison—his characters are swimming in an ocean of poison, the poison of relationships. He must give himself a precise shadow for balance. Otherwise, he couldn't survive the inner transgression. All of this is in *The Sheltering Sky*. It was his first book and there is an immediacy, a freshness. It is something very modern. It is a very simple story of very complicated people."

For Bertolucci, *The Sheltering Sky* is a departure from the historical sweep of *The Last Emperor*, but like so many of his films, it is a story of the confrontation between the inner soul of the characters and the external forces of history, society and the land. His film *1900* told of two boyhood friends who, by an accident of birth, are destined to become class enemies in prewar Italy. *The Conformist* explored the perversity of fascism. At a time of unprecedented sexual upheaval, *Last Tango in Paris* confronted barren nihilism and the emptiness of an anonymous relationship. In *The Sheltering Sky*, the alien and unforgiving landscape mirrors the desolation and tragedy of an impossibly destructive love that, like a terminal disease, cannot be shaken.

"Love is like a blackmail that condemns Port and Kit to be together," Bertolucci explains, "yet they love each other. Bowles's greatest strength is his ability to make daily life something epic. If I am able to get into the film half the poison that is in the book . . ."

Though Bowles consistently denies it, few associated with the production doubt that the book is autobiographical, or that the confused, even tormented relationship between Port and Kit was inspired by that of Paul and his beloved wife and muse, author Jane Bowles. Theirs was a complex, immensely entertaining marriage punctuated by long separations, dual residences and different partners on both sides. Jane embraced women, calling them "deep and obscene," and to this day Paul is certain that her stroke and subsequent death were brought on by poison and dark magic worked by an illiterate market woman who had become her lover. For Paul, Jane's death in 1973 meant simply that life lost all interest.

"You must understand," Bertolucci says, "that in the book Kit and Port are Jane and Paul, but for him this is something unacceptable. To admit this would expose his deep true nature. He has established a certain symmetry with life, a geometry of balance. He cannot admit that this book is a mirror of himself."

The genesis of *The Sheltering Sky* occurred in 1932 during a fifteen-month journey that Bowles took through the M'Zab, a compelling, mystical region of the Algerian Sahara. There, he met a young American, George Turner, was assisted by a Lieutenant d'Armagnac and had a strange encounter with a naked Ouled Nahil dancing girl. In writing the book fifteen years later, Bowles drew the structure and character of the landscape from these early travels, adding details as they sprang upon him as he once again made his way across North Africa: "I never knew what I was going to write on the following day because I had not yet lived through that day."

The key to the book, as to the film, is a line from Kafka: "From a certain point onward, there is no turning back; that is the point that must be reached." Bowles knew that Port would die. After that, the book would take care of itself. There would only be Kit, the desert and madness.

In describing the fever pitches that consume Port, Bowles drew on his own experience, particularly a bout with typhoid that had nearly killed him in 1932. The death itself was more problematic: "I saw it as a difficult subject to treat with anything approaching the proper style. It seemed reasonable, therefore, to hand the job over to the subconscious." So he began to experiment with *majoun,* an orally administered and potent preparation of cannabis. As he later wrote: "I lay absolutely still, feeling myself being lifted, rising to meet the sun. In another hour my mind was behaving in a fashion I should never have imagined possible." The next day, infused with his memories of fire, he wrote the death of Port, one of the most harrowing passages in modern literature.

For Bertolucci, one of the challenges is to portray the psychic transformations that for much of the novel swirl through the minds of the characters.

"I could have chosen to do a literary movie," he notes. "There are beautiful literary movies. I just saw Fassbinders *Wings of Desire* in Paris with French subtitles. It was so literary and so happy to be literary. It was fantastic to read the words on the frame—they became part of the structure of the film.

"But with *The Sheltering Sky,* I didn't want to make a literary movie, and though the script is extremely faithful to the book, I thought it best to ignore completely all the interior voices. I am not interested in the labyrinth of their minds. I want to tell their story through emotion and behaviour, letting the dry exterior of the characters be a mirror of themselves—that, combined with landscape, will reveal their isolation.

This is the chemistry of movies. Literature speaks the language of metaphor, because words are metaphorical. Cinema speaks the language of reality, because instead of words we use reality. Cinema is always *cinéma vérité*."

John Malkovich and Debra Winger are riding bicycles up a long ascending road that drops away behind them to the town of Aït Saoun and the desolate wastes of the desert. Ahead of them, the road climbs into the steepest of the Atlas ranges, then falls beyond to the fortified hamlets and casbahs of the Drâa oases, and the ancient caravan route to Mauritania and Niger. Raptors fly overhead, and on all sides the iron ridges of the Jebel Sarhro tear at a violently blue sky.

A simple but important scene, it portrays the one time in the book when Kit and Port come together, only to have their tenderness betray the distance that lies between them. In a sea of darkened stones, they encounter a naked man delicately shaving his pubic hair, and then another, cloaked silently in prayer. Port realizes that "the very silences and emptiness that touch his soul" terrify Kit. "The sky here's very strange," he tries to explain. "I often have the sensation when I look at it that it's a solid thing up there, protecting us from what's behind."

It is impossible to know what Bertolucci wants, but all afternoon the bicyclists and the bright blue car with its rear-mounted camera move up and then down a short stretch of road. The vehicle is small, packed with various crew and makeup artists. Bertolucci and cinematographer Vittorio Storaro, with their flamboyant hats and scarves, cling to the rear like gypsies. Behind them in tow on the bicycles, Debra Winger stands out in her polka-dot dress and red beret. Malkovich in khaki fuses with the haze of the desert.

Between takes, Malkovich is calm, rooted in a truly humble way. In a cluster of idle crew and hangers-on, he alone notices that the production has blocked the thoroughfare and asks that a way be cleared for the local market women. Debra Winger is the opposite. As the afternoon proceeds into twilight, she spins deeper and deeper into character. Their approach to acting is completely different. He takes on a role as a cloak; to do otherwise, he suggests, is to become psychotic. "Those who think that acting is being someone you're not invariably fail. The secret is to be someone who you are." Winger, by contrast, becomes infused by her character, drawing inspiration randomly from everything around her, in ways of which even she is unaware. Malkovich explains, "Everybody

111

needs their space to work. Debra needs to be worked up. She's not like that offstage. I'm the opposite. I've done plays on Broadway where they've practically had to wake me up when the curtain rises. They expect you to be pacing backstage, but I can't. It's not how I feel."

With each take, Debra Winger's behaviour off-camera becomes more and more charged. She cannot sit still. Like a pinball, she ricochets about, loud, boisterous, filling the set with herself. She becomes ill and stumbles off the roadway to throw up. She doesn't, but nevertheless offers "the large chunks" to anyone within earshot. She cannot know how she appears. Then, momentarily relieved, she yells an endearment to her young son, says something to his nanny, lifts a cigarette from Malkovich's breast pocket and tosses a used cup into the driver's seat of the reporters' car. Winger, who refuses to speak to the press on location, is more than anyone else aware of their presence. In a final flourish she takes possession of the press car, plopping herself in the rear seat to smoke a cigarette. She glances into the desert where her young son and his father, Timothy Hutton, are playing tenderly. In a month he will file for divorce.

At first none of this makes much sense. This cannot be the same actress who, three days before, flew headfirst from the back of a moving truck only to rebound immediately to finish the scene, even though a head injury had once nearly killed her. This cannot be the fragile person that John Malkovich speaks of. This cannot be the tender woman that Paul Bowles has fallen in love with.

"You see," Bertolucci notes, "Jane Bowles was a myth of the early feminists. Debra read all of her books at Berkeley when she was a student. Now she has done this wild identification with Jane, and I tell you for him it was irresistible. I think he is completely in love with her.

"There was one scene we shot in Tangier in which Kit watches from a hotel balcony as Port disappears in a car. It was a closeup of her face, and there is the voice of the narrator reading a few lines from the book about what she is feeling. Debra asked Paul to be there, reading from off-camera. It was a good idea. It turned out to be one of the most moving moments in the shooting. He was behind a curtain like a priest in a confessional, a little back from me. For her, it was sublime, as if it was a force from a primitive nature that she could harness and elevate to a higher plane."

It's difficult to imagine Paul Bowles being at the beck and call of a young actress, but apparently he was for the five weeks the film was based in Tangier. "I saw her all the time," he later recalled. "She was high-strung, nervous, but mainly because her little boy was always sick. Bertolucci kept telling her to look into the life of Jane. She sent letters by her driver every day. Generally, they'd ask me to go up to her villa. So I went. She's an actress," he adds, betraying a tenderness he normally reveals only when speaking of Mrs. Bowles.

John Malkovich has a completely different take on Bowles. They met for dinner only once. "Paul's a very shut-off person. He's detached, cut off. I don't mean that in a judgmental way. But I know what it's like to be cut off. I know what it's like to be charming, intelligent, well dressed. I know what that is, and the story has to be something more."

Malkovich is tentative when he speaks of his character, Port Moresby. "I'm far from a method actor, but at certain times a role has to affect you. I remember thinking *Death of a Salesman* was a great play. But when my father died a month before I started rehearsals, it didn't interest me. I work from the imagination. But it's not difficult for me to recreate extreme states. I've never had trouble having access to that. I'm not sure what that means.

"Somewhere along the way in my own life, I started to lose track of my instincts, which only now I'm sort of starting to recover. Instincts about everything. It's personal. When one goes through separation and divorce, not only do you feel the grief of the loss, you feel the loss of all things—the rituals. You're alone in the abyss. I'm strong. I wouldn't say I'm fragile, but I would say that I feel a lot. That makes this kind of movie a tough one to do."

Cinéma vérité—Malkovich and Winger stung in their own lives by the pain of separation. Port and Kit wandering in the white heat of the desert. Here on the set, up behind the roadway in the rocks, a bus stops to unload its passengers. It is sunset, and the men lay out their brown robes to face east in evening prayer.

The title of the novel was inspired by a dance-hall tune, "Down among the Sheltering Palms," that Bowles used to listen to as a child. It wasn't the song that intrigued him, it was the word "sheltering." What did the palm trees shelter the people from, and how could they be so sure of protection? Since the story was based in the Sahara, where there is only sky, the book became *The Sheltering Sky*.

For cinematographer Vittorio Storaro, sky, sun and moon are the symbolic elements around which the story must unfold. "Bernardo never sees any story in realistic terms. He always creates a duel between the conscious and the unconscious. We have worked together for so long that there is a kind of chemistry between us. With the camera, he crafts the grammar of the picture. I write with light. I take the meaning of the word 'photography literally. If someone says to me, 'You're a painter,' I don't understand. But whether it is *The Last Emperor* or *The Sheltering Sky*—the size of the canvas makes no difference—it is the ideology that is everything. We must first discover the idea.

"I then use light, colour, shadows to visualize his imagination, but not in a realistic way. I try to translate into light the two different elements of a scene, the primal forces that drive the characters, envisioning this with artificial or natural light, shadows, cold or warm colour. I try all the time to remain in a kind of conference with the two main elements driving the characterization.

"In this case I visualize Port's journey as the passage of the sun, beginning the picture with a light that heralds the waking up of the unconscious, for the first breath of the movie is his emergence from a dream that is more like a nightmare. From that moment on, it is the journey of the sun, rising through morning to the purifying light of midday. Then with the death of Port comes the end of light and the birth of the moon. There is that one moment, though, when the forces are in balance, and it is the only time of peace in the story. Kit starts to become her own person, she becomes conscious of her power as a woman.

"Then, for the first time, we see the moon rising and the colour is blue. Kit comes very close to Port as he lies dying. This is life. One is dying, the other awaiting rebirth. There is a moment when they are equal as human beings. With the arrival of night, she enters the oasis, emerging reborn.

"From this point on they start a moon journey. Port is dead, his spirit enveloped by the force of a million winds. Kit joins the caravan and follows a growing moon on a nocturnal journey across the desert. But by the time she escapes from her prison, the moon is black, the night has ended, and a new sun dawns, harsh and unforgiving of her madness.

"This is the idea. Of course, with Bernardo I have to constantly adapt my vision to the grammar of the camera. Cinematography is writing with light and movement in one specific space. The responsibility to determine that space belongs to the director—especially in Italy. This moving canvas is sometimes dominated by light. No doubt each time

Bernardo is doing a shot, some kind of light suggests to him where to start, and sometimes reading the space, we completely change the feeling, creating new conflict with light and shadows.

"Bernardo once said that a missing scene from a film is also a missing scene of light, a missing scene within a scene. Sometimes you never know until the last moment, especially with me, how much the light is going to reveal. It is a continuing transformation. That is what is great about Bernardo. The first idea is never the last. We always change. There is a kind of moving energy that takes the primitive form of words and translates them into the symphony of colour that is film."

Red grit like a veil hangs over the city of Ouarzazate, and outside the walls of the ancient casbah, the caravan of gleaming production vehicles rests after a long march from Zagora and the mouth of the Sahara. A military precision keeps this assembly of technicians, interpreters, actors and artisans rolling across much of Morocco, Algeria and Niger. Few productions pose more logistical challenges than period road pictures. Every prop, from street signs and gas pumps to camel saddles and Berber tents, must be supplied. Flatbed trucks haul a vintage Mercedes and an antique bus. For one shot, several tonnes of circa 1947 garbage had to be recreated. Another scene required the construction of a Foreign Legion fortress. Now, after a disastrous flash flood near Erfoud and a tortuous passage along the southern flank of the Atlas Mountains, the production has settled into Ouarzazate—miraculously ahead of schedule.

Thick electric cables snake up a narrow stairway into the labyrinth of the casbah, reaching a series of small chambers, one of which is made over as the hotel room in which Tunner waits in vain for word of Kit. All the frenetic energy of a film set is compressed into an impossibly small space. Orders go out in four languages, and technicians race back and forth, raising small clouds of dust that linger at knee level.

Tunner's room is infused with morning light tinged with red, brown and ochre. The furnishings are warm from years of human touch. Steamer trunks stacked in the corner of the room have the patina of a lost era of travel, before technology condensed history and transformed the meaning of geography.

In the midst of setting up the shot, Bernardo Bertolucci dips in and out of a conversation that invariably comes back to Paul Bowles. "It is fantastic that he is still here, still alive. The resonance that he has. You know, he has infected the actors with this book. They keep reading it and reading it. I have done movies from books before, but never have I seen copies of a book so present on the set during the shooting of the film."

"In the last days before shooting," Bertolucci recalls, "I was thinking of the absence of literary feeling to the script. Shooting was to begin in Tangier, so I thought, why not place Bowles in the film? His presence could give a literary resonance without the literary weight.

"I asked him to be a silent witness. On the one hand, he is the author of the story, seeing his characters come to life. But he is also the immediate present. He is an old man now, and it is as if he projects what he sees. And what appears is 1947, but he is also of today. He is like the present that comes from the pain of the past, the pain of memory. It is fantastic, even redemptive; the idea that he is here now, alive and well, seeing this image of his own past."

There is such joy in these words, such kindness. John Malkovich says that there is only one thing to know about Bertolucci. "His father was a poet. Bernardo is a poet. He has the face of a child."

Paul Bowles remembers filming the last scene in the picture, wherein Kit Moresby, white with madness, approaches Bowles in the market of Tangier. "Are you lost?" he asks. She says nothing and walks away down a long slope of garbage, flanked on both sides by street urchins tossing the rotting debris into the air, like rice at a wedding.

"Bernardo kept shooting and reshooting my eyes. He told me over and over, 'We must see in your eyes the memories of your life.' Naturally, I just sat there. Finally, he said *'Bellissima.'*"

In the room it is twilight at midday, and, as is his habit, Paul Bowles takes his meal in bed, surrounded by the small coterie of young men who care for him. Old photographs are passed around: Truman Capote, astonishingly boyish, frolicking on a sand dune, Tennessee Williams and Paul in Rome, jane Bowles in a 1950s nightclub surrounded by admirers, Bowles alone with his typewriter, William Burroughs and Allen Ginsberg on a Tangier rooftop. The window in the living room is blocked by the shade of a giant monstera, the very plant that hovered over Jane Bowles's bed until Paul discovered the sorcerer's magic bundle in its roots that contributed to her death. The film crew is far away on location in the desert. There is a lull in the waves of journalists that have so recently swept over his life.

"Writing," he once remarked, "is a superstitious way of keeping the horror at bay."

From his bed, Bowles listens to a story taken from the wind of Tangier. It concerns a woman of ethereal grace whose brother, tormented by demonic voices, entered the kitchen of their home and slit open the stomachs of his mother and grandmother. The father went mad, the family fortune was lost, and the girl, without dowry and tainted by scandal, was abandoned in her beauty.

Bowles takes in each detail with an intensity that leaves no doubt as to the truth of the tale. "That woman," he says, "must have had the eyes of a gazelle."

THE FORESTS
OF AMAZONIA

Even for those of us from Canada, a country where landscape sweeps over the imagination and defines the essence of the national soul, it is difficult to grasp the size of the Amazon. A marvellous tale is told of the explorations of Francisco de Orellana, the first European to travel the length of the river. In 1541, having crossed the Andes in search of the mythical land of El Dorado, Gonzalo Pizarro dispatched Orellana on a desperate search for food. Orellana sailed down the Napo, a swift river in eastern Ecuador, and it is said that when he finally reached the confluence of the Río Ucayali, as the upper Amazon is known in Peru, he went temporarily insane. Coming as he did from the parched landscape of Spain, he could not conceive that a river on God's Earth could be so enormous. Little did he know what awaited him 3200 kilometres downstream where the river becomes a sea and the riverbanks, such as they are, lie 160 kilometres apart.

This story, apocryphal or not, illustrates the central challenge that confronts all travellers on their first visit to the Amazon. It is the issue of scale and the impossibility of imagining rain forests of such magnitude. In the Amazon, there are 7.8 million square kilometres of forested lands, a vast expanse of biological wealth the size of the continental United States. The river itself flows for 6800 kilometres, just longer than the Nile but far more extensive, including more than 80 000 kilometres of navigable water spread across six South American nations. Within the Amazon drainage, there are twenty rivers larger than the Rhine, and eleven of these flow more than 1600 kilometres without being disrupted by a single rapid. The river delta is enormous. If the mouth of the Amazon could be superimposed onto a map of Europe, the Eiffel Tower would sit on the south bank and the north bank would support the Tower of London. Among the hundreds of islands that make up the delta, there is one named Marajo, which is itself larger than Switzerland. Sedimentary deposits at the mouth are 3700 metres deep and fresh water may be drunk from the sea 240 kilometres beyond the shore. Tidal influences reach as far up the river as Obidos, a small city located just below the mouth of the Río Trombetas, 400 kilometres from the apex of the Amazon delta and a full 725 kilometres from the sea.

The Amazon did not always flow into the Atlantic. Two hundred and fifty million years ago, the South American continent was still attached to Africa, and the predecessor of the Amazon flowed east to west, draining an arc of massive highlands, the remnants of which are now known as the Brazilian and Guiana Shields. The river reached the Pacific Ocean somewhere along the shore of contemporary Ecuador. A hundred million years later the two southern continents split apart. A mere 7 million years ago, the birth of the Andean Cordillera effectively dammed the river, creating a vast inland sea which covered much of what is now the Amazon basin. In time, these waters gradually worked their way through the older formations to the east and carved out the modern channel of the Amazon.

The Río Negro and the Río Solimòes, the two main branches that form the Amazon proper at Manaus, Brazil, are a legacy of these staggering geological events. The Río Negro drains the northern half of the Amazon basin, rising in the ancient soils of the Guiana Shield, and its dark colour is due to a high concentration of humic matter, very little silt load and a tannin content equal to that of a well-brewed cup of tea. The Solimòes and its affluents, by contrast, are born in ten thousand precipitous mountain valleys. Rich in sediments, these are the fabled milk rivers of Indian mythology, the source of nutrients that each year replenish the flood plain of the lower Amazon.

Rainfall in the Andes and water cut loose from the ice of thousands of Cordilleran glaciers drive the entire system. One of the most remarkable features of the Amazon is the fact that while the river falls 4300 metres in its first 950 kilometres, the drop in elevation over the last 4200 kilometres is but 75 metres, less than 2 centimetres per kilometre. If the Washington Monument stood at the mouth in Belem, its tip would be higher than any building in Iquitos, Peru, a sizable city 3200 kilometres upriver. The Amazon does not flow to the sea, it is pushed by the annual runoff from the Andean Cordillera.

Water, be it white or black, dominates the lives of all sentient creatures in the Amazon. In volume, the river is five times larger than the Zaire, eleven times larger than the Mississippi. The Zaire is technically the second-largest river on Earth, but within the Amazon system there are two tributaries, the Madeira and Negro, each of which is larger. In twenty-four hours the Amazon pumps as much fresh water into the Atlantic as the Thames does in an entire year. Nearly 200 000 cubic metres of water flow into the sea each second. That is enough water to provide three hundred people with a bath each week for approximately 250 million years. If the U.S. Army Corps of Engineers could figure out a way to drain Lake Ontario and divert the channel of the Amazon, the lake could be refilled in three hours.

The seasonally replenished flood plain accounts for a mere 3 per cent of the land and represents a small part of the Amazonian reality. Beyond the borders of the flood plain lies another world, *tierra firme*, the upland forests that cover so much of the basin. It is only here that you begin to sense the overwhelming grandeur, the power of the forest. It is a subtle thing—there are no cascades of orchids, no herds of ungulates such as you might encounter on the Serengeti plain. Just a thousand shades of green, an infinitude of shape, form and texture that so clearly mocks the terminology of temperate botany. If you close your eyes you can sense the constant hum of biological activity, evolution, if you will, working in overdrive.

The diversity of these tropical rain forests is staggering: 2.5 square kilometres of Amazonian forest may be home to as many as 23,000 distinct forms of life. Brazil alone harbours more primate species and, in sheer numbers, more terrestrial vertebrate animals than any other nation. There are more species of fish in the Rio Negro than in all of Europe, more species of birds in Colombia than in any other country. Whereas all of New England has perhaps 1,200 plant species, the Amazon has more than 80,000. While 400 square metres of woodland in British Columbia might have six species of trees, the same area in the Amazon could contain over three hundred.

The insect fauna is especially rich. A researcher surveyed the canopy of nineteen individuals of one tree species and found over 1,200 species of beetles. Partly on the basis of this remarkable discovery, entomologists now believe that tropical rain forests harbour over 30 million species of insects. There are ten thousand species of ants alone. At any one moment there are over 1,000,000,000,000,000 (one quadrillion) ants alive. In the

Amazon, ants comprise over 30 per cent of the total animal biomass. Harvard entomologist E. O. Wilson found in one tree stump in lowland Peru more taxa of ants than have been found in all the British Isles.

These figures, though impressive, give little indication of the biological drama constantly being played out in the tropical rain forests. Break open the trunk of a common *Cecropia* tree and find a colony of Azteca fire ants living inside the hollow internodes. The plant feeds the ants with tiny capsules of carbohydrate; the fire ants, in exchange, protect the tree from *Atta* ants, voracious leaf cutters capable of defoliating a tree in a matter of hours.

Watch for these leaf cutters in the forest. Long trails of workers scurry to unknown destinations, each toting a cut section of a leaf like a sail on its back. A closer look, E. O. Wilson reminds us, reveals the magnitude of their achievement. If you can imagine these creatures on a human scale, such that their 6-millimetre length becomes 180 centimetres, you would note that each foraging ant runs along the trail for about 15 kilometres at a speed of 26 kilometres per hour. At the end of the trail, each ant picks up a leafy burden weighing some 340 kilograms and runs back at a speed of 24 kilometres an hour. This marathon is then repeated, without pause for rest, dozens of times in the course of a day and night. The ants do not eat the leaf fragments. They turn them into mulch, which they use to grow the fungus that forms the basis of their diet. One struggles to imagine a colony of 3 to 4 million ants, dwelling underground in thousands of chambers, cultivating in the darkness a fungus found nowhere else in nature.

Consider the extraordinary pollination mechanism of the giant lily, *Victoria amazonica*. This famous plant, with its enormous leaves capable of supporting the weight of a small child, grows in side channels and standing bodies of water throughout much of the Amazonian flood plain. The simultaneous opening at dusk of its massive white blossoms is one of the most inspiring scenes in the Amazon. The exterior of the flower has four large sepals covered by sharp spines. Inside are numerous petals, arranged in a spiral, decreasing in size toward the centre. Within the petals is a whorl of thicker structures called staminodes. Next are the three hundred stamens that carry the pollen. Inside the stamens is yet another whorl of floral parts that, together with the other structures, form what amounts to a tunnel leading to a large cavity, at the base of which is the carpel, the female part of the flower. Lining the carpel is a ring of appendages that are full of starch and sugar.

When the flower buds are ready to open, they rise above the surface of the water and, precisely at sunset, triggered by the falling light, open with a speed that can be readily observed. The brilliant white petals stand erect, and the flowers fragrance, which has been growing in strength since early afternoon, reaches its peak of intensity. At the same time, the metabolic processes that generate the odour raise the temperature of the central cavity of the blossom by exactly 11 degrees Celsius above whatever the outside temperature happens to be. The combination of colour, scent and heat attracts a swarm of beetles, which converge on the centre of the flower.

As night falls and temperatures cool, the flower begins to close, trapping the beetles with a single night's supply of food in the starchy appendages of the carpel. By two in the morning, the flower temperature has dropped and the petals begin to turn pink. By dawn the flowers are completely closed, and they remain so for most of the day. In early afternoon the outer sepals and petals alone open. By now a deep shade of reddish purple, they warn other beetles to stay away. Last night's beetles, meanwhile, remain trapped in the inner cavity of the blossom. Then, just before dusk, the male anthers of the flower release pollen, and the beetles, sticky with the juice of the flower and once again hungry, are finally allowed to go. In their haste to find yet another opening bloom with its generous offering of food, the beetles dash by the anthers and become covered with pollen, which they then carry to the stigma of another flower, thus pollinating the ovaries.

This sophisticated pollination mechanism is, in its complexity, not unusual for the plants of the Amazon. Indeed, a botanist would be hard pressed to invent a strategy of pollination or seed dispersal that doesn't already exist in nature. There are fruit-eating fish, seeds that float in the wind, succulent fruits destined for birds and primates, tough woody fruits for the massive rodents, fruits that explode, fruits that are carried by bats, seeds that swim, and even seeds small enough to be dispersed by ants.

Perhaps the best symbol of the Amazon is the three-toed sloth, a gentle herbivore that dwells in the canopy of the forest. Its extremely slow movement, literally at a snail's pace, together with its cryptic colouration, protects the sloth from its only major predator, the harpy eagle. Viewed up close, the sloth appears as an ecosystem unto itself, softly vibrating with hundreds of exoparasites. The sloth's mottled appearance is due in part to blue-green algae that live symbiotically within its hollow hairs. A dozen varieties of arthropods burrow beneath its fur; a single sloth weighing a mere 4.5 kilograms may be home to more than a thousand beetles.

The life cycles of these insects are completely tied to the daily round of the sloth. With its excruciatingly slow metabolism, the sloth defecates only once a week. The animal climbs down from the canopy, excavates a small depression at the foot of the tree, voids its feces and then returns to the treetops. Mites, beetles and even a species of moth leap off the sloth, deposit an egg in me dung and climb back onto their host. After the eggs hatch, the young insects find another sloth to call home.

Why would this animal go down to the base of the tree, exposing itself to all forms of terrestrial predation, when it could just as easily defecate from the treetops? The answer provides an important clue to the immense complexity and subtlety of this ecosystem. Biologists have suggested that in depositing the feces at the base, the sloth enhances the nutrient regime of the host tree. That such a small amount of nitrogenous material might actually make a difference suggests that this cornucopia of life is far more fragile than it appears. In fact, many ecologists have called the tropical forest a counterfeit paradise. The problem is soil. In many areas, there essentially is none.

Forests have two major strategies for preserving the nutrient load of the ecosystem. In the temperate zone, with the periodicity of the seasons and the resultant accumulation of rich organic debris, the biological wealth is in the soil itself. In the tropics, it is completely different. With constant high humidity and annual temperatures hovering around 27 degrees Celsius, bacteria and micro-organisms break down plant matter virtually as soon as the leaves hit the forest floor. Ninety per cent of the root tips in a tropical forest may be found in the top 10 centimetres of earth. Vital nutrients are immediately recycled into the vegetation. The wealth of this ecosystem is the living forest itself, an exceedingly complex mosaic of thousands of interacting and interdependent living organisms. It is a castle of immense biological sophistication built quite literally on a foundation of sand.

Removing this canopy sets in motion a chain reaction of destruction with cataclysmic consequences. Temperatures increase dramatically, relative humidity falls, rates of evapotranspiration drop precipitously, and the mycorrhizal mats that interlace the roots of forest trees, enhancing their ability to absorb nutrients, dry up and die. With the cushion of vegetation gone, torrential rains cause erosion, which leads to further loss of nutrients and chemical changes in the soil itself. In certain deforested areas of the Amazon, the precipitation of iron oxides in leached exposed soils has resulted in the deposition of kilometre upon kilometre of lateritic clays, a rocklike pavement of red earth in which not a weed will grow.

What percentage of the Amazon has been compromised is a matter of debate. Estimates range from as low as io per cent to a shocking 20 per cent. The primary concern today is not the absolute amount of land that has been cleared but rather the rate at which the forests are falling. On the eve of the 1992 Earth Summit in Río de Janeiro, 11000 square kilometres were being cut each year. Since then, despite all international concern, the burning seasons have brought a threefold increase in destruction. In 1994-95, according to Brazilian government figures based on satellite images, 29 000 square kilometres, an area the size of New Jersey, were deforested. A separate Brazilian Congressional study, which took into account logging, ground fires and thinning operations proceeding beneath the canopy undetected by satellites, concluded that an area twice the size of Belgium, a total of 58 000 squares kilometres of primary rain forest, was being transformed every year.

The effects of this deforestation will be felt continentally and globally. Since fully half of the precipitation in the Amazon is generated from evapotranspiration, rainfall in the basin may be reduced by as much as 50 per cent. Worldwide clearing operations that burn the remnants of tropical forests put 52 trillion kilograms of carbon dioxide into the air each year, an amount roughly equal to 35 per cent of all industrial emissions. The result contributes to the Greenhouse Effect, a warming of the atmosphere which, even by the most conservative estimates, promises unprecedented climate change, including the possibility of an increase in sea level of as much as 2 metres, a rise that would inundate entire countries.

Perhaps most tragically, the destruction of the tropical rain forests is resulting in the massive loss of biological diversity. Although extinction is a global problem, these rain forests are particularly susceptible, because species tend to occur in low densities with restricted ranges. The impact in some regions has already been devastating. In Madagascar, where over 90 per cent of the native species are found nowhere else, only 7 per cent of the original forest remains. The Atlantic forests of Brazil, another centre of high endemism, have been reduced to less than 2 per cent of their original extent. Human activity is not only having an impact on individual species but changing the actual conditions of life itself. Acid rain, global warming, ozone depletion, the accumulation of synthetic compounds in the environment—these conditions represent changes in the actual chemistry of the biosphere.

The elimination of life, of course, is nothing new in the history of the Earth. Mass extinctions marked the end of the Permian, Triassic and Cretaceous Periods, and other crises occurred in the late Devonian and at the end of the Eocene. Shortly after the arrival of human beings in South America fifteen thousand years ago, 45 of 120 genera of mammals were lost. In general, however, over the last 600 million years, speciation has outpaced extinction and the diversity of life has steadily increased.

What has changed in a disturbing way in the last fifty years is the *rate* of disappearance. Species loss, when compensated by speciation, is a normal phenomenon. Massive, sudden species extinction and biological impoverishment are not. The current wave of extinction is unprecedented in the last 60 million years, both in abruptness and probably in the total number of species being lost. Between the years 1600 and 1900, perhaps seventy-five species were eliminated as a result of human activities. Since 1960 extinction has claimed, at a conservative estimate, upwards of a thousand species per year. E. O. Wilson believes that within the last twenty-five years of this century, one million species may disappear. That figure represents a loss of one species every thirteen minutes, no each day, 40,000 in a single year.

Does this loss of biodiversity matter? Biologists may scoff at such a question, but providing an answer that makes sense to both the public and policymakers is a critical challenge. It is and always will be difficult to argue that the value of a single species is worth more than a particular development project. Stanford biologist Paul Ehrlich explains the ecological significance of species diversity with a metaphor. Imagine, he writes, that as you are entering an airplane you notice a workman popping out rivets. The workman explains that the rivets can be sold for $2 and thus can subsidize cheaper airfares. When questioned about the wisdom of the procedure, he responds that it has to be safe, as no wings have fallen off despite many rounds of deriveting. This, in effect, is what we are doing to the biosphere through the erosion of biodiversity.

The value of a species, as Tom Lovejoy of the Smithsonian Institution has pointed out, is not simply that it may one day yield a pharmaceutical drug—though this may occur. The real issue is that there is not a single species that we can claim to understand. Our knowledge is embarrassingly rudimentary. The common fruit fly, for example, is without doubt the most studied organism on Earth. Working out its genetics and basic biology has consumed millions of dollars of research funds. Yet to date we cannot explain many of the fundamental elements of its life cycle. What's more, a species that has no apparent use today, may, as our own knowledge increases, yield astonishing benefits. Who, for example, in the nineteenth century could have realized the value of the humble *Penicillium* mold?

Consider the potential of every form of life. A single bacterium, E. O. Wilson reminds us, possesses about ten million bits of genetic data, a fungus one billion, an insect from one to ten billion, depending on the species. If the information in just one ant was translated into a code of English letters and printed in letters of standard size, the string of letters would stretch 1600 kilometres. One handful of earth contains information that would just about fill all fifteen editions of the *Encyclopaedia Britannica* since 1768. This is the true resonance of nature. Each incident of extinction represents far more than the disappearance of a form of life; it is the wanton loss of an evolutionary possibility and its irrevocable severance from the stream of divine desire.

Most of the species doomed to extinction have yet to be described by science. Estimates of the total number of species range from 3 to 100 million. Incredibly, despite two centuries of scientific research, we do not know the true number of species on the Earth, even to the nearest order of magnitude. Though approximately 1.5 million species have been taxonomically classified, most forms of life do not even have a scientific name. Virtually every time botanists or entomologists go into the tropical rain forests, they bring back species new to science.

Given this bounty and the risk to the integrity of the biosphere incumbent in the destruction of biological diversity, what do we gain from the massive exploitation of the tropical rain forests? In 1974, Volkswagen acquired 10 000 square kilometres of Brazilian rain forest, applied defoliants from the air and then torched the land, creating the largest deliberately set man-made fire in recorded history. The most optimistic agronomists working at the site estimated that cattle might be able to graze on the land for twelve to fourteen years. Each animal put out on the land requires 8900 square metres of converted forest to yield a few dozen kilograms of meat. A single Brazil nut tree left standing in the forest produces one tonne of proteinrich seeds each year. Incredibly, there is today no place in the Amazon where forest land converted to pasture before 1980 is still supporting cattle. Raising cattle is one way of utilizing the land, but considering the true potential of the rain forest, it is rather like using a van Gogh to kindle a campfire. It gets the job done, but at incalculable cost.

The result of this wanton destruction is extinction, not only of plants and animals but of human societies that have, over the course of thousands of years, developed an intimate knowledge of the forest and the natural products it contains. Largely responsible for deforestation are development programs initiated by governmental and international agencies struggling to deal with problems of massive debt and chronic population growth, poverty, unemployment and starvation. Each year the world's population increases by 90 million, much of it concentrated in the regions that contain the remaining tracts of tropical rain forest. Efforts to preserve even remnants of these forests will inevitably fail if conservation initiatives conflict with a people's fundamental struggle to survive. The ideal strategy is to learn from those who know the forest best. By turning to the indigenous peoples and by studying their use of plants, it is possible to demonstrate that the long-term income-generating potential of the standing forest equals or exceeds the short-term gain resulting from its destruction.

Ethnobotany can contribute to this effort in several ways. First, studies of indigenous people's adaptation may provide models for profitable and environmentally sound use of the forest. Among the Mebêngôkre-Kayapò of central Brazil, for example, ethnobotanists have documented a remarkably sophisticated system of integrated land management. The biological use of insects, the manipulation of semidomesticated plants, and the deliberate encouragement or transplanting of wild trees and medicinal plants along trail sides and in fields are all elements of a complex sustainable agro-forestry system that stands in marked contrast to the crude and destructive patterns of modern land use in the tropics.

Moreover, ethnobotanists can invoke the considerable economic potential of as yet undiscovered or undeveloped natural products. Plants are useful as poisons or medicines because they have evolved complex secondary compounds and alkaloids as chemical defences against insect predation. These defensive chemicals, which in certain plants may account for 10 per cent of dry weight, interact harmfully with the biochemical apparatus of the insects. The same properties, however, can be exploited by the modern chemist for therapeutic purposes. This is by no means merely an academic pursuit. In the field of medicine alone, roughly 60 per cent of modern drugs are derived from natural products. Plant ingredients valued in excess of U.S. $8 billion are included in a quarter of all prescriptions dispensed by community pharmacies in the United States and Canada. Globally, the annual sales of plant-derived pharmaceuticals exceeds U.S. $70 billion. Worldwide, there are about 121 clinically useful prescription drugs derived from 95 species of higher plants, 47 of which are native to the tropical rain forest. The majority of these—some 75 per cent—were discovered in a folk context, the gifts to the modern world of the shaman and the witch, the healer and the herbalist, the magician and the priest.

The American Indian has provided any number of vital drugs. The small patches placed by the ear to prevent seasickness contain scopolamine, a compound found in many species in the potato family, traditionally used as narcotics and medicines by Indian shaman. The essential ingredient of the first contraceptive pills, diosgenin, came from the wild yam of Mexico. Aspirin was first synthesized by Bayer, but the starting point was salicylic acid, a compound found in willow bark and first used to treat headaches by North American Indians. The Amazon and the eastern slopes of the Andes have provided such critical drugs as pilocarpine, the major treatment for glaucoma; the muscle relaxant d-tubocurarine; and quinine, the antimalarial suppressant that arguably has saved more lives than any other drug.

The daily use of medicinal plants continues to this day throughout the world. According to the World Health Organization, approximately 90 per cent of the population in developing countries relies chiefly on traditional medicine for their primary health care needs. The study of these plants remains an extraordinarily important element of modern science. Of the 3,500 new chemical structures discovered in 1985, there were 2,619 isolated from higher plants alone. Despite this concentrated effort, the potential has scarcely been tapped. To date only 5,000 out of an estimated 250,000 to 300,000 higher plants have been studied in detail for their possible medical applications.

Knowledge of the tropical rain forest flora is especially inadequate. Though 70 per cent of all plants known to have antitumour properties have been found in the tropics, over 90 per cent of plants in the rain forests of the Americas have yet to be subjected to even superficial chemical screening. Worldwide, less than 15 per cent of higher plants have been examined for anticancer activity. In the Amazon, out of

80,000 species of higher plants, a mere 470 have been investigated in detail.

Any practical strategy for expanding knowledge of this living pharmaceutical factory must include ethnobotanical work. To attempt to assay the entire flora without the collaboration of indigenous peoples would be logistically impossible, intellectually shortsighted and historically uninformed. Identifying both psychologically and cosmologically with the rain forest, and depending on that environment for virtually all their material needs, it is not surprising that indigenous peoples are exceptionally skilled naturalists. The extent of their knowledge and the sophistication of their interpretations of biological relationships can be astounding. The Waorani of the Ecuadorian Amazon, for example, not only recognize such conceptually complex phenomena as pollination and fruit dispersal, they understand and accurately predict animal behaviour. They anticipate flowering and fruiting cycles of all edible forest plants, know the preferred foods of most forest animals and may even explain where any particular animal prefers to pass the night. Waorani hunters can detect the scent of animal urine at forty paces in the forest, and can accurately identify the species from which it came.

This perspicacious knowledge of the forest, combined with an active process of experimentation, has led to the discovery of remarkable chemical properties of plants. Indigenous peoples of the Amazon, for example, employ dozens of different plant species as ichthyotoxins, biodegradable fish poisons, some of which contain up to 20 per cent rotenone in their roots. Placed into slow-moving bodies of water, these poisons interfere with respiration in the gills. The fish float to the surface and are readily gathered.

Over ninety species of plants in the Amazon yield curare, the flying death employed throughout the basin as an arrow and dart poison. The toxins are derived principally from a number of species in several genera of lianas in the Moon-seed and Logania families. The active principle of several of these plants is a muscle relaxant, d-tubocurarine, which, once isolated in the early 1940s, became an invaluable drug in modern surgery. The preparation of curare involves a number of procedures. Generally, the bark is rasped and placed in a funnel-shaped leaf compress suspended between two hunting spears. Cold water is then percolated through, and the drippings collected in a ceramic pot. This dark liquid is slowly heated over a fire and brought to a frothy boil numerous times until the fluid thickens. It is then cooled and later reheated, until a thick layer of viscous scum gradually forms on the surface. This scum is removed, the dart tips are spun in the viscid fluid, and the darts are then carefully dried by the fire. The procedure itself is mundane. The realization, however, that this orally inactive substance, derived from but a handful of the hundreds of forest lianas, could kill when administered intramuscularly, is profound.

The bounty of the tropical rain forest is by no means limited to medicinal drugs. Most of the common foods eaten in North America and Europe were first domesticated by indigenous peoples, and in many instances originated in the tropics. Indeed, if North Americans had to subsist only on cultivated plants native to the United States and Canada, our diet would consist of pecans, cranberries, Jerusalem artichokes and maple sugar. If it were not for the agricultural contributions of Central and South American Indians, Switzerland would have no chocolate, Hawaii no pineapple, Ireland no potato, Italy no tomato, India no eggplant, North Africa no chili, England no tapioca, and none of us would have vanilla, papaya or corn.

Of an estimated 75,000 edible plants found in nature, only 2,500 have ever been eaten with regularity, a mere 150 enter world commerce and a scant 20, mostly domesticated cereals, stand between human society and starvation. Yet in the Amazon, there are wild trees that yield 300 kilograms of oil-rich seeds a year; a palm whose fruits have more vitamin C than oranges, more vitamin A than spinach; and another palm, known as a living oil factory, whose seeds contain 27 per cent pure protein. There are trees in the Amazon which produce resins that, if placed raw into a fuel tank, will run a diesel engine. There are fruits containing natural compounds three hundred times sweeter than sucrose, leaves coated with industrial waxes, seeds covered by brilliant pigments and dyes, lianas impregnated with biodegradable insecticides

What economic value can we place on the potential of these plants? In certain cases the returns can be substantial and immediate. Brazil, for example, currently spends $95 million each year to import olive oil from Portugal. In the Amazon, however, there is a palm, *Jessenia bataua*, which produces an abundance of seed oil that is, in terms of taste and chemistry, indistinguishable from olive oil. The development of this plant through artificial selection could permanently free Brazil of a chronic drain on its trade balance.

Another equally dramatic example of the economic potential of wild plants is a simple discovery made by Hugh Iltis, a plant explorer from the University of Wisconsin. In 1962, on one of his botanical expeditions, Iitis collected the seeds of an apparently useless wild relative of the tomato. That plant, however, once crossbred with cultivated tomatoes, proved to have genetic traits that vastly improved the domesticated varieties. Iltis later calculated that his erTorts cost the government agency that funded his research about $40. The value of his discovery to the tomato industry has been estimated to be approximately $8 million a year, $160 million over the last two decades.

It is a strange set of values that has dictated the course of economic development in the tropical rain forests. At a time when the annual worldwide sales of plant-derived pharmaceuticals are measured in the tens of billions, Daniel Ludwig spent $1 billion levelling a stretch of Brazilian forest the size of Connecticut in a failed attempt to grow pulp fibre. His costs soared in part because so little fundamental research had been done in the tropics that his foresters and engineers had to begin from scratch, experimenting on a massive scale as they went along. Had they known, at the onset, what they discovered so painfully later on, it is unlikely the project would have ever begun. Yet in 1980, just as Ludwigs Jari project was coming to a final crisis, the total funding for global research in the basic biological sciences of ecology, taxonomy, ethnobotany and plant exploration was $30 million, a figure that then represented less than the cost of a single F-16 fighter, and perhaps the amount spent in New York City's bars on any two weekends of the year.

Ethnobotany can reveal the potential gifts of the tropical rain forest— leaves that heal, fruits and seeds that bring forth the foods we eat, plants that can transform the economies of regions and even entire nations. Yet critically, in unveiling this indigenous knowledge, we must seek not only new sources of wealth but also a new vision of life itself, a profoundly different way of living with the forest. Sensitivity to nature is not an innate attribute of indigenous peoples. It is a consequence of adaptive choices that have resulted in the development of highly specialized perceptual skills. But those choices, in turn, spring from a comprehensive view of nature and the universe in which man and woman are perceived as but elements inextricably linked to the whole. It is another vision altogether, one in which man stands apart, that threatens the forests and our world with devastation. Perhaps the greatest legacy of indigenous peoples will be their contribution to a dialogue between these two worldviews such that folk wisdom may temper and guide the inevitable development processes that today ride roughshod over much of the Earth.

WHITE BLOOD
OF THE FOREST

The day that has haunted the rubber industry for sixty years will dawn like any other. The wind along the shores of the South China Sea will pass over the land, and the sun, rising the length of Asia, will slowly burn away the haze from the plantations that are the source of 93 per cent of the world's natural rubber. In fields the size of nations, shadows will merge with the silver trunks of millions of identical trees, the most recently domesticated of all the major crops, one vast genetic clone spawned but a century ago from a handful of seeds taken from the Amazon and sown in the pristine soil of Southeast Asia.

As Chinese and Tamil workers fan out through the plantings, the wind picks up, scattering foliage which falls unnaturally from the branches. The leaves, fresh and pliant a week before, are withered and dry, blackened with lesions. The dark eruptions mean only one thing. The South American leaf blight, a fungal pestilence so virulent as to have thwarted all efforts to cultivate rubber in its native Amazonian homeland, has finally reached the shores of Asia.

In the ensuing weeks every resource will be mobilized in an attempt to isolate and contain the outbreak. On the large estates, massive applications of fungicides provide some relief, but on the scattered family farms, source of 80 per cent of the production, the disease proves impossible to control. In Kuala Lumpur, Malaysian officials hunt for the source of the infestation; so fearful have they been of this potential calamity that they have never permitted a commercial airline to fly directly to their country from any South American nation known to harbour the fungus. But it is too late; however the blight jumped the Pacific ocean, the threat is the same: the end of the natural-rubber industry as we know it.

In America, consumers lulled into complacency by faith in the wizardry of synthetic chemistry will wake to the realization that the world still moves on natural rubber. Two-and-a-half million tires are made every day, and at least a third of the rubber in every one comes from a tree. For many critical applications, there is no viable substitute. Without natural rubber, airplanes cannot land safely; the aircraft carrier is rendered obsolete. Trucking is crippled, interstate commerce severely compromised. Dismay sweeps the medical profession as doctors and hospital administrators learn that they, too, depend on natural rubber for a host of crucial products. Speculators make a killing as the price of rubber goes through the roof.

This nightmare, improbable as it may seem, is an open secret in the rubber industry. Ernie Imle, a retired pathologist, knows what could happen if the leaf blight crosses the Pacific: decades ago in Central America, he witnessed an outbreak. "It moves like a blowtorch through the plantings," he says. A wiry, soft-spoken man who devoted a good part of his career at the U.S. Department of Agriculture to finding a way to cultivate rubber in the Americas, Imle adds: "We've had a period of grace for fifty years. But eventually every disease gets everywhere. It's only a matter of time before it reaches Asia, What has saved us until now is the thinness of the fungal spore wall. It couldn't survive a long ocean voyage. But with jet travel, it's an entirely different story."

Kevin Jones, secretary of the International Rubber Research and Development Board outside London, calls the leaf blight the "AIDS of the rubber industry." Concern is intense, research difficult. "You can hope to get on top of it early, if it breaks out," he says. While scientists can test fungicides in the lab, "You cannot truly test your controls in situ for fear of actually releasing the disease into the plantations. So no one really knows what will happen. If it gets ashore, you might control it, but it would be unlikely that you could eradicate it. Eventually, it would flare up. The result could be disastrous."

Another world authority on rubber, Richard Evans Schultes, director emeritus of the Harvard Botanical Museum, believes the blight would run through the Asian plantations in five years, reducing yields, killing trees and eventually compromising the entire industry. In the words of Ernie Imle, "A sword of Damocles hangs over the neck of the industrial world. We've created a situation whereby a relatively simple act of biological terrorism, the systematic introduction of spores so

small as to be readily concealed in a shoe, could wipe out the plantations, shut down the production of natural rubber and precipitate an
economic crisis of unprecedented dimensions. And no one even knows
about it. What's more, it all could have been avoided."

This is not the worst part of the story. The worst is that we have
confronted such a crisis before, and forgotten it. In 1942 the fate of the
Allies hinged on America's ability to find new sources of rubber, after
Japan cut off supplies from Asia. Responding in spectacular fashion,
the United States raced to develop synthetics, launched a mammoth
recycling program and sent scientists to risk their lives in the Amazon
in a desperate search for latex-bearing plants.

It was synthetic rubber that was decisive in the Allied victory,
though the product was never as good as natural rubber. The plant
explorers, meanwhile, after years of frantic effort, very nearly succeeded
in giving America hardy strains that could be cultivated in the West.
Yet after the war ended, Washington discarded their work through a
combination of bureaucratic folly and 1950s-style technological hubris.
So the nation has come full circle, and once again finds itself dependent
on a natural product grown half a world away, threatened with disaster
and certain to be in short supply in the coming years.

In the Amazon it was known as the weeping tree, the white blood of the
forest, and for generations Indians had slashed its bark, letting the latex
drip onto leaves, where it could be molded by hand into vessels and
sheets, impermeable to rain. Columbus encountered Arawakans playing
games with strange balls that bounced and flew. Thomas Jefferson and
Benjamin Franklin found the material was ideal for erasing pencil
notations. Because of a general belief that it came from the East Indies,
the substance was called India rubber. In fact, the product came from
Brazil, and there the King of Portugal had already established a fledging
industry that made rubber shoes, capes and bags.

All of these products, however, had a major flaw. In cold weather
the rubber became so brittle that it cracked like porcelain. In summer
heat a rubber cape was reduced to a sticky shroud. Then in 1839, quite
by accident at his home in New Haven, Charles Goodyear discovered
vulcanization, a process that made rubber unaffected by the elements,
transforming it from a curiosity to an essential product of the Industrial
Age. In 1888 John Dunlop invented inflatable rubber tires so that his
son could win a tricycle race in Belfast. Seven years later the Michelin

brothers stunned critics by introducing removable tires in the Paris-Bordeaux car rally. By the turn of the century, there were fifty American automobile companies. Oldsmobile, the most successful, sold only 425 cars in 1901. Less than a decade later the first of 15 million Model Ts rolled off Henry Ford's assembly line. Each one needed rubber, and the only source was in the Amazon.

The flash of wealth was mesmerizing. In London and New York, men flipped coins to decide whether to go after gold in the Klondike or rubber in Brazil. At the height of the rush, five thousand adventurers a week headed up the Amazon. By 1909 merchants were shipping 500 tonnes of rubber downriver every ten days. By 1910 rubber accounted for 40 per cent of all Brazilian exports. A year later production peaked at 45 000 tonnes. It was worth, at a conservative estimate, more than $200 million. In Pittsburgh, steel tycoon Andrew Carnegie lamented, "I should have chosen rubber."

Manaus, situated at the heart of the Brazilian rubber trade, grew in a few years from a seedy riverside village into a thriving city where opulence reached bizarre heights. Rubber barons lit cigars with $100 bank notes and slaked the thirst of their horses with silver buckets of chilled French champagne. Their wives, disdainful of the muddy waters of the Amazon, sent their linens to Portugal to be laundered. Prostitutes from Tangier and St. Petersburg earned as much as $8,000 for an evenings work, fees often paid in tiaras and jewels; the citizens of Manaus in 1907 were the highest per capita consumers of diamonds in the world.

All of this wealth derived from the latex of a tree that grew scattered across 5.2 million square kilometres of tropical rain forest. In this vast expanse, an area the size of the continental United States, there were perhaps 300 million individual trees worth exploiting. Finding them was the challenge. In nature, rubber trees grow widely dispersed in the forest, an adaptation that insulates the species from the ravages of the leaf blight. This accident of biology forged the structure of the wild rubber trade, and in time determined the fate of nations.

To profit, merchants had to establish exclusive control over immense territories and secure to the yoke of the trade enormous numbers of workers. Impoverished peasants were imported by the thousands from the Brazil's northeast and absorbed into an atrocious system of debt peonage. On stud farms, Indian women were bred like cattle. Throughout the Amazon the rubber trade unleashed a reign of terror the like of which had not been seen since the Spanish Conquest. A Capuchin priest who witnessed the rubber boom recalled years later: "The best that could be said of a white man in that terrible time was that he did not kill his Indians for sport." As the workers died, rubber production soared. For each tonne produced, ten Indians perished and hundreds were left scarred for life.

In the end, what saved the native population was an act of British imperial policy. In 1877 rubber seeds taken by the English from the forests of Brazil reached Malaya, a tropical land similar in climate to the Amazon but untainted by the leaf blight. Here, there was no need for rubber trees to grow widely separated; dense, efficient plantations were possible. By 1909 Malaya (now part of Malaysia) had planted over 40 million rubber trees, spaced just 6 metres apart in neat rows that allowed a single worker to tap four hundred trees a day. Production doubled every twelve months. In a discovery that would later haunt the industry, growers learned to select high-yielding clones and propagate them by cuttings. Within a decade millions of rubber trees, all derived genetically from a handful of seeds, carpeted the hillsides of Asia.

With the success of the plantations, the Amazon rubber boom imploded. In 1910 Brazil still produced roughly half of the world's supply, but by 1918 produced only 20 per cent; the rest came from the Far East. By 1934 plantations covered more than 3.2 million hectares of Asia. In South America the industry was dead. In 1940 Brazil produced only 1.3 per cent of the international rubber supply, and the nation had become a net importer of the product she had given the world.

Dependence on plantations 21 000 kilometres away did not sit well with the leaders of American industry. With rubber by the 1920s accounting for an eighth of the value of all U.S. imports, breaking the Asian monopoly became an obsession. Harvey Firestone established a 12000-hectare plantation in blight-free Liberia. Thomas Edison surveyed seventeen thousand latex-bearing plants, exhausting his fortune as he sought new sources of rubber in North America. But the man most determined to smash the Asian growers was Henry Ford, who by then was making half the automobiles in the world. In 1927 he set in motion a multimillion-dollar scheme, in the wilds of Brazil, that came to be known as Fordlandia.

Unlike most Amazonian rivers, with their murky sloughs and

impenetrable flood forests, the Río Tapajos runs clear, its surface broken only by the flash of pink dolphins and the shimmer of distant white-sand beaches that dominate the shore. It was here in 1876 that the Englishman Henry Wickham had gathered the rubber seeds that gave rise to the Asian industry. And it was here, twelve hours by launch upriver from the Brazilian city of Santarém, that Ford chased his dream of American rubber.

On a land grant four times the size of Rhode Island, he built a town complete with kilometres of roads and railroads, a modern port, a factory, schools, churches, hundreds of brick and stucco bungalows, and a fully equipped hospital that overlooked swimming pools, tennis courts and a golf course carved from the jungle. Workers cleared thousands of hectares and planted over 5 million rubber seeds. Botanists sent to Malaya and the Dutch East Indies secured the finest, highest-yielding clones, products of fifty years of plant breeding and horticultural ingenuity. By 1934, 1. 5 million rubber saplings grew at Fordlandia. All went well initially. Then, as the foliage began to form a continuous canopy over the fields, the leaf blight struck. Within a year it had ravaged the plantation.

The plantation s namesake was not a man accustomed to failure. Nor did he think small. During World War II the Ford Motor Company would produce more industrial output than Italy. Undaunted by the debacle at Fordlandia, Henry Ford ordered his agronomists to try again, only on an even larger scale. A second concession was secured, another town built, more land cleared, and more rubber planted. The outcome was the same: dead and withered trees, bare limbs and leaves black with blight.

"Everything that was discovered at Fordlandia," Ernie Imle notes, "could have been learned on a ten-acre plot at a fraction of the cost."

Today little remains of Ford's dream. A few bungalows still stand, their scabrous façades broken and abandoned. A handful of families scratch a living from tired soil and the gnarled trunks of remnant trees. Fire hydrants stamped by a Michigan manufacturer poke incongruously from dense undergrowth. Yet despite the decay, the plantation's legacy resonates in a manner Ford would never have imagined. From the wasted fields of Fordlandia emerged a sobering lesson: by far the most sensitive and the first to die of the rubber trees were the high-yielding clones from the Far East. In selecting for yield, the breeders in Asia had inadvertently produced strains that were especially susceptible to the blight. After Fordlandia, everyone knew that if the disease ever reached Asia, it could mean the end of the industry.

The Asian monopoly took on an entirely new meaning on the morning of December 7, 1941, the day that the United States went to war. Within three months of Pearl Harbor, the Japanese, as desperate for rubber as the Allies, seized Malaya and the Dutch East Indies, taking control of 95 per cent of the world's supply and plunging America into crisis. Every Sherman tank had 20 tonnes of steel and 450 kilograms of rubber. Every battleship had twenty thousand rubber parts. Rubber was wrapped around every centimetre of wiring in every factory, home, office and military installation in America. There was no synthetic alternative. With every conceivable source taken into account, the nation had, at normal rates of consumption, roughly a year's supply. Out of this it had to fuel the largest and most critical industrial expansion in history, the arming of the Allied cause.

Washington's response was swift and dramatic. Four days after Pearl Harbor, the use of rubber in any product not essential to the war effort was outlawed. The speed limit dropped to 55 kilometres per hour, not to conserve gas but to reduce wear and tear on the nation's tires. Scrap rubber fetched a penny a pound at more than four hundred thousand depots scattered across the country. Even Fala, President Roosevelt's dog, had his toy bones melted down. It was the most extensive recycling campaign in history, and it got the Allies through 1942.

The order went out to the chemists and engineers to create a synthetic industry. The scientific initiative had already begun, but the output of the fledging enterprise was inconsequential. In 1941 total production of synthetic rubber was just over 8 000 tonnes, mostly specialty products useless for tires. The nation's survival depended on its ability to manufacture over 800 000 tonnes of a product that had barely entered the development stage. No blueprints existed for the factories that would process this immense tonnage. No facilities had been built to produce even the feed stocks from which the rubber would be made. American industry had never been called upon to handle such a task, to accomplish so much in such a short time. The engineers had two years. If the synthetic program did not succeed, America's capacity to wage war would collapse.

There was a third initiative besides recycling and synthetics: a desperate attempt to secure natural rubber from any conceivable source.

When word reached Washington that the Russians were extracting latex from dandelions, orders went out to plant them in forty-one states. The U.S. Department of Agriculture dispatched plant explorers to every corner of the free world, many to the Amazon. They were charged with securing raw supplies of latex, but also with a far greater challenge. It was their task to find a way to grow rubber in the Americas, in the hope that the nation would never again be vulnerable to a foreign powers seizing control of the Far Eastern plantations.

Out of the disaster at Fordlandia had come a stunning possibility. Among the millions of trees that died, a handful survived, all wild and native to the Amazon. This raised the prospect that in nature there might exist rare individual trees with inherent resistance to the disease. It was to locate these trees, a quixotic quest not unlike looking for a needle in a haystack, that the USDA in 1943 sent plant explorers into the basin.

Travelling by dugout canoe hundreds of kilometres down unknown rivers, living for months at a time in lands inhabited only by Indians, their bodies wracked by disease, their crews dying in rapids and consumed by the jungle, this cadre of botanists did the impossible. They not only found trees with marked resistance but also introduced them into cultivation at Turrialba, the USDA experimental station in Costa Rica. By war's end, horticultural breakthroughs, mostly the work of Ernie Imle, had solved many of the technical problems related to establishing high-yielding, disease-resistant plantations in the Americas.

"There was still much to be done," Imle cautions. "It might have taken twenty years, and forty might not have been enough. Such work never ends. Man has been improving wheat and corn for thousands of years. But with rubber we had made tremendous progress."

Yet shortly after the war's end, that work was wrecked by a single act of bureaucratic foolishness. In February 1952 the financing of the rubber research was taken over by a branch of the State Department known as the Institute of Inter-American Affairs. On March 31, Robert Rands, the botanist who had led the USDA effort since 1940, stressed the importance of the research in a memorandum sent to Rey Hill, director of the Division of Agricultural and Natural Resources, the agency that controlled the fate of the program.

"Our research has reached a crucial stage," Rands wrote. "It has provided methods and plant material that make rubber production in leaf blight areas of Latin America economically feasible. Strategically the development of sources of rubber in the Western Hemisphere is urgent to hedge against our being cut off entirely from sources of supply in the East by war, plant disease, or ideological developments."

Rey Hill and his colleagues at State did not agree. Knowing little of science, Hill had already decided on political grounds that rubber was not for Latin America. The British in Malaya were fighting a communist insurgency. American plantations would undermine the economic mainstay of the colony. Over the protests of every major rubber executive—Paul Litchfield of Goodyear, Harvey Firestone Jr., G. M. Tisdale of U.S. Rubber (now Uniroyal)—the USDA rubber research program was shut down. In Costa Rica all records of the research were lost or destroyed. The clonal gardens at Turrialba that preserved the invaluable germ plasm of an entire continent were abandoned, and in time allowed to be cut to the ground.

Recently declassified documents at the National Archives reveal the process by which the decision was made to destroy the rubber effort. What emerges is less evidence of a conspiracy than an egregious example of bureaucratic folly. That, together with blind faith in the future of synthetic rubber. The wartime synthetic rubber program had been enormously successful. At a cost of $700 million (about $5.6 billion in today's dollars), the United States had pulled off one of the most out-standing scientific and engineering achievements of all time. By 1945 production of serviceable synthetic rubber surpassed 800 000 tonnes a year and accounted for 85 per cent of U.S. consumption. Many believed that the technical innovations, which had come about so quickly, would continue indefinitely. The investment had been enormous, the infrastructure was in place, and the industrial plants had to be used or they would deteriorate. And, of course, there more votes in Texas and Louisiana where the new petrochemical industry was based than in Costa Rica and Colombia. In the fall of 1953, when the rubber program was cancelled, federal officials declared brashly that natural rubber had no future and was no longer of strategic importance.

For thirty years it seemed as though the bureaucrats had been right. Each year synthetic rubber captured a larger share of the market. Economists expected the trend to continue, and most predicted that natural rubber would be reduced to a historical footnote. They were wrong. The first blow to synthetic rubber came with the 1973 OPEC oil embargo, which quadrupled the price of raw materials for the industry.

Soaring oil prices also made consumers far more conscious of gas mileage, leading to a second and far more serious challenge to synthetic rubber: the rapid and widespread adoption of the radial tire.

Until 1968 over 90 per cent of vehicles in America ran on bias-ply tires, the same fundamental technology that had been in place since 1900. The radial tire was a radical departure. By placing the cords within the fabric of the tire at 90 degrees to the direction travelled, and later adding a steel belt for strength, engineers at Michelin created a tire that performed better, saved gas (because of its greater rigidity) and lasted twice as long. Once radials caught on in America, they swept the market, and by 1993 they accounted for 95 per cent of sales. This development provided an immense boost for the plantation industry, for only natural rubber has the strength required for the sidewalts, and the adhesive qualities necessary for the steel belt of radial tires. Here was a technological breakthrough no had predicted.

By 1996 natural rubber had reclaimed some 40 per cent of the international elastomer market, and synthetic rubber's share had declined for ten consecutive years. The United States, importing more than a million tonnes a year at cost of $1.7 billion, was more dependent on natural rubber than at any time in the previous forty years.

Washington had become concerned. Already in 1985, the National Defense Stockpile policy office had commissioned a study from Smithers Scientific Services of Akron, the largest and most highly regarded independent testing and consulting laboratory dedicated to the tire and rubber industry, on what would happen if the supply of natural rubber were to be compromised. In charge of the project for the government was industry economist Larry Hall.

"Basically, we wanted to know what would happen in a wartime scenario," Hall recalled in his office at the Federal Emergency Management Agency. "How important was natural rubber? What would be the impact of a cut off in supply on specific end use items, actual tires and other products?"

In May 1985 Smithers delivered to FEMA a document entitled "Report on the Substitutability of Synthetic and Natural Rubbers in a Wartime Mobilization." Described by Hall as the best study ever conducted on a strategic product, the document presented several disturbing conclusions. The natural rubber in a car tire could conceivably be replaced, provided the consumer was prepared to sacrifice performance and to purchase tires more often. But as demand on a tire increases, so does the importance of natural rubber. A pickup trucks tire is 50 per cent natural. The enormous tires of industrial machines are 90 per cent. So are the truck tires that carry half of America's freight. Seventy-seven per cent of all communities in the U.S. are serviced exclusively by the trucking industry, economic activity that generates $362 billion in gross revenues, roughly 5 per cent of the Gross Domestic Product. Every semi rolling down the interstate does so on rubber scraped from a tree.

The tires of every commercial and military aircraft, from the 747 to the B-2 bomber and the space shuttle, are made almost entirely of natural rubber. There is no viable substitute, no product that can match the resilience, tensile strength, and resistance to abrasion and impact. Only vulcanized natural rubber can withstand the rapid transition from the freezing temperatures of high altitude to the sudden heat of touchdown on the runway. Peter Roman, director of the Defense National Stockpile Centre (as it is now called), summed up the importance of natural rubber: "All I can tell you is this—I sure as hell wouldn't want to be in a 747 about to land on synthetic tires."

Transportation is just the beginning. There are a score of other critical needs, the most vital being human health. In the last decade, with the AIDS epidemic and the increased demand for surgical gloves and condoms, consumption of natural rubber in the medical sector has doubled. Rubbers ability to adhere to steel and glass, and to withstand heat and steam in sterilization, also makes it essential for the production of surgical tubing, blood stoppers, catheters, syringe tips and other pharmaceutical products. According to the Smithers report, there is no viable substitute. One manufacturer of drug sundries interviewed by Smithers noted flatly that without natural rubber, his operations would cease immediately, and it would be two years before he could retool his production lines and test a substitute and no doubt inferior product.

To the saga of natural rubber has been added a new chapter, a story of renewed dependence, and the very real possibility that demand will outrun supply. Economists no longer predict the demise of the industry. Instead, they forecast shortages and anticipate dramatic increases in price—even assuming that the leaf blight can be kept at bay. In the short history of its domestication, the rubber tree has proved remarkably responsive; yields have increased from 90 to 600 kilograms per 4000 square metres, with experimental plantings producing even more. Driven largely by the spread of high-yielding clones, international production reached nearly 6 million tonnes in 1995. But it is not at all clear how much higher it can go.

"Far greater yields will require a quantum leap in harvesting technology," notes Kevin Jones of the International Rubber Research and Development Board. No such innovation appears imminent.

Nor is it clear that the nations that have traditionally produced rubber will continue to do so. Asia, source of virtually all the world's supply, is in the midst of a massive economic transformation. For years Malaysia was the leading grower. But as the country industrialized, land values soared, and many planters converted to the more lucrative oil palm. Competition for labour became intense. Rubber was associated with the colonial past, and few workers wanted to collect latex if given the option, say, to build cars. Since 1988 rubber production in Malaysia has dropped nearly 40 per cent, and the trend is expected to continue.

Thailand, now the world's largest producer, has its own problems. Much of the surge in natural rubber production in recent years has been fuelled by Thailand's spectacular success in replanting high-yielding clones. But most of this work has been done. The best rubber-growing lands are in the southern peninsula, where land is limited and expensive, and tourism is booming. Many Thais would rather work in a resort than on a plantation. There is room for growth in Indonesia, but with its history of corruption and failed economic schemes, optimism is in short supply. Rubber production is expanding in Cambodia and Vietnam, and the Chinese now have 1700 square kilometres of plantations in Yunnan. New sources of supply could emerge outside Asia—in West Africa, for example—but it would be a decade at least before production could begin, even if the trees were planted tomorrow. Firestone's plantations in war-torn Liberia have been out of business since 1990 when rubber production fell 98 per cent in nine months.

Demand, meanwhile, is only increasing. The shift to radials is still underway, especially for truck and bus tires, and particularly in India, Mexico, Brazil and other developing countries. By the year 2000 the number of bias tires currently produced will drop by half, and the world will run on radials.

Global patterns of consumption are being transformed. The economic boom in Southeast Asia has led the rubber-producing nations to consume more and export less, even as vast markets for natural rubber ˅en up in China and India. In 1960 Asia consumed 12 per cent of the international production of elastomers. Today the figure is 43 per cent and rising. Within the next twenty-five years, the urban population of the Asia Pacific region will double, and the number of private cars is expected to increase nearly 600 per cent. Add to this Russia and Eastern Europe, which became major consumers of natural rubber only with the fall of the Soviet Union. Until then they got by with limited supplies from Vietnam and with Soviet-made synthetics, which may be one reason, rubber experts suggest, for Aeroflot s abysmal safety record.

Looming over everything is the spectre of disease. A 1991 Smithers report put the matter succinctly: "If the leaf blight were to affect the crops in Southeast Asia and Africa, the world's supply of natural rubber could be devastated." Of greatest concern is the relatively narrow genetic base of the plantations, a consequence of years of vegetative propagation. History is replete with examples of exotic diseases ravaging crops. The Irish potato famine was caused by a simple fungus. Another fungus destroyed the American chestnut. In the early 1970s a leaf blight wiped out 40 per cent of the American corn crop.

The South American leaf blight can be controlled with fungicides. But chemical treatments are expensive, and it is not economically practical to use them as a preventative measure. The large estates have the resources to respond aggressively to an outbreak, but should the disease spread to the small family tracts, it will be much more difficult to contain. The lion's share of the production occurs outside the large plantations. These farmers can only hope that the blight never reaches their holdings.

Ominous as these trends appear, the risk is most likely economic dislocation, not catastrophe. If the price of natural rubber rises high enough, fungicides will be applied to the plantations, despite environmental concerns. Price increases will also encourage efforts to identify so-called "escape zones," regions of Latin America beyond the range of the blight where rubber trees can still be grown. Such areas may exist, but the concept is controversial. Many agronomists believe that the blight, which has already spread from the Amazon through Central America to Mexico, will ultimately reach everywhere rubber trees are found. So far only Guatemala has managed to produce rubber commercially, and there the plantations can be established only on the west coast, where a combination of low rainfall and prevailing winds creates a microclimate that reduces the blight's virulence. Efforts to identify and exploit escape zones elsewhere in the Americas, most notably in Brazil, have met with far less success.

The great hope of the rubber industry lies with the synthetic chemists. No one has forgotten the miracle of 1942-45, and there is a quiet confidence that scientific ingenuity unleashed by urgency will once again rise to the occasion. Of the dozens of different synthetic rubbers that have been developed since the war, only one comes close to replicating the complex polymer created by nature. Introduced commercially in 1960 and sold by Goodyear under the trade name Natsyn, it has the same empirical formula (1-4 cis-polyisoprene) and nearly the same molecular structure as natural rubber. If supplies of natural rubber are compromised, the industry will turn to synthetic polyisoprene.

But Natsyn is by no means a perfect substitute. As Bill Schloman, a rubber chemist at the University of Akron, explains: "It is the same but different. Natsyn is not a perfect structure. There is some branching (in the molecule), and this manifests itself in the final product in subtle differences in performance. Polyisoprene is what the Soviets had. They made over a million tons a year. If it's as good as natural rubber, you have to ask why they jumped to our formula of tire making as soon as they had the chance."

Cost and capacity are even bigger problems. The isoprene monomer, Natsyn's basic building block, is expensive and difficult to make. Good-year operates the only facility in North America capable of transforming it into polyisoprene. Located in Beaumont, Texas, the plant produces roughly 60000 tonnes a year, less than a sixteenth of the tonnage of natural rubber consumed annually. In an emergency, some of the factories currently making other synthetic rubbers could be converted to polyisoprene production, but this strategy would only transfer the shortage to other types of rubber. And even if every factory capable of making polyisoprene was converted, the process would take eighteen to twenty-four months and still absorb less than half of the shortfall that would result from a loss of natural rubber. And that scenario assumes adequate supplies of the isoprene monomer are available. As Bill Schloman put it, "If we needed to replace natural rubber with synthetic polyisoprene, Goodyear would have to clone its plants, as opposed to cloning its trees."

In 1942 the fate of the free world hinged on America's ability to find new sources of a commodity that had entered the economy less than a century before. Now, once again, we find ourselves dependent on a natural product certain to be in short supply in the coming years. If rubber trees in Asia begin to die, history will repeat itself. The industry will scramble to build up production capacity for polyisoprene and other synthetic stopgaps. It will try to salvage some of the crop, blanketing the plantations with toxic fungicides, overriding any environmen tal considerations.

But common sense would suggest another possibility. The path of caution, indeed of wisdom, leads back to the dream of the plant explorers who during and after the war came so close to providing South and Central America with a plantation industry. "There is still time," Ernie Imle notes. "The world cannot afford to give up on a plant that produces millions of tons of superior rubber, a crop benign to soils and the environment, a tree that at the end of its life furnishes a fine lumber to help finance the replanting of even higher yielding selections."

Scattered across the United States, living out the final years of their lives, are many of the men once dispatched into the Amazon to do the impossible. Their field notes are deposited in archives, their collections rest in herbaria. It is not too late to rekindle their work, to apply the genius of agricultural science to finding a way to develop high-yielding and blight-resistant rubber trees for the Americas. This strategy alone will end the nightmare that has loomed over the rubber industry since its inception and will assure the world of a growing supply of natural rubber adequate to meet the needs of the twenty-first century.

THE ART OF
SHAMANIC HEALING

In 1981 I was engaged in ethnobotanical work in the Northwest Amazon near the Río Ampiyacu—the river of poisons. It was the rainy season and rising waters had forced the forest animals to high ground. As a result, the Bora and Huitoto villages where I was working became infested with poisonous snakes. Late one evening, while I was writing up my field notes, a boy came to my hut, his face flushed with panic. He told me that a young man at the other end of the village had been struck by a deadly fer-de-lance and now lay dying in his mother's home.

Because of my interest in plants, the villagers assumed that I was a doctor and requested my help. By the time I arrived at the young man's side, a shaman was already hard at work, rubbing the patient with urticating nettles and blowing tobacco smoke over his brow. A small poultice of renealmia leaves covered the wound. If the shaman resented my arrival, he gave no such indication; his attention was focussed on the patient, who had begun to spit up frothy blood. I realized that both the patient and the shaman expected me to intervene, so I did my best to mimic a physician. I felt the young man's pulse, examined his wound and placed my hand on his forehead—all the time struggling to look as grave as possible.

It was a long night of serious work for the shaman and earnest gesticulations for myself. By dawn the crisis had passed and the young man's condition began to improve; his subsequent recovery was complete. Both the shaman's prestige and my reputation as a doctor were significantly enhanced—and my curiosity aroused. Was either of us in any way responsible for the patient's recovery? Neither of us had interacted with him in a manner that a scientist would define as meaningful, and at no time had we physically extracted the venom from his wound. However, there was a vast difference between my antics and the ritual behaviour of the shaman, who invoked a spiritual tradition that reached back millennia. Was it possible that he had actively assisted the patient in other, less tangible ways? If so, what had been the nature and essence of his therapy?

A year or two later I found myself in central Haiti, living at the temple of a prominent *mambo*, or Vodoun priestess, noted for her skills as a healer. One day a young woman arrived at the temple, carrying a chicken. After two years of marriage, she had yet to conceive a child. That evening the mambo invoked the gods, calling forth the spirit Erzulie, the goddess of love. Erzulie took possession of the patient's body and proceeded to slice the chicken's neck and offer to the earth a gift of blood, the vital essence that brings forth life. The spirit then left and the young woman collapsed. Two months later she became pregnant.

Years later, in North Africa, I met a Moroccan *sherifa* family, descendants of the prophet Mohammed, who told me of a mystical experience involving their daughter. As a young girl, she had fallen into a coma after a mysterious stranger had entered her home. Though no expense had been spared, every medical treatment had failed. Then, after the family had given up all hope of breaking the sorcerer's spell, another stranger appeared, touched the sleeping girl and left. The girl recovered on the following day. The family attributed her miraculous healing to her grandfather's prayers and the intervention and blessing of the wandering holy man.

These anecdotes, drawn from a decade of ethnographic and ethnobotanical field research, have one important theme in common. In each case, the healing process was facilitated by a recognized specialist whose power was derived not from an ability to manipulate the body but from a culturally perceived capacity to intervene directly on the spiritual or nonmaterial plane. This ability to mediate personally between the ordinary world and other realms of spirits and supernatural forces—a profound skill evident around the world in a thousand distinct and culturally rooted manifestations of the human imagination—lies at the very heart of the art of shamanic healing.

Shamanism is, arguably, the oldest of human spiritual endeavours, born at the dawn of our species' awareness. For our Paleolithic ancestors, death was the first teacher, the first pain, the edge beyond which life, as they knew it, ended, and wonder began. Religion was nursed by mystery, but it was born of the hunt, from the need on the part of humans to rationalize the fact that to live they had to kill that which they most revered, the animals that gave them life. Hunting myths developed as an expression of the covenant between animals and humans, a means of eliminating the guilt of the hunt and maintaining a certain essential balance between the living and the spirits of the animal dead. Illness, so often the harbinger of human death, lay heavily upon primitive hunters, a foreboding disruption of the normal processes of life that brought in its wake fever and delirium, perhaps madness and despair. Coming to terms with the inexorable separation of death and understanding the source of illness and disease were undoubtedly among the earliest of human intellectual and spiritual pursuits.

The shamanic intuition emerged from this ancient era, and, even today, shamanism is practised most commonly by individuals in small egalitarian hunting and gathering societies. The agrarian transformation and the advent of sedentary village life, which led in turn to the first organized religious hierarchies, generally meant the end of shamanic traditions. As agriculture overthrew the hunt, so the priest displaced the shaman. With religious leaders serving as mere functionaries of established religious theologies, the shaman's poetry was turned into prose.

For, unlike the priest who is a socially inducted and initiated member of a recognized religious organization, the shaman is one who, as a consequence of a completely personal psychological crisis, has gained a certain power of his or her own. Whereas the priest is concerned with integrating the individual into a firmly ordered and well established social context, the shaman seeks the release of his or her own wild genius, wherever that may lead. Almost invariably, an overwhelming mental crisis is part of the vocational summons. Indeed, for the seeker of shamanic wisdom, it is a fine line between mystical initiation and psychological breakdown.

Yet, though this crisis may resemble a mental breakdown, it cannot be dismissed as one. For it is not a pathological but a normal event for the gifted mind in these societies, the realization and intuition of a level of spiritual depth that gives the world a sacred character. In seeking the solitary vision, the shaman breaks not with the other traditions of his tribe but with the comparatively trivial attitude toward the spirit realm that seems to satisfy the majority. By following this most difficult path, the shaman becomes a master of death and resurrection, of health and well-being.

Before attempting to understand how extraordinary healing abilities manifest themselves in certain small indigenous societies, we must first recognize that a chasm exists between the spiritual world of the shaman and our own secular tradition, in which science, as author Saul Bellow put it, "has made a housecleaning of belief." For the modern physician, medicine is a science and, like all sciences, it is based on an intellectual tradition that, at least since Descartes, has molded the Western worldview. According to our scientific paradigm, phenomena that cannot be positively observed or measured cannot exist. As a result, Western medicine has come to view the body essentially as a machine, an exceedingly complex mechanism that can be understood and, as appropriate, modified and repaired. Specificity is the tradition's greatest asset. As long as there is a discrete disease vector that can be identified and eliminated, or an acute trauma that may be surgically addressed, modern medicine is unsurpassed. As a doctor friend of mine always says, anyone who severs a limb wants to be taken to a modern emergency room, not to a herbalist.

Indeed, the development within the last century of a modern, scientific system of medicine represents one of the greatest episodes in human endeavour. The achievements are astonishing: the elimination of diseases through immunology, parasitology, and the discovery of antibiotic drugs and vitamins; the advances in surgery made possible by antiseptics and anesthesia; and the discovery of insulin and human growth hormones. To appreciate the significance of this revolution in knowledge, we need only recall that, as recently as 1919, an outbreak of influenza took the lives of over 15 million people, many more than died during the First World War.

Yet the narrow focus of modern medicine is both a strength and a weakness. In much of the world, Western medicine is too expensive, unavailable or presented in a way that is inconsistent with traditional beliefs. What is more, there is an increasing sense that certain ancient and esoteric healing practices, long ignored by modern science, may in fact represent profound insights into the very nature of well-being.

Long before the miraculous dexterity of modern surgery, before the development of medical technologies, men and women sought the source of illness and the elixir of good health. The Chinese, who discovered smallpox immunization a thousand years before Europeans did, saw humankind as a mirror of the universe, infused with *ch'i*, vital energy that courses through channels in the body. Disease, by definition, involved impediments placed in this flow of cosmic energy. Treatment called for the ch'i to be redirected, and this led to the practice of acupuncture. The main diagnostic of the Chinese was the pulse, and the procedure was so complex that it took a trained practitioner more than three hours to obtain a reading. From this, the healer made remarkable predictions, identifying the site of a disease or forecasting the time of anticipated recovery. Early European diagnostics were somewhat cruder. The practice of tapping a patient s lungs to check for fluid levels was devised by a Viennese physician, the son of an inn-keeper who used the method to gauge the level in his wine casks.

For patients in these early days, treatment could be worse than any conceivable ailment. In pre-Columbian Peru, holes were cut into the skulls of the living to provide diseases with an avenue of escape. Cosmetic surgery began in ancient India, where the standard punishment for adultery was the amputation of the nose; primitive surgical techniques grew out of attempts to graft pieces of the cheek to the stump. As late as the eighteenth century, Europeans and Americans believed that bad blood was the source of disease. Benjamin Rush, an American physician and signer of the Declaration of Independence, bled one patient eighty-five times in six months. George Washington's doctors, on the day that he died, drained at least four pints of blood from his veins, having already given him a large dose of mercury—his only ail-ment was a sore throat. Early in this century, physicians latched onto radioactivity as a panacea. Leather belts that had pouches designed to hold chunks of radioactive ore over the kidneys came into vogue. Water coolers were designed to ensure that hospital patients had a constant supply of radioactive water. Such folly persists to this day, exemplified by the more subtle, but, in fact, more pernicious, practice of dispensing antibiotics in the treatment of viral ailments.

However ridiculous, and indeed horrendous, some of these interventions now appear, in their time they were considered the apogee of medical knowledge. No doubt they were administered with the same professional confidence we have come to expect from our own doctors. Given this checkered history, it behooves us to be wary of our own hubris, particularly our tendency to dismiss, out of hand, healing practices that we know nothing about. This is especially important when we consider that almost 90 per cent of the world's population depends on traditional healers for their basic medical needs.

In contemporary secular society, life and death are defined in strictly clinical terms that are determined by physicians, and the fate of the spirit is relegated to the domain of religious specialists who, significantly, have nothing to say about the physical well-being of the living. By contrast, in most shamanic traditions, the physician is also the priest, and the condition of the spirit is as important as—and, in fact, determines—the body's physical state.

Shamanic medicine is based on a non-Western conception of the etiology of disease, in which health is defined as a coherent state of equilibrium between the physical and spiritual components of the individual. Sickness is disruption, imbalance and the manifestation of malevolent forces in the flesh. Health is a state of harmony, and, for the shaman, it is something holy, like a perfect reunion with the gods. The maintenance or restoration of this balance is the shaman's duty, and it accounts for his or her unique role as healer.

As a form of medicine, shamanic healing does not ignore the existence of pathogens; it simply notes that pathogens are present in the environment at all times and then focusses, instead, on why certain individuals succumb when they do. Good or bad health results not just from the presence or absence of pathogens but from the proper or improper balance of the individual. Shamanic medicine consequently operates on two quite different levels—the spiritual and the physical.

Typically, shaman recognize an entire range of ailments that may be treated symptomatically, much as is done in Western medicine, and they use medicinal plants and folk preparations, many of which are pharmacologically active. From the shamanic perspective, however, purely physical ailments that can be treated with herbal remedies are less serious than the troubles that arise when the spiritual harmony of an individual is disturbed. Because disharmony will affect all aspects of me individual's life, he or she may surfer from both physical and psychological ailments, as well as from other troubles such as chronic bad luck, marital stress or financial difficulties. In such cases it is the source of the disorder, not its particular manifestation, that must be treated—and that responsibility falls strictly within the domain of the religious specialist.

Restoring the patient's health may involve a number of techniques. At the material level, treatments may include herbal baths and massage, administration of medicinal plants, physical isolation of the patient in a sacred space and, in certain traditions, animal sacrifice, whereby the patient returns to the earth a gift of life's vital energy. But, invariably, it is intervention on the spiritual plane that ultimately determines the patient's fate, and for this the healer must employ a specific technique of ecstasy to achieve an altered consciousness. Indeed, the very power of a shaman rests in the ability to enter a trance. Critically, the shaman is never a victim of that trance. Rather, he or she commands it, deftly utilizing the rhythm of the drums, the power of dance or some other means to elevate the spirit to those distant realms where spiritual healing takes place.

Tibetan healers mediate the fate of their patients by ritualistically transforming themselves into Tantric deities capable of influencing the passage of time. For Native American shaman, the vehicle to the gods may be the sweat lodge, the pain of ordeal, the rhythm of sacred drums or the arrows of magical plants. The Huichol of Mexico ingest peyote, the tracks of the little deer, in order to take on the identity of ancestral gods. The Tukanoan peoples of the Northwest Amazon drink a bitter preparation known as *yagé* or *ayahuasca,* the vine of the soul, in order to confer with the spirits of the forest. Yanomami shaman in the Venezuelan Amazon inhale *epená,* the semen of the sun, an extremely potent hallucinogen derived from the resin of several trees in the nutmeg family. In the high Andes of Peru, traditional healers, or *curanderos,* divine the future and diagnose ailments by reading coca leaves, a sacred practice reserved for those who have survived a lightning strike.

In virtually all Native American healing traditions, the role of the shaman is pivotal. As the repository of tribal lore, the shaman weaves a protective cloak of ritual around the patient, gives metaphysical form to subtle visionary stimuli and skilfully interprets a complex body of belief—all in order to rebalance the forces of the universe. For the people of these societies, there is no rigid separation between the sacred and the secular. Every act of the healer becomes a prayer, every ritual a form of collective preventative medicine.

The idea that true healing occurs on a spiritual plane accessed through trance states is also prevalent in West African and Afro-Caribbean cultures. In Haiti, for example, acolytes of the Vodoun faith move in and out of the spirit realm with an impunity that has always impressed ethnographic observers. In place of psychoactive drugs, however, the conduit to the gods is spirit possession. As in Native American traditions, health is considered a matter of equilibrium. Disease and misfortune result from disharmony, more often than not caused by sorcery, the vehicle for the dark forces of the universe. Counteracting these forces and achieving balance between good and evil is not only the central duty of the Voudoun priest, it is the fundamental goal of the religion and, indeed, of most traditional healing practices.

One of the most impressive manifestations of the Vodoun faith is the capacity of possessed initiates to endure extremes of pain and exposure to fire. In Haiti, I frequently observed possessed individuals dance on fire and place burning embers in their mouths without suffering physical damage. For Vodounists, this remarkable ability is but a logical extension of their belief system. When possessed, one is a god, and a god, by definition, cannot be harmed.

In many religious societies, acolytes affirm their faith by exposing themselves to fire. In Brazil, hundreds of Japanese celebrate the Buddha's birthday by walking across beds of burning coals. In Greece, tourists regularly watch firewalkers at the village of Ayia Eleni; these Orthodox Christians believe that the presence of St. Constantine protects them. Firewalking occurs in many traditions throughout Asia and the Far East. People have been documented walking unharmed across beds of coals that have been measured at temperatures up to 315 degrees Celsius.

What is fascinating about the phenomenon of firewalking is not its sensational character but rather what it says about human potential. That individuals remain physically unharmed when exposed to temperatures that would—and do—result in serious damage if experienced in ordinary states of consciousness has profound implications. It suggests that trance states may potentiate certain innate yet exceptional powers of the mind. Though the exact mechanism remains to be identified, the remarkable ability to withstand fire appears to lie in areas of mind/body interaction that neurophysiologists have yet to fathom.

The ability to walk on fire and to handle burning embers are but examples of human potential unleashed by profound states of altered consciousness. Numerous reputable observers have witnessed the capacity of individuals in trance states to endure physical mutilation with no apparent signs of pain: Tu shaman pierce their cheeks with spikes, and Filipino healers allow nails to be driven through their feet and hands. Other remarkable feats are often associated with extreme states of spiritual excitation: Korean *mudang* walk on sharp knives; Tibetan *tumo* practitioners are able to withstand freezing temperatures for long periods of time; and some Hindu yogis can consciously slow their breathing and heart rates to almost imperceptible levels.

Once we accept the reality of firewalking and other extraordinary abilities, it does not require a great leap of faith to understand how shamanic rituals may be capable of eliciting unexpected physiological responses, particularly when both the healer and the patient share an absolute faith in the practice. Moreover, the fact that individuals in our secular culture have been able to induce trance states that allow them to walk on hot coals without harm, suggests the exciting possibility that all humans might share the same latent potential. Taking advantage of this potential, and using altered states of consciousness to manipulate the human capacity, is precisely what the higher levels of shamanic healing are all about.

At the core of shamanic medicine is the conviction that the mind can affect the body that bears it. In the West, we embrace this notion in the term *psychosomatic*, which does not mean fake but rather is derived from the Greek words for "mind" and "body." Intuitively, we know there is something to this. No one falls ill the day after falling in love. Many of us become sick in the wake of intense emotional stress. Still, even as we accept that the psychological and biological components of the individual are two parts of a whole, the weight of our own tradition leaves many of us quietly skeptical. Not so the Haitian or the Amazonian Indian. Shamanic healing in these cultures becomes potent precisely because of the power and authority of their beliefs.

Those who serve the gods in Haiti or ingest ayahuasca under an Amazonian sky move through a metaphysical landscape that is alive and that responds in a multitude of ways to their spiritual readiness. They believe that spirits are real, that souls exist, that magic has potency. Critically, the inevitable cognitive steps that their societies take, and must take, to protect those beliefs from doubt give rise to closed, circular systems of thought. All their magical and mystical ideas weave together into a web that is not an external structure in which these believers are trapped but is rather the very texture of their thoughts. They cannot think that their thoughts are wrong. Even if they were skeptics, they could express their doubts only in the terms of the beliefs shared by all their peers.

The shaman and his or her people therefore share a set of magical ideas which form a collective worldview that dominates the psychological and physical experience of any one individual. A world of few alternatives, however, not only makes for an absolute acceptance of established tenets but also assures that they have an absolute and exclusive validity. There is no incentive for agnosticism. Within these confines, the believer can manoeuvre with some intellectual ingenuity, but beyond the limits of belief, there is only chaos.

Needless to say, most shamanic ideas concerning the nature of disease and healing are not currently endorsed by the medical establishment. Many of the ideas that lie at the very core of shamanic healing—ideas concerning the spiritual realm, mind/body interactions, and the interplay among humanity, the environment and the cosmos—are summarily dismissed by Western medicine because they do not fit into its scientific model, even though some of these themes nourished the roots of our own healing tradition and remain profound metaphysical questions.

For many, there is a growing intuition that the art of healing involves not only a scientific understanding of the mechanisms of the body but a consideration of other less tangible issues. To the shaman, health and illness involve complicated mysteries that lie at the heart of existence— mysteries of balance, of the mind, of faith and belief, of death and the dream of rebirth. No doubt people throughout the world will continue to benefit from modern medicine. But medicine, in turn, will gain by drawing into its fold new possibilities, lessons derived from traditional healers who, lacking the technical ability to dissect the human body, learned long ago to embrace the human being as a whole.

PLANTS OF
THE GODS

Many years ago, while living among the Barasana Indians on the banks of the Río Piraparana in the Northwest Amazon of Colombia, I was invited one night to drink *ayahuasca*, the vine of the soul, the most revered and celebrated of Amazonian shamanic preparations. The tribal leader, a man named Rufino, described it as the jaguar's nectar, a magical intoxicant that could free the soul, allowing one to wander in mystical encounters with ancestors and animal spirits. He cautioned that the potion, like any sacred medicine, could be many things, but pleasant was not one of them.

We were sitting on four small wooden stools placed around the men's circle in the *maloca*, the community longhouse. Rufino, like his father, Pedro, was wearing a loincloth, as was a third man whose name was Pacho. All three had carefully decorated their bodies, tracing lines of red and black dye on their faces, and painting their legs with small wooden rollers which left geometric patterns on the skin. Each wore a seed anklet and a simple headdress that had a corona of green and yellow parrot feathers, tufts of eagle down and a long tail feather taken from a scarlet macaw. In the centre of the circle was a large red ceramic vessel, with swirling designs around the rim. Inside was a frothy liquid. Near the base of the pot were rattles, panpipes and other musical instruments made from turtle shells and deer skulls. Already the men had danced, shoulder to shoulder in a line, singing as they circled the pillars of the longhouse. Now they waited quietly. The women and children had long since retired, and the only light came from a resin torch burning at the base of one of the house posts.

Pedro stood up and began a solemn chant. When it was over, he dipped a black calabash into the ayahuasca and passed it to his son.

Rufino grimaced as he drank the potion, as did we all. The taste was bitter and nauseating. There followed more singing and dancing, high tremulous voices, and the sound of rattles and anklets. Then always a hush of expectation as Pedro prepared the next allotment of the brew.

I sat quietly among them, unable to participate yet conscious of the power and authority of their ritual. The plant took them first. In soft murmurs, Rufino spoke of a red sun, a red sky, a red rain falling over the forest. Nausea came quickly and he vomited. Immediately, Pedro offered another draught of ayahuasca, which Rufino took, spitting and gasping. Until then I had felt nothing, but the sound of his retching caused me to turn aside and throw up in the dirt. Pacho laughed and then did the same. We all took more ayahuasca, several more cycles. An hour or more passed. I looked up and saw the edges of the world soften, and felt a resonance coming from beyond the sky, like the intimation of a hovering wind, pulsating with energy.

At first it was pleasant, a wondrous sense of life and warmth enveloping all things. But then the sensations intensified, became charged with a strange current, and the air itself took on a metallic density. Soon the world as I knew it no longer existed. Reality was not distorted, it was dissolved, as the terror of another dimension swept over the senses. The beauty of colours, the endless patterns of orblike brilliance, were as rain falling away from my skin. I caught myself and looked up, saw Rufino and Pacho gently swaying and moaning. There were rainbows trapped inside their feathered headdresses. In their hair were weeping flowers and trees attempting to soar into the clouds. Leaves fell from the branches, with great howling sounds. The sky opened. There was a livid scar across the heavens, stars throbbing, a great wind scattering everything in its path. Then the ground opened. Snakes encircled the posts of the maloca and slipped away into the earth. The rivers unfolded like the mouths of blossoms. Movement became penetration. Then the terror grew stronger, as did my sense of hopeless fragility. Death hovered all around. Ravenous children, and animals of every shape and form, lay sick and dying of thirst. Their nostrils plunged into the dry earth. Their flanks lay bare and exposed. And all around rose a canopy of immense sorrows.

I tried to shake away the forms from the luminous sensations. Instead, my thoughts themselves turned into visions, not of things or places but of an entire dimension that in the moment seemed not only real but absolute. This was the actual world, and what I had known until then was a crude and opaque facsimile. I looked up and saw my companions. Rufino and Pacho sat quietly, heads down, hunched around a fire that had not been there before. Pedro stood apart, arms outspread as he sang. His face was upturned, and his feathered corona shone like the sun. His eyes were brilliant, radiant, feverish, as if focussed into the very nature of things.

Slowly, as the night moved forward, the colours faded and the terror receded. I felt my hands running over the dirt floor of the maloca, saw dust tinged with green light, heard the voices of women laughing. Dawn was coming. I could hear it in the forest. My companions remained by the hearth, but the fire had died and the air was cold. I stood and stretched my muscles. Tired but no longer afraid, I slipped into my hammock. For the longest time I lay awake, wrapped in a cotton blanket, like a drained child waiting to sweat out the end of a fever. The last thing I saw before drifting off to sleep was a placid cloud of violet light softly descending on the maloca.

Some hours later, I was awakened by the roar of an airplane passing just over the roof of the longhouse. I looked up and saw narrow shafts of light cutting through the thatch. My head ached and I was thirsty, but other than that I was fine. I felt clean, as if my body had been washed inside and out. Sitting up, I found myself surrounded by young boys who followed me outside into the sunlight and down the path that led to the river. The water was cool and refreshing, delicious to drink. There was a shout and one of the boys pointed to the riverbank. It was the missionary pilot who had dropped me off at the village a fortnight earlier. Beside him stood Rufino and his father. They had packed away their regalia, but their legs still bore decorative motifs and black genipa dye was smeared across their faces. The pilot had his hands on his hips.

"Gone native have we," he called out. "I wouldn't touch that water if I was you."

"You're early," I said.

"Actually, I'm two days late."

"Oh."

"Well, come on then. I don't have all day. I've got to be in Miraflores by noon."

It made for an awkward departure. I gathered my gear and specimens, left what remained of the trade goods with Rufino, and within twenty minutes was airborne, soaring above the maloca and over the forest toward the small town of Mitú. The sudden shift in perspective was startling. The streams fell behind, grew into rivers, and the rivers spread like serpents through a silent and unchanging forest. Rufino had likened ayahuasca to a river, a journey that takes one above the land and below the water to the most remote reaches of the Earth, where the animal masters live and lightning is waiting to be born. To drink ayahuasca, anthropologist Gerardo Reichel-Dolmatoff once wrote, is to return to the cosmic uterus and be reborn. It is to tear through the placenta of ordinary perception and enter realms where death can be known and life traced through sensation to the primordial source of all existence. When shaman speak of facing down the jaguar, it is because they really do.

On Earth, there are some eight hundred thousand species of plants feeding on the light of the sun. Of these, only a few thousand yield food and medicines, and only a mere hundred or so contain the compounds that transport the mind to distant realms of ethereal wonder. Strictly speaking, a hallucinogen is any chemical substance that distorts the senses and produces hallucinations—perceptions or experiences mat depart dramatically from ordinary reality. Academics call these drugs *psychotomimetics* (psychosis mimickers), *psychotaraxics* (mind disturbers) and *psychedelics* (mind manifesters). These dry terms quite inadequately describe the remarkable effects the compounds have on the human mind. Indeed, the sensations are so unearthly, the visions so startling, that most hallucinogenic plants acquired a sacred place in indigenous cultures. In rare cases, they were worshipped as gods incarnate.

The pharmacological activity of the hallucinogens arises from a relatively small number of chemical compounds. While modern chemistry has been able, in most cases, to successfully duplicate these substances or even to manipulate their chemical structures to produce novel synthetic forms, nearly all such drugs have their origins in plants. In the plant kingdom, they occur only among the advanced flowering plants and the more primitive spore-bearing fungi. Most hallucinogens are alkaloids, a family of about five thousand complex organic molecules that also account for the biological activity of most toxic and many medicinal plants. These active compounds may be found in various concentrations in different parts of the plant—root, leaves, seeds, bark and flowers—and they may be absorbed by the human body in a number of ways, as is evident in the wide variety of folk preparations. Psychoactive plants have been smoked or snuffed, swallowed fresh or dried, drunk in decoctions and infusions, absorbed directly through the skin, placed in wounds or administered as enemas.

In the worldwide distribution of hallucinogens, there is a remarkable anomaly that illustrates the role that they play in traditional societies. Of the 120 or more such plants found to date, over 100 are native to the Americas; the rest of the world has contributed fewer than 20. In part, this uneven distribution is a reflection of the emphasis of academic research. A good many of these plants were first documented by my former professor Richard Evans Schultes and his students at the Harvard Botanical Museum and elsewhere. His interest has been predominantly in the New World. Still, were the hallucinogenic plants a dominant feature of traditional cultures in Eurasia, Africa, Australia and the South Pacific, surely they would have shown up in the extensive ethnographic literature and in the journals of traders and missionaries. With few notable exceptions, they do not. Nor is this discrepancy due to floristic peculiarities. The rain forests of West Africa and Southeast Asia, in particular, are exceedingly rich and diverse. Moreover, the peoples of these regions have most successfully explored them for pharmacologically active compounds for use both as medicines and poisons. In fact, as much as any other material trait, the manipulation of toxic plants is a consistent theme throughout sub-Saharan African societies.

The Amerindians, for their part, were certainly no strangers to plant toxins. They commonly exploited them as fish, arrow and dart poisons. Yet while the peoples of Africa consistently used these toxic preparations on each other, the Amerindians almost never did. And whereas the Amerindians successfully explored their forests for hallucinogens, the Africans did not. The use of any pharmacologically active plant is firmly rooted in culture. If the African peoples did not exploit their environment for psychoactive drugs, it is because they had no cultural need or desire to do so. In many Amerindian societies, by contrast, the use of plant hallucinogens lies at the very heart of traditional life.

In searching for hallucinogenic plants, indigenous peoples have shown extraordinary ingenuity. In experimenting with them, they have demonstrated signs of pharmacological genius. They have also, quite evidently, taken great personal risks. Peyote *(Lophophora williamsii)*, for example, has as many as thirty active constituents, mostly alkaloids, and is exceedingly bitter, not unlike most poisonous plants. Yet the Huichol, Tarahumara and numerous other peoples of Mexico and the

American Southwest discovered that, sun-dried and eaten whole, the cactus produces considerable psychoactive effects.

With similar tenacity, the Mazatec of Oaxaca discovered, in a mushroom flora that contains numerous deadly species, two dozen that are hallucinogenic. These, they believed, had ridden to Earth upon thunderbolts and were reverently gathered at the time of the new moon. Elsewhere in Oaxaca, the seeds of a morning glory (*Turbina corymbosa*) were crushed and prepared as a decoction that we now know contained alkaloids closely related to LSD. This was *ololiuqui*, the vine of the serpent, a sacred preparation of the Aztec.

The group of plants that shaman approach with the greatest trepidation are in the potato family, species of *Datura* and *Brugmansia*— the Holy Flowers of the North Star and the Trees of the Evil Eagle. These plants contain tropane alkaloids that, though useful in the treatment of asthma, can in higher dosage induce a frightening state of psychotic delirium marked by burning thirst and visions of hellfire, and ultimately stupor and death. Sorcerers among the Yaqui of northern Mexico anoint their genitals, legs and feet with a salve based on crushed datura leaves and thus experience the sensation of flight. Many believe that the Yaqui acquired this practice from the Spaniards, for throughout medieval Europe, witches commonly rubbed their bodies with hallucinogenic ointments made from belladonna, mandrake, henbane and datura. In fact, much of the behaviour associated with witches is as readily attributable to these drugs as to any spiritual communion with demons. For women, a particularly efficient means of self-administering the drug is through the moist tissue of the vagina; the witch's broomstick or staff was considered a most effective applicator. The common image of a haggard woman on a broomstick comes from the belief that the witches rode their staffs each midnight to the sabbat, the orgiastic assembly of demons and sorcerers. It now appears that their journey was not through space but across the hallucinatory landscape of their own minds.

Lowland South America has provided several important and chemically fascinating hallucinogenic preparations, notably the intoxicating *yopo* and *epená* snuffs of the upper Orinoco in Venezuela and adjacent Brazil, and *ayahuasca*, found commonly among the rain forest peoples of the Northwest Amazon. Yopo is prepared from a tall forest tree, *Anadenanthera peregrina*, in the bean family. The seeds are roasted and ground into a fine powder, which is then mixed with some alkaline substance, often the ashes of certain leaves.

The sacred powder known as epená, the semen of the sun, is a tryptamine-based hallucinogen that induces not merely the suspension of reality but the complete dissolution of the material world as we know it. The source of this most remarkable hallucinogen is the blood-red resin found in several tree species in the genus *Virol·* of the nutmeg family. Preparations vary. The nomadic Makú ingest the resin directly, while other tribes, notably the Huitoto and Bora, swallow pellets made from a paste of the resin. The drug is taken as a snuff by the Barasana, Makuna, Tukano, Kabuyaré, Kuripako and Puinave of eastern Colombia, and various groups of the Yanomami in the upper Orinoco. To prepare the snuff, the bark is removed from the trees in early morning, and the soft inner layers are scraped off. The shavings are kneaded in cold water, which is subsequently filtered and boiled down to a thick syrup that, when dried, is pulverized and mixed with the ashes of the bark of wild cacao. As with many shamanic preparations, several admixture plants may be added to enhance the snuff.

In the case of ayahuasca, it is the sophistication of the preparation that is most impressive. The drug is derived from two species of forest lianas, *Banisteriopsis inebriam* and, more commonly, *Banisteriopsis caapi*. The potion is made in various ways, but generally the fresh bark is scraped from the stem and boiled for several hours until a thick, bitter liquid is produced. The active compounds are the beta-carbolines harmine and harmaline, whose subjective effects are suggested by the fact that, when first isolated, they were known as telepathine. Taken alone, an infusion of the plant induces subtle visions, blues and purples, slow undulating waves of colour.

Long ago, however, the shaman of the Northwest Amazon discovered that the effects could be dramatically enhanced by the addition of a number of subsidiary plants. This practice is an important feature of many folk preparations and it stems, in part, from the fact that different chemical compounds in relatively small concentrations may effectively potentiate one another. In the case of ayahuasca, some twenty-one admixtures have been identified to date. These include roots and leaves, the bark of lianas, flowers and seeds derived from a host of species in a wide range of botanical families. Two of the admixtures are of particular interest. *Psychotria viridis* is a shrub in the coffee family. *Diplopterys cabrerana* is a forest liana closely related to ayahuasca, *Banisteriopsis caapi*. Unlike ayahuasca, both these plants contain tryptamines, powerful psychoactive compounds that when smoked or snuffed induce a very rapid, brief and intense intoxication marked by astonishing visual imagery. Taken orally, however, these potent compounds have no effect because they are denatured by an enzyme, monoamine oxidase (MAO), found in the human gut. Tryptamines can be taken orally only if combined with a MAO inhibitor. Amazingly, the beta-carbolines found in ayahuasca are inhibitors of precisely this sort. Thus, when ayahuasca is combined with either one of these plants, the result is a powerful synergistic effect, a biochemical version of the whole that is greater than the sum of the parts. The visions, as the Indians say, become brighter, and the blue and purple hues are augmented by the full spectrum of the rainbow.

When I first witnessed and experienced this remarkable example of shamanic alchemy, what astonished me was less the raw effects of the drug—stunning as they were—than the intellectual process underlying the creation of these complex preparations. The Amazonian flora contains literally tens of thousands of species. How did the Indians learn to identify and combine in such a sophisticated manner these morphologically dissimilar plants with such unique and complementary chemical properties? The standard scientific explanation, trial and error, may well account for certain innovations; but at another level, it is but a euphemism disguising the fact that ethnobotanists have very little idea how Indians originally made their discoveries.

The problem with trial and error is that the elaboration of the preparations often involves procedures that are exceedingly complex or that yield products of little or no obvious and immediate value. *Banisteriopsis caapi* is an inedible, nondescript liana that seldom flowers. True, its bark is bitter, but scarcely more so than a hundred other forest vines. An infusion of the bark causes vomiting and severe diarrhea, hardly conditions that would encourage further experimentation. Yet not only did the Indians persist, they became so deft at manipulating the various ingredients that individual shaman developed dozens of recipes, each yielding potions of various strengths and nuances for specific ceremonial and ritual purposes.

The Indians have their own explanations, rich cosmological accounts that from their perspective are inherently logical. Sacred plants which had journeyed up the Milk River in the belly of anaconda, potions created by primordial jaguar, the drifting souls of shaman dead from the beginning of time. As a scientist I had been taught not to take these myths literally. But they do suggest a certain delicate balance, the thoughts of a people who do not distinguish the supernatural from the mundane. The Indians believe in the power of plants, accept the existence of magic, acknowledge the potency of the spirit. Magical and mystical ideas enter the very texture of their thinking. Their botanical knowledge cannot be separated from their metaphysics. Even the way they order and label their world is fundamentally different.

There are tribes in the Northwest Amazon that do not distinguish green from blue, for the canopy of the forest is the very sky that shelters them. This strange concept lingered in my imagination when I first worked in the tropical lowlands. It surfaced whenever I confronted yet another botanical enigma, the manner in which the Indians classify their plants. The Ingano of the upper Putumayo in Colombia, for example, recognize seven kinds of ayahuasca. The Siona have eighteen varieties, which they distinguish on the basis of the strength and colour of the visions, the trading history of the plant, the authority and lineage of the shaman, even the tone and key of the incantations that the plants sing when taken on the night of a full moon. None of these criteria make sense botanically and, as far as modern science can distinguish, all the plants are referable to one species, *Banisteriopsis caapi*. Yet the Indians can readily differentiate their varieties on sight, even from a considerable distance in the forest. What's more, individuals from different tribes, separated by large expanses of forest, identify these same varieties with amazing consistency. It is a similar story with other stimulants, such as the caffeine-rich liana *Paullinia yoco*. In addition to *yoco blanco* and *colorado*, the Ingano recognize black yoco, jaguar yoco, *yagé-yoco*, yoco of the witches. Fourteen categories in all, not one of which can be determined based on the rules of our own science.

Like most ritual hallucinogens, ayahuasca is a sacred medicine and a vital component of the shaman's repertoire, enabling him to communicate across great distances in the forest to diagnose illness, ward off evil, prophesy the future. But for the peoples of the Northwest Amazon, it is far more. Ayahuasca is the visionary medium through which human beings orients themselves in the cosmos. Under the cloak of the visions, die user of ayahuasca encounters the gods, the primordial beings and the first humans, even as he or she embraces, for good and for bad, the wild creatures of the forest and the powers of the night. Lifted out of his body, the shaman enters a distant realm, soaring like a bird to beyond the Milky Way or descending the sacred rivers in supernatural canoes manned by demons to reach distant lands where lost or stolen souls can be found and mystical deeds of spiritual rescue may be accomplished.

To begin to understand the role that all these powerful plants play in these societies, it is essential to place the drugs themselves in proper context. For one, the pharmacologically active components do not produce uniform effects. On the contrary, any psychoactive drug has within it a completely ambivalent potential for good or evil, order or chaos. Pharmacologically, it induces a certain condition, but that condition is mere raw material to be worked by particular cultural or psychological forces. Andrew Weil, a physician who has written a great deal about the cross-cultural use of drugs, illustrates this point with an example from our own society. In the rain forests of Oregon, there are a number of native species of hallucinogenic mushrooms. Those who go out into the forest deliberately intending to ingest these mushrooms generally experience a pleasant intoxication. Those who inadvertently consume them while foraging for edible mushrooms invariably end up in the poison unit of the nearest hospital. The chemical effects of the mushrooms have not changed. What does vary is the interpretation of the intoxication and the individual's expectations of what the drug will do.

Similarly, the hallucinogenic plants consumed by the Amerindian induce a powerful but neutral stimulation of the imagination. They create a template upon which cultural beliefs may be amplified a thousand times. What individuals see in the visions is dependent not on the drug but on other factors: the physical and mental states of the users; their expectations based on a rich repository of tribal lore; and, above all, the authority, knowledge and experience of the leader of the ceremony. The role of this figure, be it man or woman, shaman, *curandero, payé, maestro* or *brujo,* is pivotal. It is the shaman who tackles the bombardment of visual and auditory stimuli and gives it order. It is the shaman who must interpret a complex body of belief, reading the power in leaves and the meaning in stones, skilfully balancing the forces of the universe and guiding the play of the winds. The ceremonial use of hallucinogenic plants is a collective journey into the unconscious. It is not necessarily, and in fact is rarely, a pleasant or an easy journey. It is wondrous and it may be terrifying. But above all, it is culturally purposeful.

Amerindians enter the realm of hallucinogenic visions not out of boredom or to relieve restless anxiety but rather to fulfil some need of the group. In the Amazon, for example, hallucinogens are taken to divine the future, track the paths of enemies, unveil the medical properties of healing plants. The Amahuaca of Peru drink ayahuasca in order that the nature of the forest animals may be revealed to their apprentices. The Huichol of Mexico eat their peyote at the completion of long, arduous pilgrimages through a landscape of the spirits, that they may experience in life the journey of the soul of the dead to the underworld. In eastern North America, during puberty rites, the Algonquin confined adolescents to a longhouse for two weeks and fed them a beverage based, in part, on datura. During the extended intoxication—and the subsequent amnesia, a pharmacological feature of this drug—the young boy forgot what it was to be a child so that he might learn what it meant to be a man.

Whatever the ostensible purpose of the hallucinogenic journey, Amerindians generally take the sacred plants in a highly structured manner which places a ritualistic framework of order around their use. Moreover, the experience is explicitly sought for positive ends. It is not a means of escaping from an uncertain existence. Rather, it is perceived as a means of contributing to the welfare of all of one's people.

SMOKING TOAD

Scientific research is a wondrous journey, a path of unexpected delights that leads only to new questions, each posed to challenge what has been learned and to expose the ignorance of the curious. In a field as eclectic as ethnobiology, which embraces everything from plants to the poetics of culture, the horizon is limitless. A simple intuition, a single observation, can open vistas of unimagined potential. Once caught in the web of an idea, the researcher is happily doomed, for the outcome is always uncertain, and the resolution of the mystery may take years to unfold. Such was the case in my encounter with the magic toads of the Americas.

The story began innocently enough in Haiti in the spring of 1982, in the temple of a Vodoun sorcerer as he and a companion gathered materials for a poison reputedly used by the secret societies to create zombies, the living dead. At the time I was a graduate student at the Harvard Botanical Museum, working under the legendary ethnobotanist Richard Evans Schultes. Schultes had sent me to Haiti to secure the formula of the zombie powder, document its preparation and collect samples of the various ingredients. I had entered the sorcerer's compound on a cool and clear morning, to find hanging from a clothesline a macabre assortment of dried animals and plants, all components of the poison. Among them was the flattened carcass of an enormous toad. From size alone, I suspected it to be *Bufo marinus,* a native of the American tropics, quite common and certainly poisonous.

Twenty-five centimetres across and weighing as much as 3 kilograms, *Bufo marinus* is the world's largest toad, a strange toothless creature incapable of breathing when its mouth is open, and noted for the peculiar habit of shedding and swallowing its own skin. Its mating patterns

171

also tend toward the eccentric. A pod of obsessive males will sometimes envelop a single female, and cling to her raddled flesh long after she is dead and her body decomposed. This odd inclination, a sort of amphibian necrophilia, is often observed in road kills as males attempt to copulate with the squashed corpses of the female dead. On the back of the heads of both females and males are large parotoid glands that secrete highly toxic chemicals. Just to touch the glands is to risk nausea, severe headache and violent retching. To consume the venom is to court death. Formidable animals, they seemed a highly appropriate ingredient for a folk preparation said to be capable of causing the living to appear dead, and the dead to be reborn in the realm of the living.

On Easter Sunday, 1982, I passed through United States Immigration at Kennedy Airport in New York, carrying a kaleidoscopic Haitian suitcase constructed from surplus soft drink cans. The specimens inside included lizards, a polychaete worm, two marine fish and several tarantulas—all preserved in alcohol—as well as several bags of dried plant material. Two rum bottles contained the antidote; the zombie powder itself was in a glass jar wrapped in a red satin cloth. There were also several seed necklaces, a dozen unidentified powders and two Vodoun *wangas*, or protective charms, and one dried toad. A human tibia and skull were at the bottom of the case. I also had with me a cardboard box full of herbarium specimens, and concealed inside a duffel bag was a live and rather active specimen of *Bufo marinus*. The customs agent opened the metal suitcase, took a quick look and violently slammed it shut.

"Look," he said in a voice tempered by the back alleys of Brooklyn, "it's Easter Sunday. I didn't even want to work today. I don't know who the fuck you are. Just get the fuck out of here."

He never found the toad.

The following morning I walked through the dark corridors of the Museum of Comparative Zoology at Harvard and deposited the animal specimens with various specialists for identification. Then I returned to my office at the Botanical Museum to have a look at the plants. My initial concern, as it would be in any such ethnopharmacological investigation, was to determine whether or not the ingredients contained chemical compounds that either alone or in combination might account for a particular outcome. In the case of the Haitian zombie, I was looking for a drug that might induce a state of apparent death so profound that it could fool a Western physician. Once the specimens were identified, the real work could begin in the library, the primary site, along with the mind, of ethnopharmacological exploration. From the herpetologists, I learned that the toad was indeed *Bufo marinus*, and as I poked around the literature, I discovered that the curious creatures had quite a story. What I didn't realize at the time was that long after the zombie problem had been resolved, the toads would remain a source of mystery and intrigue.

Native to the Caribbean, *Bufo marinus* thrives in low swampy habitats ranging from Florida west along the Gulf Coast to Mexico, and south to Panama and northern South America. In the mid-fifteenth century, in the wake of European contact, it dispersed throughout tropical America along the Pacific coast, as well as inland into the Amazon basin. The large parotoid glands at the back of its head have been described as "veritable chemical factories"; they produce and secrete at least twenty-six compounds, all of which are biologically active. Some of them—such as dopamine, epinephrine, norepinephrine and serotonin—are benign and occur naturally in human tissues. However, the glands secrete other compounds of considerably greater interest, including bufotenine, a purported hallucinogen, and two classes of highly toxic cardiac glycosides, bufogenin and its derivative bufotoxin. These compounds are found in the skin and glands of a number of toads, including the common European species *Bufo vulgaris*, and it is their properties that have earned these animals a notorious place in the repertoires of poisoners and practitioners of black magic throughout the world.

The Roman satirist Juvenal described women using toads, presumably *Bufo vulgaris*, to kill unsuspecting husbands. The toxicity of the venom provided the basis upon which the Talmud differentiated between frogs and toads, classifying the latter with all animals that were poisonous to the touch—an idea that persists to this day in Western societies. European sorcerers believed that toads derived their venom from the earth by eating mushrooms—hence the English word *toadstool* —and they commonly prepared potions using toads mat had macerated in menstrual blood for a month or more. It is to these "menstruums" that Shakespeare referred in *Macbeth:*

> Toad, that under the cold stone,
> Days and nights hast thirty-one
> Swelter'd venom sleeping got,
> Boil thou first i' the charmed pot!

Medieval witchcraft boasted a complete collection of such recipes. One from the court astrologer and alchemist for Frederick II reads: "Five toads are shut up in a vessel and made to drink the juices of various herbs with vinegar as the first step in the preparation of a marvellous elixir for the purposes of transformation." Soldiers in the Middle Ages believed that a discreet way of killing an enemy was to rub his skin or wounds with the secretions of *Bufo vulgaris*.

The more toxic *Bufo marinus* reached Europe soon after the voyages of Columbus, and poisoners quickly discovered that by placing the toad in boiling olive oil, they could skim the secretions of the glands off the surface. In early sixteenth-century Italy, poisoners devised sophisticated processes for extracting toad toxins in salt, which could then be sprinkled on the intended victim's food. So highly regarded was the toxicity of toad venom that at the beginning of the eighteenth century it was added to explosive shells and mixed with saltpetre to make gunpowder. Presumably, the military commanders believed that if the cannon did not kill their enemies, the toad toxins would.

European physicians incorporated toad venom into their *materia medica* at a very early date. Michael Etmuller (1644-1683), professor of medicine at Leipzig, noted that "living toads aroused to the point of fury are venomous, but found dead they are entirely devoid of poison. Transfixed alive in the month of July, dried, powdered and administered in doses of twelve grains on alternate days, they furnish an excellent cure for dropsy. Powdered toad is also an effective remedy against incontinence of urine, and is said to be efficacious because of its anodyne character while its volatile, penetrating salt acts as a diuretic." Toads remained an important therapeutic agent throughout the eighteenth century and as late as 1833 were mentioned in a medical compilation, *Pharmacologia*, by J. A. Paris.

Chinese physicians were even more inventive than their Western counterparts. For centuries, they had formed the toxic secretions into smooth disks named *ch'an su*, meaning "toad venom" in Mandarin. According to the *Pentsao Kang*, a famous herbal guide written at the end of the sixteenth century, this preparation was used to treat toothache, canker sores, inflammations of the sinus and bleeding gums. It was also said to cure the common cold. From this list of rather mundane afflictions, it may not be apparent that the Chinese were, in fact, using an extremely toxic preparation. Although early medical reports are uncertain as to the species of toad used, analysis of ch'an su (probably

Bufo gargarizans) has revealed the presence of both bufogenin and bufotoxin. Separate studies suggested that ch'an su was fifty to a hundred times more potent than digitalis, a powerful substance derived from the common European foxglove, which had been used as a heart stimulant in Britain since the tenth century. In one modern experiment, a cat was injected with as little as 0.02 gram of crude toad venom; its blood pressure tripled almost immediately, and it collapsed following massive heart failure. This could mean that as little as half a gram of dried venom, injected intravenously, would do similar damage to a 70-kilogram human.

Like its Chinese cousin, *Bufo marinus* secretes venom that can kill. But both the pharmacological action of the toxin, which induces fatal arrhythmia in the heart, and the manner in which the toads are prepared in Haiti, grilled and pounded to dust, made it highly unlikely that it played more than a symbolic role in the elaboration of the zombie powder. Still, symbols are touchstones, and the pursuit of one mystery often unveils another.

Even as I eliminated the toad as a suspect in the zombie investigation, I was astonished to learn that anthropologists have long speculated that the Maya and other ancient civilizations of Mesoamerica may have used *Bufo marinus* as a ritual intoxicant. Though on the face of it the idea seemed biologically untenable, given the toxicity of the venom, I was nevertheless intrigued. The discovery of a psychoactive toad would be extraordinary. All known and deliberate human uses of natural hallucinogens involve derivatives of higher plants and fungi. No hallucinogenic agent had yet been found in the animal kingdom.

To be sure, there had been numerous scattered reports of psychoactive drugs derived from animals. An early nineteenth-century travel account from eastern Brazil, for example, suggested that the Malalis Indians may have used *bichos de tacuara,* the larvae of a moth tentatively identified as *Myelobia smerintha,* as a hallucinogen. The late peyote specialist Weston La Barre once referred in passing to a narcotic bamboo grub of Amazonian origin, a hallucinogenic dream fish of Melanesia and a black and red *oconenetl* bird from Tlaxcala, Mexico, whose flesh was reputedly hallucinogenic. Hallucinogenic fish poisoning, involving four species of mullet and goatfish, as well as the silver drummer fish found off Norfolk Island, had been reported from the Pacific and Indian Oceans. Robert Carneiro, an anthropologist associated with the American Museum of Natural History, described in

1970 the use of an unidentified frog in the hunting magic of Peruvian Indians in the Northwest Amazon.

The Brazilian report, I discovered, though provocative, was based strictly on hearsay. No voucher specimens had verified the identity of the moth, no chemical analysis had been undertaken, and, in the original 1824 report by the French traveller Saint-Hilaire, the correspondent did not observe anyone experiencing psychoactive effects. La Barre's "narcotic bamboo grub" may well be a reference to the same moth larvae. When I contacted Professor La Barre just before his death, he could not recall the provenance of his references to either the grub or the purportedly hallucinogenic oconenetl bird of Mexico.

Hallucinogenic fish poisoning had been reported from Hawaii, South Africa and Melanesia. In Hawaii, the toxin evidently is found in the head of a fish which is considered poisonous only in June, July and August. According to one early report, forty Japanese labourers became delirious and "mentally paralysed" after eating *weke pahala*, a goatfish also known by the name "nightmare *weke*." On Molokai, local fishermen maintain that both the head and tail of these fish cause vivid dreams which are not necessarily pleasant. Similar effects are apparently induced by the "dream fish" from Norfolk Island near Australia. Those who eat this fish before sleeping reputedly suffer terrifying nightmares.

Whether these fish are truly hallucinogenic and whether indigenous peoples have deliberately sought out the intoxication and interpreted it in culturally meaningful ways remains unknown. In most instances, the symptoms of the intoxication—dizziness, loss of equilibrium, partial paralysis of the legs, an itching or burning sensation in the throat, hallucinations and mental depression, delirium, a subjective perception of imminent death—appear to be highly unpleasant and are difficult to distinguish from poisoning. The chemistry and pharmacology of the phenomenon remain unknown, and attempts to replicate the intoxication in controlled experiments have failed. From the isolated reports, it appears that outbreaks are sporadic and unpredictable in their occurrence. Evidently, many of those who have experienced hallucinogenic fish poisoning have done so quite inadvertently, whilst seeking out fish that under most circumstances are perfectly edible.

The Peruvian frog reported by Carneiro turned out to be *Phyllomedusa bicolor*, and analysis of its secretions revealed the presence of a number of biologically active proteins. Amahuaca and Matse Indians along the border of Peru and Brazil collect and dry the skin secretions of this frog, then mix the powder with saliva and introduce it into lines of fresh burns on the arms or chest, producing a rapid, violent intoxication. Although behavioural effects are reported, it remains to be proved that this species is truly hallucinogenic. Adrian Morgan, an English author and toad expert, described the effects of the secretions in a recent letter:

> A young explorer Benedict Allen traveled with the Matses Indians to a lake held to be sacred. Along the journey his two native companions decided to do a spot of hunting. To this end, they took a frog and stretched it across upright sticks. Unlike other recorded practices with this frog, the venom was scraped from the frog's back but not processed by drying or heat. Instead the spatula was passed to each individual to consume raw, orally. Mr. Allen turned an interesting shade of green and after reeling about, threw his guts up.

Of all the possible animal hallucinogens, none had excited more interest than *Bufo marinus*. The argument in favour of the toad as a hallucinogen is based on several lines of evidence. First, throughout Central America the toad was a prominent symbol, particularly in Olmec, Mayan and Aztec iconography. Numerous artifacts, including small ceramic serving bowls, bear obvious toad representations with especially graphic portrayals of the distinctive parotoid glands. Second, at a number of Olmec and Maya sites, *Bufo marinus* bones have been found in great abundance and often in ritual context. Indeed, it was the concentration and distribution of *Bufo marinus* remains at the Olmec site at San Lorenzo that led Michael Coe, a noted Mesoamerican archaeologist at Yale, to first suggest that the toad may have been used as a drug. Third, one of the substances secreted by the toad is bufotenine, a compound found in a hallucinogenic snuff known as *yopo*, made today by South American Indians from the seeds of *Anadenanthera peregrina*. This tree, a member of the bean family, occurs in the plains and grasslands of the Orinoco basin of Colombia and Venezuela, in the light forests in southern Guiana and in the Río Branco area of northern Amazonian Brazil. One report in the medical literature, an experiment conducted in the 1950s by a physician, Howard Fabing, suggested that pure bufotenine, injected intravenously into human subjects, induces hallucinations. Finally, all the proponents of the hallucinogen hypothesis cite an unpublished account by an anthropologist,

Timothy Knab, of the contemporary use of *Bufo marinus* in a hallucinogenic preparation in Veracruz, Mexico.

On the face of it, however, this cumulative evidence struck me as being far from conclusive. Even if Mayan iconography does represents *Bufo marinus,* that does not necessarily mean the Maya used the toad as a hallucinogen. Symbols, in particular ritual symbols, incorporate a wide range of meanings. Given the remarkable fecundity of the toad, one could speculate with equal assurance that toad motifs relate to fertility, to water or rain, or even, given the life cycle of the creature, to some notion of sacred metamorphosis and renewal.

By the same token, there is not always a direct relationship between a decorative motif applied to ceramic wares and the purported use of the object. In a critical review of the hallucinogen hypothesis, one anthropologist noted that in the central market in Guatemala City, native women today sell a great variety of modern toad-shaped artifacts. Does this imply, he asked wryly, that "these little old ladies secretly imbibe mind expanding doses of toad-juice cocktails under their counters?" Although certain investigators, most notably Richard Evans Schultes, have drawn conclusions from the provocative shapes and motifs of archaeological artifacts, they have done so only when the purported ancient use of a hallucinogen is corroborated by ethnohistorical records or ethnographic evidence of contemporary use. No such evidence has been found for *Bufo.*

The paucity of historical evidence is another flaw in the argument for the hallucinogenic use of toads. If, in fact, the extensive icono-graphic representation of *Bufo marinus* indicates its role as a drug in a state religion, there ought to be some record of its use in the early chronicles. Throughout the Americas, the Spanish zealously ferreted out and described in their writings the "diabolical" use of hallucinogens, along with other indigenous religious practices, if only as a way of rationalizing their own nefarious actions. They left extensive accounts of virtually all of the major hallucinogenic plants now known to have been used in the territories they conquered.

While it is true that the Spanish tried to suppress the use of psychotropic drugs throughout the Americas, they mostly succeeded in driving these practices underground. In many cases, it is possible to demonstrate the continuity and subsequent modifications of pre-Columbian practices through colonial times to the present. So what happened to *Bufo marinus?*

At least one ethnohistorical source does mention the use of toads in a Mayan potion. Peter Furst, a leading scholar of Mexican ethnography and prehistory, notes in a paper that the "17th century English friar, Thomas Gage, described the Pokoman Maya practice of steeping venomous toads in fermented beverages used for ritual intoxication to give them extra potency." When I consulted the original source, however, I found the reference somewhat less precise. It speaks of a *chicha* consisting of water, honey or sugar cane, tobacco leaves, various roots "which they know to be strong in action," and, in certain localities, a live toad. This mixture was placed in a sealed container "till all that they have put in be thoroughly steeped, the toad consumed, and the drink well strengthened." From the original syntax, it is not clear whether the Pokoman Maya attributed the potency of the preparation to the addition of the unidentified toads, the plant constituents or the month of underground fermentation. The practice of steeping toads in chicha to make a more potent beverage continues to this day and has been reported from the Quiché Maya, but there is no evidence that a hallucinogenic preparation is the result. Similarly, there is no indication in the journals of Thomas Gage that the fermented potions of the Pokoman Maya were hallucinogenic. They were, evidently, highly toxic, and "certainly the cause of many Indians' death, especially where they use the toad's poison with it."

The anthropologists who believe that *Bufo marinus* was the source of a drug also draw attention to the distribution of toad remains at a number of archaeological sites. In discussing his discoveries at San Lorenzo, for example, Michael Coe noted: "These toads are a puzzle, as they cannot be skinned without an extremely dangerous poison getting into the meat. We are now looking at the possibility that the Olmecs used them for a hallucinogenic substance called bufotenine, which is one of the active ingredients." As it turns out, a survey of the archaeological literature shows that a significant quantity of *Bufo marinus* bones have been found in middens throughout Central America, leading other archaeologists to believe that pre-Columbian Indians used the toad for meat after carefully cutting away the skin and parotoid glands. In spite of Goes cautionary words, Richard Cooke, an archaeologist working in Panama, himself butchered and cooked several specimens, which he was pleased to note tasted rather pleasantly like smoked chicken. On the basis of temporal and spatial distribution of *Bufo marinus* remains, he proposed that the toad was not used as a drug but as a survival food, a suggestion partially corroborated by the fact that it is today employed for precisely that purpose by the Campa Indians of the lower Apurimac River in Peru.

The central weakness of the hallucinogen hypothesis seemed to be the inability of proponents to demonstrate how any preparation of *Bufo marinus* could be safely consumed. It is true that the glands secrete bufotenine, a methylated derivative of serotonin and a known constituent of certain South American hallucinogenic snuffs. However, also present in the toad venom are bufotoxin and bufogenin. Both are highly toxic. Ingesting a straight maceration of the parotoid glands would almost certainly cause heart failure long before the recipient had a chance to experience any useful states of consciousness induced by bufotenine. It seems unlikely that the Maya would have wanted to poison vast numbers of their people, let alone their priests, who presumably would have been among those taking the drug. Only if some process had been developed that selectively neutralized the toxic constituents could *Bufo marinus* have been an orally administered hallucinogen. Folk healers have often demonstrated a sophisticated biological and chemical knowledge, as is evident in their ability to enhance certain hallucinogenic preparations by the careful use of various admixtures. However, eliminating both bufotoxin and bufogenin from an oral toad preparation would be a formidable achievement.

Though such a process is not altogether inconceivable, the explanations offered by the anthropologists left something to be desired. Allison Kennedy, perhaps the most emphatic proponent of the hallucinogen hypothesis, suggested that the Maya used ducks as bioprocessors of the toxins. In her scheme, the Maya raised toads on a large scale, fed the toads to ducks and then ritually consumed the birds' flesh, which she claimed would now be safely psychoactive. She demonstrated that ducks could safely eat the toads, but she failed to take the obvious next step of butchering the birds and assaying their meat.

A more promising attempt was made by an intrepid explorer, Timothy Knab, who searched the back country of Mexico for evidence of a contemporary *curandero* who might have preserved ancient knowledge of a toad preparation. His unpublished account was heralded by Allison Kennedy. "Knab," she writes, "has penetrated the arcana of several *curanderos* in the Veracruz area and details the recipe for the preparation of *B. marinus* parotoid glands which eliminates the most toxic compounds."

When I tracked down Knab, who happened to be teaching in Boston at Tufts University, I found that he had been somewhat more modest in reporting his own discovery. After considerable effort, he had located an old curandero in the mountains of southern Veracruz who claimed to know the formula of a preparation that had not actually been used by his people for fifty years. The old man ground the glands of ten toads into a thick paste, to which he added lime water and the ashes of certain plants. The mixture was boiled all night, or until it no longer smelled foul, and then was added to corn beer and filtered through palm fibre. The liquid was mixed with cornmeal and placed in the sun for several days to ferment. Finally, the mixture was heated to evaporate the remaining fluid, and the resulting hardened dough was stored until the time came to mix it with water to produce the final potion.

Although Knab had persuaded the curandero to prepare the drink, under absolutely no conditions would the old man sample it. Only very reluctantly did he consent to give a dose to Knab. From what happened, it appears that he knew something the anthropologist did not. Knab's intoxication was marked by sensations of fire and heat, convulsive muscle spasms, a pounding headache and delirium. He writes of the experience:

> The drink starts to take effect within a half hour; profuse sweating is noted along with a sudden increase in heart beat. The heart beat becomes continuously harder and stronger. A pronounced chill sets in with twitching of the facial and eye muscles. A pounding headache and delirium shortly follow the onset of twitching. During this delirium, the individual is unable to walk, sit up, or move about, as he lies in a specially excavated depression in front of the fire. This state usually lasts from three to five hours and wears off slowly.

Knab reports no hallucinations, and from what he told me when we met, it appears that he merely suffered the symptoms of severe poisoning. He never found out whether the preparation neutralized any of the toxic compounds, for it was never analysed. Asked whether he would describe the preparation as hallucinogenic, he replied, "Hell, no! The shit nearly killed me."

The principal unresolved issue in this controversy is the pharmacological activity of the purported hallucinogenic agent itself, bufotenine. Virtually every report that characterizes it as a hallucinogen dates to a single experiment completed by a medical doctor, Howard Fabing, in the 1950s. Fabing obtained permission to inject bufotenine intravenously into a number of inmates at the Ohio State Penitentiary. The recipient of the mildest dose complained of nausea, prickling sensations in the face and slight difficulty in breathing. With a higher dosage, these symptoms became more pronounced, and the subjects face and lips became purplish. The final dose caused mild hallucinations and delirium, and the skin turned "the color of an eggplant." The hallucinations were ephemeral. Three minutes after injection, the subject vomited and "saw red spots passing before his eyes and red-purple spots on the floor. Within two minutes, these visual phenomena were gone, but they were replaced by a yellow lens filter." That is the extent of the hallucinations experienced by any of the recipients of the bufotenine injections.

Later investigators attempted but failed to replicate these results. Harris Isbell, a researcher at the Public Health Service Hospital in Lexington, Kentucky, experimented with bufotenine as a snuff. Neither inhalation of pure bufotenine in aerosol suspension nor oral ingestion of bufotenine in doses as high as 100 milligrams elicited any psychoactive effect. W J. Turner and S. Merlis tried injecting bufotenine intramuscularly. They noted that with a dose of 40 milligrams, the recipient "suddenly developed an extremely rapid heart rate; no pulse could be obtained; no blood pressure measured . . . onset of auricular fibrillation . . . extreme cyanosis developed." Massive resuscitative procedures were immediately implemented, and fortunately the pulse eventually returned to normal. After the failure of this and other experiments, investigators concluded that, though bufotenine was present in the hallucinogenic snuffs used by the Indians of the Orinoco, the drug was not itself "capable of producing the acute phase of intoxication."

This conclusion is supported by other experimental evidence. One measure of the ability of compounds to penetrate the nervous system is lipid solubility. Experiments have shown that bufotenine has a very low lipid solubility and is relatively incapable of crossing the blood-brain barrier, making it unlikely that the drug would have any effect on the central nervous system. The visual effects reported after injections of high doses of bufotenine most likely result from oxygen starvation of the optic nerve, caused by the drug's effect on the heart. Therefore, even assuming that a folk preparation could eliminate the toxic constituents in the toad venom, it is very doubtful that bufotenine itself is psychoactive.

After a week in the library, I was convinced the anthropologists were wrong. Chemical and pharmacological evidence left little doubt that the ancient peoples of Mesoamerica did not use *Bufo marinus* as a hallucinogen, at least not in any manner consistent with what we know of the contemporary use of such substances by indigenous societies of the Americas. *Bufo marinus* venom may have been employed as an ordeal poison and the physiological effects caused by its action on the cardiovascular system may conceivably have been interpreted in culturally meaningful ways by religious practitioners. But it was not a hallucinogen.

In 1988 I published these conclusions in the *Revista Academia Colombiana de Ciencias Exactas Fiskas y Naturales,* a journal sufficiently obscure to guarantee that I would never again have to think about toad venom. But then, a year or two later, my phone rang in the middle of the night. At the time, I was living in Vancouver. The call came from a reporter in Toronto. A grown man had raised a pet toad for eight years and *then* decided to suck its venom glands. Evidently, I had not been the only one reading the anthropological literature.

Picking up on the mistaken idea that *Bufo marinus* could get you high, he and a friend had squeezed the glands and ingested the toxic secretions. Both had become violently ill. One suffered near-lethal seizures and remained in the intensive care unit of the North York General Hospital. The toad, whose name was withheld from the press presumably for privacy reasons, was donated to the Metro Toronto Zoo. The police were confused. The Canadian Criminal Code contained nothing about licking toads. The Americans, however, apparently knew all about the potential danger of a new drug craze. With characteristic zeal, the Drug Enforcement Agency had identified the milky white toad venom as bufotenine, a "dangerous new hallucinogen." The fact that there was not a shred of evidence suggesting that the compound was psychoactive had not deterred the U.S. government from placing bufotenine in Schedule 1 of the Controlled Substance Act, along with LSD. Though it would come as a surprise to pet shop owners all over America who sell the homely creatures for $20 to $50, possession of *Bufo marinus* is a criminal offence, subject to the same sanctions reserved for heroin and crack cocaine.

The Toronto toad-licking episode was part of a small wave of *Bufo* mania that made its way to North America from Australia in the late

1980s. The Aussies have always had a complex love/hate relationship with *Bufo marinus*, ever since the toad was introduced Down Under in 1935. The original hope was that the fertile and voracious toads would consume the greyback beetles which were then destroying sugar-cane fields all over Queensland. Unfortunately, the only thing in Australia the toad did not eat was the insect pest. Christened "cane toads" in memory of this agricultural folly, the creatures found themselves in a tropical paradise, devoid of predators and flush with prey. Before long, they multiplied in the millions and began to spread inland at a rate of 25 kilometres a year.

Though local press reports described the toads as "one of nature's ugliest little beasts," some Aussies found them cute and kept them as pets, dressing them in little outfits, skirts and shirts made of calico cloth. But the toxic toads also killed dogs and wild things. For many Australians, there could be no greater pleasure than driving down an open road across a migrating horde of cane toads, weaving the vehicle back and forth until the tires grew thick with the remains of flattened amphibians. Between these two extremes, isolated from the world at large, were some hippies of the northern rain forest who had chosen life in the wild over civilization. They had found in the toads a pathway to oblivion. An Australian film crew recorded this testimonial from an avid, if less than articulate, toad acolyte:

> You use a little qua ... use a little quantity at first ... then larger ... little bit first ... then ... Well, er, Don Juan, er, says that, er, some of the South American Indians, they, er, when they get the mescaline out of the cactus they say that ... that you actually start to see what the world looks like through the eyes of the cactus ... er, your toad's the same. I am seeing the world ... er ... through the consciousness of a toad.

Why one would want to experience the world from the perspective of a toad was not a question posed to this self-confessed cane-toad drug abuser. Still, the authorities could not ignore this egregious violation of the norm. When the Drug Squad of Brisbane discovered a Heinz baby food jar full of crystallized venom, they sprang into action. "The conservative Queensland government," reported Reuters on April 15, 1988, "renowned for its curbs on pleasures of the flesh, has classified toad slime as an illegal substance under its Drug Misuse Act." Rob Endean, the Queensland University zoologist quoted in the story, remarked that the toads were just one of a long list of bizarre tropical goodies that were boiled, smoked, ground or chewed by the hippies of the rain forest. "They'll try anything, plants, mushrooms, toads," he said. "They've got nothing better to do."

In North America, the media caught wind of the scandal. *Discover* magazine reported that Australians were forsaking "traditional illegal drugs for Cane toads, which they boil for a slimy, potentially lethal cocktail." In May 1988 the *Weekly World News* ran several tabloid articles under the banner headlines "Rare Toad Keeps Druggies Hopping," "Toad Licking Poses Threat to Youth in America" and "Druggies Find Sick New Way to Get High—They Lick Toads!" The mainstream newspapers soon followed. "Terror Toads" proclaimed the *New York Times.* "A Dark Invasion in the Sunshine State" warned the *Chicago Tribune.* A sampling of other headlines suggests the tenor of the reporting: "Monster Drug Toad Invasion Feared," *Vancouver Province;* "Drug Addicts Licking Giant Toads to Get High," *Palm Beach Post;* "Minds Go Loose from Toad Juice," *Albany Times Union.* Although it was not at all clear precisely how many young Americans were likely to find sucking toad glands an attractive recreational pursuit, all these articles took the breadth of the alleged problem as a given. As a cultural phenomenon, toad-licking had arrived. Or at least it had in the media. The popular television show *L.A. Law* did an episode about a man charged with using toads illegally to get high. In San Francisco, a rock-and-roll band changed its name to Mojo Nixon and the Toad Lickers. American pop culture may have reached a new low on the night *Beavis and Butt-Head touted* toad licking on MTV.

By this point, politicians were beginning to stir. In Georgia, Representative Beverly Langford introduced legislation in the State General Assembly, urging lawmakers to consider "the extreme dangers of toad licking becoming the designer drug of choice in today's sophisticated society." Ms. Langford did not specify what might become the new drug of choice among the unsophisticated. Next door in South Carolina, Representative Patrick Harris introduced similar legislation. Noting that toad licking was "repulsive," he recommended sentencing criminal offenders to "sixty hours of public service in a local zoo." Canadians were not about to be left behind. Vancouver police urged politicians to ban the import of the "lethal giant toad" and prohibit possession by "outlawing them under the Federal Narcotics Control Act."

Though fuelled by hysterical reports in the media, and misinformation and paranoia on the part of antidrug crusaders, the toad-licking saga revealed more than anything the extraordinary lengths to which people would go to get intoxicated. Missing from the heated rhetoric, however, was one obvious fact: an animal venom that contained no hallucinogenic agent but that did contain lethal poisons was not likely to inspire a new drug craze. Whenever I had a chance, I tried to make this clear. Finally, totally frustrated, I gave up and turned to the one individual I knew who might be able to make sense of the situation.

Though known today as Americas wellness doctor, Andrew Weil established his reputation as a thoughtful voice in a noisy debate about the nature and character of human drug use. In a series of books, he noted that the desire to change consciousness, and the use of stimulants to do so, was so common in the ethnographic record that it had to be considered a basic part of the human appetite. Given this natural impulse, it was naive and historically uninformed to expect people to cease the ritualistic and recreational use of stimulants. The primary goal of drug policy should not be a drug-free world, he argued, but a better understanding of the economic and social forces that lead certain individuals to use potentially dangerous substances in an unconscious and self-destructive manner. For those with an ideological stake in the War on Drugs, this was heresy. When Andrew published *From Chocolate to Morphine,* a dispassionate assessment of the pharmacology and history of legal and illegal drugs, it was singled out by the Christian right as a book to be banned.

Andrew and I had been friends for years, both of us having studied ethnobotany with Richard Evans Schultes at Harvard. By overnight mail, I sent to his home in Tucson a copy of my paper which dismissed the possibility of *Bufo marinus* being hallucinogenic. A few days later, I had a message from him on my answering machine.

"It's a great paper," he said, "but there's just one problem. I keep hearing about all these freaks around here going into the desert and smoking toad. I know this guy who does it all the time."

That evening, I called him back and told him I'd be right down. The next weekend, I flew to Arizona. The toad caper was on.

With the sun going down over the Sonoran desert, Andrew led me down a dusty trail toward a narrow draw that opened onto a flat enveloped by mesquite trees and looming cacti. In the middle of the clearing was a large fire, heaped with red-hot stones. To one side was a traditional sweat lodge, a willow arbour low to the ground and half-covered with dark canvas. Just beyond was a trampoline. Tending the fire was the person we had come to see, White Dog, Andrew's main toad man. At 194 centimetres, with beard and dreadlocks to the waist, he towered over the burning coals, a barefoot desert wizard in red sweatpants and a lilac shirt that fused seamlessly with the setting sun.

With a warm embrace, he greeted Andrew, and then turning to me, asked, "So, have you tasted toad?"

"No," I replied.

"It's a tool for meditation," he noted sagely, getting right to the point. "It's for meditation because it will make you meditate whether you like to or not."

"How often have you taken it?"

"Not often. Seventy-five, maybe a hundred times," he replied. I gasped.

"White Dog thinks it's the ultimate vehicle for mapping the limits of consciousness," Andrew remarked.

"It's an astral propeliam," White Dog added, as if the phrase would explain all.

"Just where did you come up with all this?" I asked. His voice trailed off in a laugh as he moved away from the fire and made his way into the sweat lodge.

The story of White Dog and the magic toad unfolded through a long evening of searing heat. He grew up in Minnesota, acquired a taste for psychedelics as a youth, and later hooked up with the Peyote Way Church of God, a legally sanctioned religious descendant of the peyote cult that swept the Great Plains in the late nineteenth century. His name came to him in a vision. For a time he considered establishing his own religious group, Migrant Agricultural Gypsies International, but the mass suicide in Jonestown and his own restless character made him fear the power and horrors of a private cult. He elected to work instead "on a cellular level," individual to individual, spreading the word through personal revelation.

It was at this point that he stumbled upon an obscure pamphlet, published anonymously by a mysterious author who identified himself by the pseudonym Albert Most. The document described precisely how a toad could be milked, the venom dried and then smoked for intoxication. It was a technique of ecstasy that appealed to White Dog.

The idea was repulsive, the concept obscure, and the high by all accounts intense beyond imagining. Best of all, the toads were legal, common denizens of the Arizona desert, and presumably beyond reach of the law. Or so he thought.

"You say these toads are from here?" I asked.

"Yeah. You see them all the time when the rains come in summer, when all the people who hate the desert but live here for the suntans split for other places and the land returns to what it once was."

I turned to Andrew. "It can't be *Bufo marinus.*"

"No. It's not," he said. "It's *Bufo atvarius.*"

It was then that I realized that for thirty years the anthropologists had been thinking about the wrong species of toad.

Over the next few days, Andrew and I, with the help of colleagues and reference librarians scattered across the country, pieced together the story. *Bufo marinus,* native to the Yucatan and lowland rain forests of Guatemala and found there in great abundance, had naturally drawn the attention of the Mayanists. *Bufo alvarius,* by contrast, is found only in the Sonoran Desert, an area of approximately 300 000 square kilometres extending from southeastern California across the southern half of Arizona and south approximately 650 kilometres into Mexico. Nocturnal in habit, it avoids the desert heat by burrowing beneath the ground during the day, emerging at dusk to congregate around streams, springs and moist riverbeds. For most of the year, from September through April, me toads remain underground in a dormant state. Beginning in June, before the summer rains begin, the species is highly active, and the desert comes alive with thousands of the animals.

One of more than two hundred species *of Bufo,* the Sonoran toad is a large amphibian, and like *Bufo marinus* it has prominent parotoid glands that secrete a viscous, milky white venom. The two species are morphologically similar, and iconographic representations would be impossible to distinguish. The secretions of *Bufo atvarius,* however, are distinctly different from those of its better known relative. Toad venom is chemically complex, with particular combinations of constituents peculiar to each species, a sort of biochemical fingerprint useful for taxonomie delineation. *Bufo atvarius,* as we learned from the literature, is unique within the genus in its possession of an unusual enzyme, O-methyl transferase, which, among other reactions, converts bufotenine (5-0H-DMT) to the extraordinarily potent hallucinogen 5-methoxy-

N,N-dimethytryptamine (5-MeO-DMT). In fact, the activity of this enzyme leads to the production and accumulation of enormous amounts of 5-MeO-DMT, up to as much as 15 per cent of the dry weight of the parotoid glands. Such a concentration of a pure drug in a living creature is virtually unheard of, and this was no ordinary compound.

One of the most powerful hallucinogens known from nature, 5-MeO-DMT is the compound responsible for the hallucinogenic properties of the South American snuffs derived from *Anadenanthera peregrina* and from various species of *Virola·*, a genus of trees in the nutmeg family. In the plant kingdom, it usually occurs together with N,N-dimethytryptamine (DMT), another strong drug. Orally inactive as the result of the activity of an enzyme in the human gut, monoamine oxidase, these compounds are usually smoked and rarely injected. They may be ingested orally if taken in combination with monoamine oxidase inhibitors, as in the case of certain sophisticated indigenous preparations reported from the Northwest Amazon. Both DMT and 5-MeO-DMT are easily synthesized compounds that appeared as recreational psychedelics in the American drug subculture during the 1960s. DMT is a controlled substance under U.S. federal law, but its 5-methoxy derivative is not. Some chemical supply houses sell 5-MeO-DMT, and quantities are occasionally diverted to human users.

The disparity in the law probably has to do with the different reputations of these two drugs. When smoked, DMT produces a very rapid, brief and intense intoxication marked by vivid visual imagery. These effects made it popular among users of LSD, psilocybin and other well-known psychedelic drugs, and thus drew the attention of authorities. By contrast, smoking pure 5-MeO-DMT, a more potent substance, produces an overwhelmingly powerful experience that can be unnerving. It is like taking a rocketship into the void. Whereas most hallucinogens, including LSD, merely distort reality, however bizarrely, 5-MeO-DMT completely dissolves reality. One user described it as being shot out of a rifle barrel lined with baroque paintings and landing on a sea of electricity. The experience need not be negative, but it is not for the novice. As a result, 5-MeO-DMT never gained the street popularity or notoriety of its chemical cousin. Over the years, it has remained an obscure drug taken mostly by small groups of psychiatrists and explorers of consciousness.

The first published analysis of the venom of *Bufo alvarius* appeared in 1965, followed in 1967 by a more comprehensive study in a journal of pharmacology. The research was later reported in a book on the evolution of the genus *Bufo*. These publications probably inspired experimentation with the venom of *Bufo alvarius* that led to the appearance in 1984 of the underground pamphlet found by White Dog. Written by "Albert Most" and titled *"Bufo alvarius,* the Psychedelic Toad of the Sonoran Desert," it gave detailed instructions for collecting and drying the venom. The document, which reads like a recipe from a cookbook, suggests useful tools and techniques, notes the glands worth milking, and even provides guidelines as to the frequency with which the toads can exploited. One learns, for example, that each gland, "can be squeezed a second time for an additional yield of venom if you allow the toad a one-hour rest period. After this the glands are empty and require four to six weeks for regeneration."

These instructions seemed remarkable given the toxicity of the Sonoran toad. *Bufo alvarius* is hardly benign. There are many instances of dogs being poisoned after mouthing the animal. In one case, an owner reported that he removed the toad from his dog's mouth within ten seconds. Nevertheless, after thirty minutes, the dog began to salivate profusely, quickly went into convulsions and died, apparently in respiratory arrest. Human poisonings had also been reported. Andrew knew of a terrible case of a five-year-old boy admitted to a hospital in southern Arizona in 1986. On the edge of death, he suffered from intense seizures, induced within fifteen minutes of his licking a toad, later identified definitively as *Bufo alvarius.* The child survived, but it took a full week of constant medical care for him to return to normal.

Clearly, the venom of *Bufo alvarius* taken orally is highly toxic, as is that of its Caribbean cousin, *Bufo marinus.* But from the testimony of White Dog and interviews conducted with other toad lovers, it seemed that the venom could be safely smoked. The toxic constituents would be denatured and the full potential of the hallucinogenic component, 5-MeO-DMT, would be realized. On the strength of this deduction, we felt confident in initiating a series of self-experiments with *Bufo alvarius* venom obtained from White Dog.

Both Andrew and I had previously smoked synthetic 5-MeO-DMT and were familiar with its effects. When we burned the venom, we found the odour and taste of the smoke to closely resemble the very distinctive odour and taste of the vapour of the pure compound. We prepared a small chip of dried venom, the size of a paper match head.

Within fifteen seconds of a single deep inhalation of the vapourized material, both of us experienced pronounced psychoactive effects. We later recorded our impressions. I wrote:

> In comparison to the pure compound the toad venom appears longer lasting and, because one does not completely lose contact with reality, far more pleasant, even sensual. Shortly after inhalation I experienced warm flushing sensations, a sense of wonder and well-being, strong auditory hallucinations, which included an insect-cicada sound that ran across my mind and seemed to link my body to the earth. Though I was indoors, there was a sense of me feel of the earth, the dry desert soil passing through my fingers, the stars at midday, the scent of cactus and sage, the feel of dry leaves through hands. Strong visual hallucinations in orblike brilliance, diamond patterns that undulated across my visual field. The experience was in every sense pleasant, with no disturbing physical symptoms, no nausea, perhaps a slight sense of increased heart rate. Warm waves coursed up and down my body. The effects lasted only a few minutes but a pleasant afterglow continued for almost an hour.

Andrew's remarks were somewhat more clinical:

> Profound alteration of consciousness within a few seconds of exhaling. I relax into a deep, peaceful interior awareness. There is nothing scary about the effects and no sense of toxicity. I try to describe my feelings but am unable to talk for the first five minutes and then only with some difficulty. This is a powerful psychoactive drug, one that I think would appeal to most people who like the effects of hallucinogens. For the next hour I feel slow and velvety, with a slight pressure in my head. No long-lasting effects to report.

We repeated the experiment with a sample of venom that Andrew had collected two years earlier in Gila County, Arizona. This material, which had been kept in a closed vial at room temperature, had darkened over time but was quite active.

Experiencing this powerful psychoactive drug, easily obtained from a common and conspicuous toad, forced us to reconsider some of the issues raised in the anthropological literature. One question begged consideration. Given that the toxic constituents of *Bufo alvarius* are evidently denatured by smoking, might *Bufo marinus* also be benignly hallucinogenic if smoked or administered by some means other than by mouth? It was conceivable, provided that *Bufo marinus* contained a psychoactive substance. But clearly it did not. To experiment with a known poison that had no potential upside would be the height of folly. There was nothing in the chemical constituents of the glands of *Bufo marinus* to suggest that under any circumstances, now or in the past, it could be employed as a psychoactive agent. If the ancient civilizations of Mesoamerica had a hallucinogen derived from a toad, the source would have had to be *Bufo alvarius.*

Over the next days, as Andrew and I walked the ancient desert landscape that surrounded his home, we pondered the significance and potential of what we had found. It was, of course, one thing to show that the toad venom was psychoactive. It was quite another to prove that the substance had actually been used in the Americas in pre-Columbian times.

Indigenous peoples of the Sonoran desert would certainly have recognized the toxicity of *Bufo alvarius.* The animal has no predators and poisons dogs. We also knew that these properties would not have deterred experimentation but, on the contrary, would have drawn attention to the toad. The record of folk experimentation suggests that Amerindian peoples consistently underwent considerable risk, marked no doubt by the occasional deaths of individuals, in their search for pharmacologically active substances. Some psychoactive plants, employed ritually now or in the past, are highly toxic. The ingestion of datura, for instance, induces psychotic delirium marked by violent visions and burning thirst, with the possibility of stupor and death. The use of mescal bean, prominent in the Great Plains before the arrival of the peyote cult, was a pharmacological equivalent of playing Russian roulette.

From Tucson, we phoned Peter Furst at the University of Pennsylvania to let him know the results of our experiments and seek his advice on the possible use of the toad in prehistoric Mexico. Peter was a lone voice among anthropologists. As long ago as 1972, in a paper that I had initially overlooked, he had drawn attention to the Sonoran toad. Delighted to learn of our successful self-experiments, he faxed a copy of his early paper. "The area to which *Bufo alvarius* is presently native," he had written, "was once inhabited by archaic desert cultures; it is also the putative homeland of the Uto-Aztecans, from which they expanded southward into Mexico as early as 1500 B.C. Was it the shamans of the pre-agricultural desert cultures who discovered the potent psychotomimetic effects of toad poison and whose ecstatic trance experiences gave rise to the now widespread beliefs in the toad as a transforming shamaness ... ?"

At the time, Peter told us, he had thought that Indians would have had to ingest the toxin of *Bufo alvarius* by steeping the toad in some sort of potion. He did not know that taken alone 5-MeO-DMT is orally inactive, or that the venom could be collected, dried and smoked. In fact, smoking was a practice well known throughout the Americas and was intimately associated with ritual activities. Many Indians regarded smoke as a sacred essence, a vehicle to the spirit world. The use of tobacco established a pattern of consuming psychoactive drugs by smoking. Admixtures to tobacco preparations abound, and it is at least conceivable that toad venom would have been among them.

Extensive trade routes through the Sonoran Desert to Mesoamerica have been well documented, and dried venom would have been an excellent object of trade. It is an axiom of long-distance commerce that the ideal trade item is one that is highly esteemed, easy to transport, durable, readily available at the source, and difficult or impossible to find at the point of exchange. *Bufo alvarius* venom meets all requirements. One toad yields 0.25 to 0.5 gram of dried venom. Since concentrations of 5-MeO-DMT may be as high as 15 per cent, one toad may yield 75 milligrams of a hallucinogenic drug that, when smoked, is effective in humans at doses of 3 to 5 milligrams. In other words, a single toad produces twelve to twenty-five doses of one of the most potent psychoactive drugs found in nature. A container the size of a matchbox could hold thousands of effective doses.

At this point we believed but had no proof that the ancient peoples of Mesoamerica used *Bufo alvarius* as a hallucinogen. On the basis of solid chemical and pharmacological evidence, we were quite certain that they did not use *Bufo marinus*. Still, there was the puzzling issue of the distribution of *Bufo marinus* bones at various Mayan sites. While the archaeologist Richard Cooke was no doubt correct in suggesting that *Bufo marinus* was consumed as food, the fact remains that the toad is often found in ritual contexts. At Seibal, for example, archaeologists encountered a partially intact *Bufo marinus* skeleton inside a Late Classic burial vessel. A *Bufo marinus* skull turned up in a Classic burial at Dzibilchaltun. At Mayapan, the skeleton and skull of a single specimen of the toad was found in a sealed chamber containing two human burials. At Cozumel, archaeologist Nancy Hamblin discovered that *Bufo marinus* bones made up as much as 99 per cent of the amphibian component of the remains. The overwhelming majority of the material was excavated from ritual burials or found in association with ceremonial artifacts, primarily from the Late Postclassic.

As Andrew and I discussed the matter, several plausible explanations emerged. The most obvious is that the toads were ritual offerings not because they were hallucinogenic but because they embodied a wealth of powerful symbolic meanings. The toad as the Great Earth Mother, an image of transformation, death and regeneration, a harbinger of the seasonal rains and protector of crops, is a potent mythic complex found throughout the Americas. In Aztec cosmology, the toad is Tlaltecuhti, the mediator, the image of fecundity and cannibalism, at once creator and destroyer of life. In Mayan religion, toads or frogs are the attendants and musicians of the Chacs, the Yucatec rain gods. Representations that could be either toads or frogs appear with some frequency in the Maya Codices. Given these mythological and religious associations, it should not be surprising that *Bufo marinus,* the largest and most conspicuous toad in Mesoamerica, is found in ancient Mayan burials.

There was one other intriguing possibility. Both *Bufo marinus* and *Bufo alvarius* are enormous toads, readily distinguished from many other species of the genus by their size. In studying the remains from various Mayan sites, archeologists would have no difficulty separating *Bufo marinus* bones from the remains of the other toads native to the region and would not think to compare them with *Bufo alvarius,* an obscure species found in a completely different habitat several hundred kilometres away.

When I returned from Tucson to Vancouver, I wrote to Elizabeth Wing at the University of Florida, who had identified the amphibian remains at San Lorenzo and other ancient sites. Could it be, I asked, that some of the toad remains found in ritual context and identified as *Bufo marinus* were, in fact, *Bufo alvarius? Wet* response was fascinating. "I am sure," she wrote, "that *Bufo alvarius* was not considered a possibility in the identifications I made from material in Vera Cruz and Belize. I am sure I looked just at the regional species and the large size of *Bufo marinus* separated it easily." Intrigued, she examined the one large specimen of *Bufo alvarius* in the collections at the Florida Museum of Natural History:

> The results of a quick look at whether skeletal remains of *Bufo marinus* and
> *Bufo alvarius* can be easily distinguished are inconclusive . . . *Bufo alvarius* is

separable from all our *Bufo marinus* specimens with respect to the relative size of the dorsal projection on the blade of the illium though this is a variable character and what I do not know is whether our one *alvarim* specimen is just on the large end of the continuum . . . This issue of the possible introduction of *alvarius* into Mexico and south needs to be closely examined but more comparative material than I have at the moment is necessary to do this.

Clearly, it would be premature to conclude that the ancient peoples of Mesoamerica used *Bufo alvarius* as a sacred intoxicant. However, having proved beyond doubt that a psychoactive toad does exist and was available in pre-Columbian America, Andrew and I were keen that others more knowledgeable in the field of Mesoamerican studies should re-examine the archaeological and iconographic record with this revelation in mind. In particular, we hoped to inspire a careful review of the osteological remains in order to determine whether *Bufo alvarius* had not, in fact, already been found at various Mayan sites.

To this end, we published a paper in the anthropological journal *Ancient Mesoamerica*. Both of us felt good about our results. We had opened up new ethnographic and ethnohistorical vistas for anthropologists and decisively laid to rest the deeply flawed and dangerous notion that *Bufo marinus* is hallucinogenic. With luck, word might spread, and fewer individuals would end up in hospital emergency rooms. In addition, we had demonstrated that the secretions of *Bufo alvarius,* though known to be toxic when consumed orally, may be safely smoked and are powerfully psychoactive by that route of administration. Our experiments represented the first documentation of a hallucinogenic agent from the animal kingdom, as well as providing clear evidence of a psychoactive toad that could have been employed by pre-Columbian peoples of the New World.

The response to our paper was somewhat surprising. Though it was generally well received, Andrew and I nevertheless became the fulcrum of an ongoing debate about the legitimacy of self-experimentation in science. On June 3, 1994, the *Globe and Mail,* Canada's national newspaper, ran an article, "Taking their own medicine," which focussed on our toad work. Some scientists were deeply offended that we had sampled the venom, as opposed to employing the analytical capability of a modern laboratory. Our position was unequivocal. We had entered the experiment with care and consideration. As far as we knew, the Uto-Aztecans, not to mention the Mayans, had not had white-frocked technicians, precisely calibrated scales or white rats caged in laboratories. Since our goal had been to test whether or not *Bufo alvarius* toad venom was psychoactive in humans, the experiment was, by definition, subjective. Also, we considered it to be more ethical to test the venom on ourselves than to use, for example, unknowing prison inmates, as had been done in the past. Moreover, we were acting in a manner consistent with an established tradition of self-experimentation that through the years has resulted in some of the most important discoveries in pharmacology. As Andrew explained to the media, "I think the kind of inspiration which comes from experience makes for the best kind of science."

This did not quiet our critics. A reviewer writing for the *Journal of Ethnobiology* concluded that our paper "seems to amount to little more than an endorsement for abuse of an hallucinogenic material with potentially deadly side effects." In unveiling the truth about the potentially deadly *Bufo marinus*, we were apparently guilty of fomenting a new drug craze. Even had we wanted that honour, it would have been too late. A front-page story in the *Wall Street Journal*, "Toad Smoking Gains on Toad-Licking Among Drug Users," revealed what was really going on among toad aficionados. Our research was discussed, but the genesis of the report lay elsewhere.

On Monday, January 24, 1994, California drug agents arrested Robert Shepard, a forty-one-year-old teacher and naturalist in Angels Camp, about 160 kilometres east of San Francisco. Shepard's wife Connie, thirty-seven, was also nabbed in the sting, along with Hans, Franz, Peter and Brian, their four pet *Bufo alvarius* toads. The War on Drugs had hit a new low. Shepard was not, in the words of the narcotics agent who busted him, "your average maggot-looking dope dealer on the corner." To the contrary, by all accounts, he was a model citizen with no previous criminal record. An Explorer Scout leader and thirteen-year volunteer with the Calaveras County Sheriff Department's search-and-rescue squad, Shepard made a living teaching elementary schoolchildren about the wonders of nature. His arrest was big news in a county already partial to toads. The year marked the sixty-fifth anniversary of the Calaveras County Fair and Jumping Frog Jubilee, the annual celebration inspired by Mark Twain's short story, "The Celebrated Jumping Frog of Calaveras County."

The authorities were not sure what to do with the suspects or the family toads. "Here's some guy who squeezes toads, for Christ's sake," remarked John Schlim, a veteran narcotics agent. "We don't really get much training in this area." Nor was there was much legal precedent. The Shepards were the first to be charged with possessing a toad for illicit purposes since 1579. That was the year Mother Dutton of Cleworthe Parish in England was accused of frolicking intimately with a toad in her flower garden. Declared a witch, she was executed. Bob Shepard was condemned to make an instructional video for the county's Narcotics Enforcement Team. Viewing the final film, remarked one agent, was "like watching the Discovery Channel. He's very pleasant." Meanwhile, Matt Campoy, task force commander of the antidrug unit, was becoming fond of the incarcerated toads. Asked about their fate, he replied, "I don't want these poor guys sent to a delicatessen. You get attached to them after a while." Dangerous and subversive cracks were appearing in the monolithic façade of the antidrug warriors.

Bob Shepard lost his job and was ordered into drug rehabilitation for the crime of possessing a toad. Ironically, what made his activity illegal was the fact that the venom contained bufotenine, a compound with no hallucinogenic properties. As the New Mexico-based *Entheogen Review* noted, bufotenine is universally regarded in the drug subculture as the "ultimate bummer." Outlawing it makes about as much sense as banning the ingestion of drain cleaner. It wasn't bufotenine that allowed Bob Shepard to hear, as he put it, "electrons jumping orbitais in his molecules." It was 5-methoxy-N,N-dimethytryptamine, arguably the most powerful hallucinogen in nature and a compound as legal in America as apple pie. No one said that the War on Drugs was supposed to make sense.

In the years since Bob Shepards arrest, the worst fears of drug enforcement agents have not been realized. Smoking toad has not swept the nation and young people have not succumbed en masse to a *Bufo alvarius* cult. True, there have been isolated incidents. In New York, a performance artist named Zero Boy was caught with venom while rehearsing his latest production, aptly named *Amphibia*. In Arizona, a man was found with dozens of *Bufo alvarius* toads in his living room, far in excess of the quota of ten permitted under state law. John Romero, the enforcement manager of the Arizona Department of Fish and Game, was stumped by the case until, as he recalled, "the light came on" and he realized that the toads were being kept as a source of drugs.

In general, however, the practice of milking the toxic glands of a living animal, drying the venom on glass and inhaling a substance that sends one into a netherworld of oblivion did not catch on. The toad's moment of fame was short-lived. Still, somewhere out there in the deserts of the Southwest, White Dog and his friends remain hard at work "mapping the limits of consciousness." They are not at all depraved. They are simply curious, inspired by a spirit of wonder that has propelled experimentation with mind-altering substances since the dawn of human awareness. This impulse, embraced by Neolithic shaman, honoured by the ancient Maya and invoked today by solitary seekers like White Dog, will never be extinguished. We may never know whether or not the ancient peoples of the Americas discovered the bizarre properties of *Bufo alvarius*. But of one thing we can be sure. They too were on the lookout for magic potions and would have envied White Dog his good fortune.

BREAKING TRAIL

Imagine yourself on the edge of a high plateau in the late afternoon sun. Before your eyes, down the snowmelt gulleys and past the tangled spruce, beyond the rivers, lakes and jagged peaks, lie uninhabited valleys larger than entire countries. Imagine moving across the tundra, a cornucopia of colour and sound, of whistles and birdcalls, of rust and ginger splashed onto a canvas that stretches to the horizon— and there, forests of mountains wrapped in ice fields, seething masses of rock and snow in an ocean of clouds. In every direction space yields to the infinite.

To the east is Spatsizi, land of the red goat, the largest and most remote wilderness park in British Columbia and the birthplace of the Stikine, the wildest river remaining on the western shore of North America. To the west, beyond the soaring uplands of the Klastine Plateau, is Edziza, sacred mountain of the Tahltan Indians, a towering dormant volcano veiled perpetually in cloud and capped with an ice field 10 kilometres across. Overhead, raptors scrape the sky, and in the distance goat trails lead off the plateau and into the forest. There are signs of the wild everywhere—a flush of ptarmigan, the twisted scat of wolves, fireweed crushed by the weight of grizzly. In all this land there is nothing of human scale, except for a thin highway running north-south up the valley bottom and, by the roadside, a cluster of buildings which, seen from this height, appear toylike and fragile.

If you ever drive north to the Yukon on the dirt surface of the Stewart-Cassiar Highway, you will almost certainly stop at this ramshackle collection of cabins known as the Tatogga Lake Triangle Resort. About 1600 kilometres north of Vancouver, it will be the first sign of gas you've seen in four hours, the first decent shelter in six. Unlike most places encountered on the way north—heaps of galvanized metal, trailers bolted together on a pad of gravel, souvenir stands where books sell by the pound—Tatogga Lake is built of wood, logs mostly, propped up with enough moose antlers to give a person an appetite.

There will probably be a caravan of RVS backed up at the gas pumps, a couple of parked semis, helicopters coming and going overhead, slinging loads of gear destined for the spikecamps of the gold prospectors. There's an illuminated Exxon sign where people from Florida who are afraid of bears ask to park at night and a meadow where Betsy Robinson, a welder from Detroit, used to rest her mobile whorehouse each spring as she made her way north to the pipeline. Inside the main lodge, pelts and traps drape the walls, and bush pilots, truckers, trappers, native guides and tourists gather around a stone fireplace beneath the watchful gaze of a signed portrait of Loretta Lynn.

For the last fifteen years Tatogga Lake was run by Mike Jones, a fisheries biologist who settled in the valley because, as he once told me, it was the kind of place where you could hide Yosemite and the Americans would never find it. He had first stopped by while collecting data for a salmon study and had overheard Leon Fleming, then the owner of Tatogga, complaining about his life. Leon couldn't decide whether to go fishing or drift down the lake to nail this big bull moose he'd been watching from the dock. Mike said he wished he had Leon's problems; Leon said, "You can." The deal went down with a handshake, and with it at least one marriage. Mike Jones walked away from one life and into another.

Mike, besides being as good a bush pilot, riverboatman and hunting guide as the country had ever seen, knew how to spin stories that, as the old Indians said, could make the stars shift in the sky. Many had to do with people he'd bailed out of trouble, like the three German canoeists who shoved off on a suicide run down the wrong river, or all those eastern reporters from *Fish, Fur and Feather* magazine with the thigh-length knives with the little compasses on top. He often told of his travels across the north—it seemed there was nowhere he hadn't been. In the evenings, people from all over the valley would end up at Tatogga gathered around Mike's fireplace. People felt good to be in a place—in a country—that Mike called home.

To know a people, British writer Lawrence Durrell once said, you need only a little patience, a quiet moment and a place where you might listen to the whispered messages of their land. Landscape, he thought, held the key to character. He wrote that you could depopulate France, resettle it with Tartars, and within a few generations find, to your astonishment, that the national characteristics had re-emerged: the restless, metaphysical curiosity, the passionate individualism, the affection for good living. It is what he called the invisible constant of a place. Canadian writer Margaret Atwood understood this when she wrote that if you had to choose three words to distil the essence of Britain, America and Canada, the words would be island, frontier and survival. She was getting at something that travellers have always understood. Just as landscape defines a people, culture springs from a spirit of place. Quebec songwriter Gilles Vigneault expressed the muted Canadian patriotism perfectly when he wrote, "My country is not a country, it is the winter."

Space, land and winter—these are the overwhelming realities of Canada. Tiresome though they can be, the numbers tell an impressive story. A country 7200 kilometres across, spanning six time zones and encompassing over 10 million square kilometres of the Earth. A country that has more lakes than people, a nation that could swallow all of Britain in British Columbia, a land where winter determines the mood of the entire year.

Yet the American preoccupation with self, and the Canadian obsession with America, conceal the most compelling feature of Canada's geography. Demographers are forever pointing out that 80 per cent of Canada's population resides within 160 kilometres of the American border, that Newfoundland lies closer to Dublin than to Vancouver, that Calgary is nearer to Mexico City than to Halifax. But turn the map on its side, and you'll see the real story. The distance from the American border to the northern tip of Canada is more than 4800 kilometres, a greater distance than between New York and Los Angeles. Within that immense space is a forest six times the size of France, and an expanse of tundra larger than Western Europe with fewer people in it than you might find in the Rose Bowl. The territories of the north, a homeland to the Native peoples mostly unknown land to the rest of us, make up 40 per cent of Canada, and lie perpetually bound by permafrost.

This depth is what makes Canada so enticing—the idea that at the border you can start walking north and disappear into a land that rolls on to some impossibly distant shore. Perhaps only the Sahara and parts of the Amazon also evoke this feeling—the sense that a journey, once initiated, need never end. Yet those are completely exotic landscapes. The Canadian north holds a certain familiarity—the memory of winter, the character of the fauna and flora—that reminds Europeans and Americans of things long forgotten in their own homelands.

The weight of the north hovers in the imagination of every Canadian child. The strongest memories of my youth in Quebec are of ice storms roaring out of the Arctic, snapping elms and maples at the base. I remember boys playing hockey on the St. Lawrence River, slapshots disappearing over the ice floes, the black spire of the Catholic church dissolving in the winter winds that turned sky and land into an infinite whiteness, all without contour or relief. This is something that all Canadians know, the feel of the wild even in the heart of the city. In Vancouver, where I live, salmon spawn in the neighbourhood creeks and black bears descend from the coastal mountains to feast on them. There are bald eagles in the city parks, and ravens tumbling through the air each spring.

Perhaps the best way to understand the role of landscape in the Canadian imagination, and indeed the difference between the American and Canadian ethos, is to look at the writings of two men, Henry David Thoreau and Frederick Philip Grove. Thoreau's prose is beautiful, his message eternal, yet he could write about the wilderness as he did only because he never experienced anything truly wild in his life. Grove, by contrast, was wholly absorbed by the drama of living in the wild. His classic, *Over Prairie Trails,* tells of the trips he made one winter between the school where he taught and his family, who lived 55 kilometres away across the Manitoba prairie.

Unlike the supremely self-conscious Thoreau, Grove wrote as a form of meditation, his stories intended only for the eyes and ears of his wife and child, to be read aloud by the evening fire during the weeks of his absence.

Each of Groves accounts, each journey, is unique. There is movement as dream, the poetry of silence as sleigh runners pass over soft snow. There is the terror of winter storms, the temperatures dropping so low the horse's leather halters snap and human breath freezes instantly with a crackling sound like the voices of stars. Grove tells of wondrous passages through daylight into the shadow of a winter moon, of marsh fogs fading to reveal the northern lights. He tells of desperate journeys with injured children and dying women across landscapes shaped by snow and wind where the carcasses of dead animals form

202

dark outlines on the prairie. For Grove, nature is not an entity but a condition, something to be endured rather than heralded.

Grove experienced Canada not as a wilderness but as a remote and wild, vibrantly beautiful, homeland. To him it was a neighbourhood, albeit an odd one, where caribou outnumbered people, but a neighbourhood nevertheless, where man, woman and nature had long ago come to terms with one another; those terms involved a set of relationships to the land that demanded the luxury of space. Within that vast territory of the spirit, in the solitude of the prairie, he discovered what it meant to be of this place.

For Canada's Native peoples, this sense of place, this topography of the spirit, at one time informed every aspect of existence. I once met in the Yukon an elderly Sekani man who was completely confounded by a missionary's notion of heaven. He couldn't believe anyone could be expected to give up smoking, drinking, swearing, carousing and all the things that made life worth living in order to go to a place where they didn't allow animals. "No caribou?" he would say in complete astonishment. He couldn't conceive of a world without wild things.

Mike Jones often told of the time in northern Ontario when he hired a Cree trapper, Peter Whitehawk, to assist him with an environmental assessment study. For several weeks and in growing frustration, the Indian watched as Mike set out tiny traps to capture small rodents. Finally, unable to restrain himself, Whitehawk left camp one morning before dawn. Mike awoke to find one of his mousetraps on the breakfast table. Placed beside it was a carefully excavated wolf track. Taught since childhood to avoid direct criticism, Whitehawk had nevertheless felt compelled to warn Mike that he would never catch anything worthwhile with a trap that small.

This simplicity of gesture, like the privilege of silence, is part of the language of a people for whom actions count far more than words. In northern British Columbia, some years ago, I worked in a hunting camp with Alex Jack, an old Gitxsan man, wrangling horses and repairing fences, guiding the odd hunter in search of moose or goat. Each day I would ask Alex to tell me the stories of the old days, the myths or tales of his people and his land. Though he happily told of his youth, of the daily hunting forays that brought meat to the village and of the winter trading runs by dogsled to the coast, Alex never said a word about the legends.

He preferred to speak of survival, of winters when the winds blew so hard the caribou froze, dogs died, people were reduced to eating spruce bark, and parents had to choose which of their young would live and which would be abandoned to die. I remember once when we passed an encampment where his Bear Lake people had settled for several years. Alex didn't describe it as a place where they had lived. "Here," he said with the carefully chosen words of one speaking a foreign language, "is where we survived."

Months later, long after I had given up on hearing the origin myths, I paddled out to salvage a moose carcass that a trophy hunter had abandoned in the bush. When I returned after two days with a canoe full of meat, Alex was waiting for me at the dock. As we walked back across the pineflat with our loads, he said very quietly that he remembered a story. That night I began to record a long series of We-gyt Creator tales.

Some nights later I asked Alex how long it took to complete the cycle of tales. He replied that he had asked his father that very question. To find out, they had strapped on their snowshoes and walked the length of Bear Lake, a distance of some 25 kilometres, telling the story as they went along. They reached the far end and returned all the way home, and the story, as Alex recalled, "wasn't halfway done."

Twenty years have passed since that season in the forest, and though I now live in the valley with Alex for part of each year, I have yet to comprehend the landscape that he knows so well. I do understand something of the medicine power, and I know what happened on the night that We-gyet flung his arrows past the moon. I know of the day when the Meat Mother spread her robe between the peaks and tossed the animals skyward, each to land in its favoured habitat. I cannot walk with the mountain goats without remembering the story of the child who rescued the people from their greed, and each time I see the northern lights I think of the warriors fallen in battle, their blood staining the sky and the sighs of their widows whistling in the darkness. Bear droppings on a trail, aspen leaves spinning in the breeze, hawks dipping and diving with the wind—all these sights are now reminders of ancient tales of balance and honour, of laughter and tears, in a land where the Old Ways were once revered and the children nursed on the magic of the white winds.

Canada has not been kind to its Native peoples. Yet their spirit still lingers, now intermingled with the lives of the newcomers: the wranglers and guides in the mountains of the west, the fishermen and women working the nets in the salt chuck off the coast of Nova Scotia, the trappers who disappear with the frost into the forests of Saskatchewan, the prospectors scratching for gold from Labrador to the Yukon, the men and women of Newfoundland who have died on the ice hunting seals. They live on the trails of the Rockies, in the Gaspé, by the lakes and streams of Ontario's woodlands and across the limitless tundra—ordinary Canadians, drawn together in a landscape whose very indifference breeds tolerance and respect. They have little in common save some random mutation in their family past that coded for stubbornness—and a deep conviction that Canada is a paradise that cannot be improved upon.

If you get as far as Tatogga Lake this summer, you won't find Mike Jones. Last winter it got so cold that mountain goats ate their own hair and caribou browsed on willow branches thick as a man's thumb. More than 30 metres of snow fell on the coast mountains. Sometime just before Christmas, Mike disappeared on his trapline at Bowser lake. The Mounties found his dog, Chinook, 15 kilograms underweight, and judging from the few pelts found in the line cabin, they figure Mike went through the ice not long after he reached his trapline. They didn't find his body until spring. The entire valley went numb with grief and disbelief. Mike knew the bush as well as anyone. He understood the whispered messages of the wild.

When you get to Tatogga, or the cliffs of Cape Breton, or the Alberta badlands, pause long enough to find an open ridge where the sky seems to shelter the earth, or a valley where horses shake manes that quiver like sheets of distant rain. Watch for pollen in the wind, an eagle circling, ice forming on a summer lake. When you find a place where the clouds and mist envelop the peaks, creating that special illusion of depth that grants meaning to all travel, tip your hat to those who have come before you, breaking trail.

IN THE SHADOW
OF RED CEDAR

In the shadow of red cedar, along a stream coloured by salmon, in a place where plants draw food from the air and small creatures living on dew never touch the forest floor, it is difficult to imagine a time when the coastal temperate rain forests of North America did not exist. Today, these immense and mysterious forests, which in scale and wonder dwarf anything to be found in the tropics, extend in a vast arc from northern California 3200 kilometres north and west to the Copper River and the Gulf of Alaska. Home to myriad species of plants and animals, a constellation of life unique on Earth, they spread between sea and mountain peak, reaching across and defying national boundaries as they envelop all who live within their influence in an unrivalled frontier of the spirit.

It is a world anchored in the south by giant sequoias, the most massive of living beings, and coast redwoods that soar 90 metres above the fog banks of Mendocino. In the north, two trees flourish, western hemlock, with its delicate foliage and finely furrowed bark, and Sitka spruce, most majestic of all, a stunningly beautiful species with blue-reen needles that are salt tolerant and capable of extracting minerals and nutrients from sea spray. In between, along the silent reaches of the midcoast of British Columbia, behind a protective veil of Sitka spruce, rise enormous stands of Douglas fir. Intermingled with hemlock and fir, growing wherever the land is moist and the rains abundant, is perhaps the most important denizen of the Pacific slope, the western red cedar, the tree that made possible the florescence of the great and ancient cultures of the coast.

To walk through these forests in the depths of winter, when the rain turns to mist and settles softly on the moss, is to step back in time. Two hundred million years ago vast coniferous forests formed a mantle across the entire planet. Dinosaurs evolved long supple necks to browse high among their branches. Then evolution took a great leap, and flowers were born. What made them remarkable was a mechanism of pollination and fertilization that changed the course of life on Earth. In the more primitive conifers, the plant must produce the basic food for the seed with no certainty that it will be fertilized. In the flowering plants, by contrast, fertilization itself sparks the creation of the seed's food reserves. In other words, unlike the conifers, the flowering plants make no investment without the assurance that a viable seed will be produced. As a result of this and other evolutionary advances, the flowering plants came to dominate the Earth in an astonishingly short time. Most conifers became extinct, and those that survived retreated to the margins of the world, where a small number of species maintained a foothold by adapting to particularly harsh conditions. Today, at a conservative estimate, there are over 250,000 species of flowering plants. The conifers have been reduced to a mere seven hundred species, and in the tropics, the hotbed of evolution, they have been almost completely displaced.

On all the Earth, there is only one region of any size and significance where, because of particular climatic conditions, the conifers retain their former glory. Along the northwest coast of North America the summers are hot and dry, the winters cold and wet. Plants need water and light to create food. Here in the summer there is ample light for photosynthesis but not enough water for most deciduous trees, except in low-lying areas where broad-leafed species such as red alder, cotton-wood and vine maple flourish. In the winter, when both water and light are sufficient, the low temperatures cause the flowering plants to lose their leaves and become dormant. The evergreen conifers, by contrast, are able to grow throughout the long winters, and since they use water more efficiently than broad-leafed plants, they also thrive during the dry summer months. The result is an ecosystem so rich and so productive that the biomass in the best sites is easily four times as great as that of any comparable area of the tropics.

Indeed it is the scale and abundance of the coastal rain forests that overwhelms the visitor. White pine, the tallest tree of the eastern deciduous forests, barely reaches 60 metres; in the coastal rain forests there are thirteen species that grow higher, with the redwoods reaching nearly 120 metres, taller than a twenty-five storey building. Red cedars can be 6 metres or more across at the base. The footprint of a Douglas fir would crush a small cabin. The trunk of a western hemlock, a miracle of biological engineering, stores thousands of litres of water and supports branches festooned with as many as 70 million needles, all capturing the light of the sun. Spread out on the ground, the needles of a single tree would create a photosynthetic surface ten times the size of a football field.

These giant trees delight, but the real wonder of the forest lies in the details, in the astonishingly complex relationships. A pileated wood-pecker living in the hollow of a snag, tiny seabirds laying their eggs among the roots of an ancient cedar, marbled murrelets nesting in a depression in the moss in the fork of a canopy tree, rufous humming-birds returning each spring, their migrations timed to coincide with the flowering of salmonberries. In forest streams dwell frogs with tails and lungless salamanders that live by absorbing oxygen through their skin. Strange amphibians, they lay their eggs not in water but on land, in moist debris and fallen logs.

Invertebrate life is remarkably diverse. The first survey to explore systematically the forest canopy in the Carmanah Valley of Vancouver Island yielded fifteen thousand species, a third of the invertebrates known to exist in all of Canada. Among the survey's collections were five hundred species previously unknown to science. Life is equally rich and abundant on the forest floor. There are twelve species of slugs, slimy herbivores that in some areas account for as much as 70 per cent of the animal biomass. A square metre of soil may support 2,000 earth-worms, 40,000 insects, 120,000 mites, 120,000,000 nematodes and millions upon millions of protozoa and bacteria, all alive, moving through the earth, feeding, digesting, reproducing and dying.

None of these creatures, of course, live in isolation. In nature, no event stands alone. Every biological process, each chemical reaction, leads to the unfolding of other possibilities for life. Tracking these strands through an ecosystem is as complex as untangling the distant threads of memory from a myth. For years, even as industrial logging created clearcuts the size of small nations, the coastal rain forests were among the least studied ecosystems on the planet. Only within the last decade or two have biologists begun to understand and chart tbe dynamic forces and complex ecological relationships that allow these magnificent forests to exist.

One begins with wind and rain, the open expanse of the Pacific and the steep escarpment of mountains that makes possible the constant cycling of water between land and sea. Autumn rains last until those of spring, and months pass without a sign of the sun. Sometimes the rain falls as mist, and moisture is raked from the air by the canopy of the forest. At other times, the storms are torrential and daily precipitation is measured in centimetres. The rains draw nutrients from the soil, carrying vital food into rivers and streams that fall away to the sea, and support the greatest coastal marine diversity on Earth. In the estuaries and tidal flats of British Columbia, in shallows that merge with the wetlands, are six hundred types of seaweed, seventy species of sea stars. Farther offshore, vast underwater kelp forests shelter hundreds of forms of life, which in turn support a food chain that reaches into the sky to nourish dozens of species of seabirds.

The land provides for life in the sea, but the sea in turn nurtures the land. Birds deposit excrement in the moss, yielding tonnes of nitrogen and phosphorus that are washed into the soil by winter rains. Salmon return by the millions to their native streams, providing food for eagles and ravens, grizzly and black bears, killer whales, river otters and more than twenty other mammals of the sea and forest. Their journey complete, the sockeye and coho, chinooks, chums and pinks drift down-stream in death and are slowly absorbed back into the nutrient cycle of life. In the end there is no separation between forest and ocean, between the creatures of the land and those of the sea. Every living thing on the rain coast ultimately responds to the same ecological rhythm. All are interdependent.

The plants that dwell on land nevertheless face unique challenges, especially that of securing nutrients from thin soils leached by rain throughout much of the year. The tangle of ecological adaptations that has evolved in response is nothing short of miraculous. As much as a fifth of the biomass in the foliage of an old-growth Douglas fir, for example, is an epiphytic lichen, *Lobaria oregana*, which fixes nitrogen directly from the air and passes it into the ecosystem. The needles of Sitka spruce absorb phosphorus, calcium and magnesium, and their high rate of transpiration releases moisture to the canopy, allowing the lichens to flourish.

On the forest floor, thick mats of sphagnum and other mosses filter rainwater and protect the mycelia of hundreds of species of fungi; these elements form one of the richest mushroom floras on Earth. Mycelia are the vegetative phase of a fungus, small hairlike filaments that spread through the organic layer at the surface of the soil, absorbing food and precipitating decay. A mushroom is simply the fruiting structure, the reproductive body. As the mycelia grow, they constantly encounter tree roots. If the species combination is the right one, a remarkable biological event unfolds. Fungus and tree come together to form mycorrhizae, a symbiotic partnership that allows both to benefit. The tree provides the fungus with sugars created from sunlight. The mycelia in turn enhance the tree's ability to absorb nutrients and water from the soil. They also produce growth-regulating chemicals that promote the production of new roots and enhance the immune system. Without this union, no tree could thrive. Western hemlocks are so dependent on mycorrhizal fungi that their roots barely pierce the surface of the earth, even as their trunks soar into the canopy.

The story only gets better. All life requires nitrogen for the creation of proteins. Nitrates, a basic source, are virtually absent from the acidic, heavily leached soils of the rain forest. The mycorrhizae, however, contain not only nitrogen-fixing bacteria that produce this vital raw material but also a yeast culture that promotes the growth of both the bacteria and the fungus. There are scores of different mycorrhizae—the roots of single Douglas fir may have as many as forty types—and like any form of life, the fungus must compete, reproduce and find a means to disperse its spore. The fruiting body in many cases is an underground mushroom or a truffle. When mature, it emits a pungent odour that seeps through the soil to attract rodents, flying squirrels and redbacked voles, delicate creatures that live exclusively on a refined diet of truffles. As the voles move about the forest, they scatter droppings, neat little bundles of feces that contain yeast culture, fungal spores and nitrogen-fixing bacteria—in short, all that is required to inoculate roots and prompt the creation of new mycorrhizae.

Fungi bring life to the forest both by their ability to draw nutrients to the living and by their capacity to transform the dead. In old-growth forests 20 per cent of the biomass—as much as 600 tonnes per hectare—is retained in fallen debris and snags. There is as much nutrition on the ground as there is within it. The moss on the forest floor is so dense that virtually all seedlings sprout from the surface of rotting wood, stumps and logs, which may take several hundred years to decay.

When a tree falls in the forest, it is immediately attacked by fungi and a multitude of insects. The wood provides a solid diet of carbohydrates. To secure proteins and other nutrients, the fungi deploy natural antibiotics to kill nitrogen-fixing bacteria. Chemical attractants emitted by the fungi draw in other prey, such as nematode worms, which are dispatched with exploding poison sacs and an astonishing arsenal of microscopic weapons. The assault on the log comes from many quarters. Certain insects, incapable of digesting wood directly, exploit fungi to do the work. Ambrosia beetles, for example, deposit fungal spores in tunnels bored into the wood. After the spores germinate, the tiny insects cultivate the mushrooms on miniature farms that flourish in the dark.

In time, other creatures appear—mites and termites, carpenter ants that chew long galleries in the wood and establish captive colonies of aphids that produce honeydew from the sap of plants. Eventually, as the log progresses through various stages of decay, other scavengers join the fray, including those that consume white cellulose, turning wood blood-red and reducing the heartwood to dust. Two centimetres of soil may take a thousand years to accumulate. Organic debris may persist for centuries. Dead trees are the life of the forest, but their potential is realized only slowly and with great patience.

This observation leads to perhaps the most extraordinary mystery of all. Lush and astonishingly prolific, the coastal temperate rain forests are richer in their capacity to produce the raw material of life than any other terrestrial ecosystem on Earth. The generation of this immense natural wealth is made possible by a vast array of biological interactions so complex and sophisticated as to suggest an evolutionary lineage drifting back to the dawn of time. Yet all evidence indicates that these forests emerged only within the last few thousand years. In aspect and species composition they may invoke the great coniferous forests of the distant geologic past, but as a discrete and evolving ecosystem the coastal temperate rain forests are still wet with the innocence of birth.

Some twenty thousand years ago, what is today British Columbia was a place of turmoil and ice. The land was young, unstable, given to explosive eruptions that burst over the shore. A glacial sheet more than 1800 metres thick covered the interior of the province, forging mountains and grinding away valleys as it moved over the land, determining for all time the fate of rivers. On the coast, giant tongues of ice carved deep fjords beneath the sea. The sea levels fell by 90 metres, and the sheer weight of ice depressed the shoreline to some 230 metres below its current level. Fourteen thousand years ago, an instant in geologic time, the ice began to melt and the glaciers retreated for the last time. The ocean invaded the shore, inundating coastal valleys and islands. But the land, freed at last of the weight of eons, literally sprang up. Within a mere thousand years, the water drained back into the sea, and the coastline became established more or less as it is today.

Only in the wake of these staggering geological events did the forests come into being. At first the land was dry and cold, an open landscape of aspen and lodgepole pine. Around ten thousand years ago, even as the first humans appeared on the coast, the air became more moist and Douglas fir slowly began to displace the pine. Sitka spruce flourished, though hemlock and red cedar remained rare. Gradually, the climate became warmer, with long seasons without frost. As more and more rain fell, endless banks of clouds sheltered the trees from the radiant sun. Western hemlock and red cedar expanded their hold on the south coast, working their way north at the expense of both fir and Sitka spruce.

For the first people of the rain coast, this ecological transition became an image from the dawn of time, a memory of an era when Raven slipped from the shadow of cedar to steal sunlight and cast the moon and stars into the heavens. Mythology enshrined natural history, for it was the diffusion of red cedar that allowed the great cultures of the Pacific Northwest to emerge. The nomadic hunters and gatherers who for centuries had drifted with the seas along the western shores of North America were highly adaptive, capable of taking advantage of every new opportunity for life. Though humans had inhabited the coast for at least five thousand years, specialized tools first appear in the archaeological record around 3000 B.C., roughly the period when red cedar came into its present dominance in the forests. Over the next millennium, a dramatic shift in technology and culture occurred. Large cedar structures were in use a thousand years before the Christian era. A highly distinct art form developed by 500 B.C. Stone mauls and wooden wedges, obsidian blades and shells honed to a razor's edge allowed the highly durable wood to be worked into an astonishing array of objects, which in turn expanded the potential of the environment.

Though in time some five hundred plants would be used on the coast, red cedar was from the beginning the tree of life. Its soft and pliant inner bark provided cordage and the fibre that was woven into clothing. Steamed, the wood could be bent into boxes that allowed for the efficient storage of food, especially salmon, berries and eulachon oil. Cedar provided armour and weapons for war, hewn planks for housing, dugout canoes for transportation, fishing and hunting whales and seals. It also provided the template upon which dreams could be brought into daylight, families celebrated, and mythological time remembered in the form of crests, memories of the dead displayed for generations of the living.

With cedar as the material foundation of culture, and salmon and other marine resources providing the mainstay of the diet, the seafarers forged the most complex civilization ever to emerge without benefit of agriculture. Although living in permanent settlements, in a stratified world of commoners, slaves, shaman and noble elite, the people remained foragers, nomads of the open seas, hunters whose lives depended on their relationship with the wild. Unlike so many who had succumbed to the cult of the seed, the nations of the coast believed in the power of animals, accepted the existence of magic, acknowledged the potency of the spirit. The physical world presented but one face of reality. Behind it existed an inner world of meaning, a place reached through transformation, a passage familiar to shamans and recalled by all during the great winter dances and ritual celebrations.

Living from nature, and lacking the technology to dominate it, the people watched the Earth for signs. The flight of eagles helped fishermen track salmon. Sandhill cranes heralded the onset of herring runs. The flowering of certain plants brought families to the shore to gather clams, but if ravens and crows abandoned the beach, so did the people, for it was a sure indication that the shellfish were toxic. Between humans and animals there was a constant dialogue, expressed in physical action, in gesture and repartee, but also in myths and stories that resonated with magical and mystical ideas. The Tlingit addressed plants as spirits, offering prayers before harvesting a tree. Nuu-chah-nulth ceremonies sought protection for the hunter and beseeched whales to give freely of their lives. When raging currents threatened Haida war parties, the paddlers scattered swan feathers upon the water to calm the sea. Encounters with grizzly bears brought power to the Gitxsan. The Kwagiulth dispatched initiates into the forest to seek Huxwhukw and the Crooked-Beak of Heaven, cannibal spirits living at the north end of the world.

Though neither sentimental nor weakened by nostalgia, these indigenous cultures forged through time and ritual a traditional mystique of the Earth that was based not only on deep attachment to the land but also on far more subtle intuition—the idea that the land was breathed into being by human consciousness. Mountains, rivers and forests were not perceived as inanimate, as mere props on a stage upon which the human drama unfolds. For these societies, the land was alive, a dynamic force to be embraced and transformed by the human imagination. Whether this was true in some absolute sense is not the point. Rather, the significance lies in the manner in which the conviction played out in the day-to-day lives of the people. A child raised to revere the forest as the domain of the spirits will be a fundamentally different person from a child brought up to believe that a forest exists to be cut.

I was fifteen when I first learned that all of these ancient forests, from California to Alaska, were dying. This startling information was presented to my school biology class in a documentary film sponsored by Weyerhaeuser and featuring as host and narrator the actor Eddie Albert, famous for his role as the husband of Eva Gabor in the television hit *Green Acres*. It was difficult news to swallow. The script called for Mr. Arnold to make his pronouncement while walking along a trail in a verdant grove of hemlocks and cedars. The trees were massive, 3 metres or more across at the base, and all were draped in lichens which fused with the dense and lush moss of the forest floor. Mist hung in the air. From fallen logs sprouted wisps of red huckleberry and salal. A stream ran through the frame, and on either bank grew dense thickets of sword ferns and salmonberry.

"True, it looks healthy," Arnold cautioned, "but don't let it fool you. This forest is dying."

Our teacher, a flaccid individual with a brilliant shock of red hair, explained the scientific foundation for Arnold's astonishing assertion. Science had shown that the annual increment of cellulose in a young tree plantation was greater than that of an ancient forest. The old growth was, by definition, a forest in decline. The trees were overmature. To see evidence of decadence, one had only to look at the dead-fall, tonnes of rotting timber wasted on the forest floor. The goal of proper management was to replace these inefficient stands with fresh and productive new forests. A regime of carefully monitored clearcut logging would eliminate the old growth, the debris would be burned, and the land sown with a uniform plantation comprised of only the most up-to-date conifer seedlings. In short, modern forestry would clean up the mess inherited from nature.

Even as a teenager, sitting in a classroom overlooking the forested slopes of Vancouver Island, I had the sense that somebody was playing with a short deck. Industrial logging on a massive scale had been underway in British Columbia since the end of the Second World War. The rotation cycle—the rate at which forests were to be cut across the province, and thus the foundation of sustained-yield forestry—was based on the assumption that all of the old growth would be cut and replaced with tree farms. The intrinsic value of the ancient forests had no place in the calculus of forest planning. The science of forestry provided the rationale for eradication. The obvious beneficiaries of such ideas and policies were the large timber concerns, including the sponsor of the film we had been obliged to watch.

Some years later, soon after graduating from university, I experienced firsthand the actual practice of modern forestry. Working for one of the largest timber companies in British Columbia, I spent a long winter in a logging camp near the west coast of Haida Gwaii, or the Queen Charlottes, as the islands were then commonly known. Hired as a forestry engineer, I worked as a surveyor, which meant that I spent most of my time in the primary forest, far ahead of the fallers and loggers, laying out roads and falling boundaries, determining the pattern in which the trees would come down. In the depth of winter our small crew moved through stands of red cedar, hemlock and Sitka spruce, trees as tall as cathedrals.

Inevitably, there was, at least for me, an almost surreal quality to life in our remote camp, where men lived away from their families and earned a wage cutting down in minutes trees that had taken centuries to grow. The constant grinding of machinery, the disintegration of the forest into burnt slash and mud, the wind and sleet that froze on the rigging and whipped across the frozen bay, etched patterns into the lives of the men. Still, no one in our camp had any illusions about what we were doing. All talk of sustained yield and overmature timber, decadent and normal forests, we left to government bureaucrats and company foresters. We used to laugh at the little yellow signs stuck on the sides of roads that only we would ever travel, announcing that 8 hectares had been replanted, as if it mattered in a clearcut that stretched to the horizon.

With haunting regularity, winter gales swept through the islands, and along the face of the forest exposed by the clearcut, it was not unusual to encounter hectares of timber brought down by the wind.

The result was a nightmare of overlapping trunks and roots, thousands of tonnes of wood weighted down with immense pressure and ready to explode with the first cut of a saw. Salvaging blowdown was dreaded work, dangerous and sometimes deadly. To mitigate the hazard and avoid the loss of fibre, government foresters permitted us to expand our cutblocks with wind-firm boundaries as the goal. As a result, openings grew to encompass entire valleys, with the edge of the clearcut reaching to the ridge line of distant mountains. If a slope was deemed too steep to be logged, it was only because machinery could not get to it. Trees left standing by the edge of lakes or along streams inevitably blew over in the next storm. So these too were cut. My immediate boss used to joke about getting rid of the forest so that we could see something. Once, when questioned about the wisdom of logging across a salmon stream, he replied, "Hell, that's no creek, just a draw with a little bit of water in it."

Everyone knew, of course, that the ancient forests would never come back, at least not in any meaningful time frame. The tangle of half-hearted trees that grew up in the slash no more resembled the forest they had displaced than a wheat field resembles a wild prairie meadow. But nobody was worried about what we were doing. It was work, and living on the edge of that immense forest, people simply believed that it would go on forever.

If anyone in the government had a broader perspective, we never heard about it. Our camp was 30 kilometres by water across an inlet from a back road that ran 65 kilometres to the nearest forestry office. The government had cut back on overtime pay, and what with the statutory coffee and lunch breaks, the forestry employees had no way of travelling to our camp and back in less than seven-and-a-half hours. So they rarely came. The bureaucracy within the company was not much better. The mills down south often complained that our camp was sending them inferior grades of Douglas fir, which was surprising since the species does not grow on the islands of Haida Gwaii.

There were, of course, vague murmurs of ecological concern that filtered through to our camp. One morning in the cookhouse I ran into a friend of mine, a rock blaster named Archie whose voice had been dusted by a lifetime of cigarettes and the dirt from a dozen mine explosions. He was reading an old newspaper, and the headline said something about Greenpeace.

"Sons of bitches don't know a damn thing about pollution," Archie said. He then proceeded to tell me about working conditions in the hardrock uranium mines of the Northwest Territories shortly after the Second World War. Concerned about the impact of radioactivity, the companies used to put the workers, including Archie, into large sealed chambers and release a gas with particles of aluminum suspended in it. The idea was that the aluminum would coat the lungs, and at the end of the shift the men would gag it up, together with any radioactive dust.

"Now that," growled Archie, "was environmental pollution."

In truth, it is difficult to know how much life in the midst of such destruction actually affected the men working in the forest. Some clearly believed blindly in the process and were hardened by that faith. Others were so transient, moving from camp to camp, sometimes on a monthly basis, that they never registered the full measure of the impact of any one logging show. Some just didn't care. Because the entire industry was so itinerant, no one ever developed a sense of belonging to a place. There was no attachment to the land, nor could there be, given what we were doing. In the slash of the clearcut, there was little room for sentiment.

Talk for the most part was of wages and survival. Logging is among the most perilous of occupations. Were a government office of five hundred employees to suffer the injury rate typical of a west coast logging camp, the office workers would see someone carried out on a stretcher virtually every day. Six or seven times a year there would be a death. In the year I worked in the woods I heard of a faller killed by a snag that pierced his hard-hat and exited his groin. Another returned to camp covered in blood; his saw had kicked back and ripped a trench in his face. In a neighbouring camp, a trigger-happy rigging slinger blew in the main line before the chokermen were clear of the bight. The logs hung up, nose-dived into the ground and then, torn by the force of the yarder's two-thousand horsepower, swung about like a giant scythe. One man was crushed beneath a hundred tonnes of spruce. Another miraculously escaped unscathed, losing only his hard hat. The third and youngest was struck in the back of the head. No one was able to find his face.

The fallers were a breed apart, the elite of the camp, rough-cut individuals willing to risk their lives in exchange for the highest industrial wages in the province. They loved the solitude of the forest, even when its silence was broken by the whine of their saws. In their massive hands these formidable machines could appear almost toylike. But each weighed nearly 14 kilograms, packed the power of an outboard motor and at full throttle drove 30 metres of sharpened steel chain around a 120-centimetre bar every second. Such a tool cuts through a 90-centimetre log in a minute, a leg in the wink of an eye. In time, the vibration affects the circulation in the hands. Several old fallers in camp could get to sleep at night only by tying their hands above their heads to reduce the pain. Others had nightmares of trees that twisted and split as they fell, or hollow snags that collapsed and exploded. One spoke of a friend who never returned from a shift. Buried by blow-down, his body was not found until the setting was logged.

It was impossible not to admire these men, but it was equally difficult to ignore the consequences of what we were doing. Week by week, month by month, the edge of the clearcut spread, consuming the forest and leaving in its wake a torn and desolate landscape, pounded by winter rains that carried away the thin soil in dark torrents to the sea. What ultimately happened to the land was irrelevant. It was simply abandoned to nature. In the nine months I spent in the camp I never saw a tree planted, let alone evidence of a sustained program of modern silviculture. I cannot recall a single decision that was influenced in any way by an ecological concern. The priority and focus of every aspect of the logging operation was the extraction of timber. Roads were built as cheaply and efficiently as possible and, with the exception of mainline corridors, expected to last only long enough to access the wood. Streams clogged by riprap, mountain sides etched with erosion and scarred by landslides, clearcuts piled high with wood, wasted and abandoned—these were the norm, the inevitable result not just of an economic imperative but of a way of thinking that viewed the forest as but a resource to be exploited. As surely as a miner rips coal from the earth, we were cutting away the rain forest. It was a one-time deal, and we all knew it.

Like everyone in camp, I was there to make money. On weekends, when our survey crew was down, I picked up overtime pay by working in the slash as a chokerman, wrapping the cables around the fallen logs so the yarder could drag them to the landing where they were loaded onto the trucks. Setting beads was the most miserable job in a logging show, the bottom rung of the camp hierarchy.

One Saturday I was working in a setting high up on the mountain that rose above the camp. It had been raining all day and the winds were blowing from the southeast, dragging clouds across the bay and up the slope, where they hung up in the tops of the giant hemlocks and cedars that rose above the clearcut. We were working the edge of the opening, but the landing was unusually close by. It took no time at all for the mainline to haul the logs in and for the haulback to fling the chokers back to us. We had been highballing all day, and both my partner and I were a mess of mud, grease and tree sap. He was a young Nisga'a from New Aiyansh on the Nass River, but that's all I knew about him.

Late in the afternoon something got fouled up on the landing and the yarder shut down. Suddenly, it was quiet and you could hear the wind that had been driving sleet into our faces all day. My partner and I abandoned the slash for the shelter of the forest. We found a dry spot out of the wind in a hollow at the base of an enormous cedar and waited for the yarder to start up. We didn't speak. He kept staring off into the forest. All hunched up with the cold, we looked the same— orange hard-hats, green-black rain gear, rubber corkboots. We shared a cigarette. I was watching his face as he smoked. It struck me as strange that here we were, huddled in the forest in silence, two young men from totally different worlds. I tried to imagine what it might have been like had we met but a century before, I perhaps a trader, he a shadow in the wet woods. His people had made a home in the forest for thousands of years. I thought of what this country must have been like when my own grandfather arrived. I saw in the forest around us a world that my own children might never know, that Nisga'a children would never know. I turned to my partner. The whistle blew on the landing.

"What the hell are we doing?" I asked.

"Working," he said. I watched him as he stepped back into the clearcut, and then I followed. We finished the shift and, in the falling darkness, rode to camp together in the back of the company crummy. That was the last I saw of him.

Twenty years have passed since I left that camp, and much has changed in the forest industry. I've often wondered what became of that Nisga'a youth. It is a good bet that he is no longer working as a logger. Native workers rarely get promoted beyond the landing, and what's more, over the last two decades a third of all logging jobs have been lost. Industry blames environmentalists, but the truth lies elsewhere. All the conservation initiatives have not cost the unions more than a few hundred jobs, if that. In many sectors of the forest economy, new regulations have in fact enhanced employment by mandating, for example, labour-intensive restorative efforts on cutover lands. Jobs have been sacrificed on a massive scale because industry, in an intensely competitive global marketplace, has consistently chosen efficiency and profit over employment.

In the last thirty years, the volume of timber logged has increased threefold, but the number of jobs generated per unit of wood has been cut in half. Modern mills consume wood at twice the rate but use half the labour to produce the same volume. In many camps, grapple yarders have eliminated rigging crews; two men now do the work of six. Automation, together with dwindling timber supplies, has put almost thirty thousand people out of work in British Columbia alone, and their jobs will not be replaced. Over fifty years ago exclusive timber rights to the most productive lands in British Columbia were granted to private companies on the condition that they would provide employment to the people of the province. This social contract, the foundation of a tenure system that ultimately locked up 94 per cent of the commercially viable provincial forests in timber supply, has been broken and betrayed.

Still we keep cutting. In Oregon and Washington, only 10 per cent of the original coastal rain forest remains. In California only 4 per cent of the redwoods have been set aside. In British Columbia, roughly 60 per cent has been logged, largely since 1950. In the two decades since I stood in the forest with that Nisga a youth, over half of all timber ever extracted from the public forests of British Columbia has been taken. At current rates of harvest, roughly 4 square kilometres of old growth per day, the next twenty years will see the destruction of every unprotected valley of ancient rain forest in the province.

In truth, no one really knows what will happen to these lands once they are logged. Forests are extraordinarily complex ecosystems. Biologists have yet to identify all of the species, let alone understand the relationships among them. Although we speak with unbridled confidence of our ability to reproduce the ecological conditions of a forest and grow wood indefinitely, there is no place on Earth that is currently cutting a fourth generation of timber on an industrial scale. The more imprecise a science, the more dogmatically its proponents cling to their ability to anticipate and predict phenomena.

Forestry as traditionally practised in the Pacific Northwest is less a science than an ideology, a set of ideas reflecting not empirical truths but the social needs and aspirations of a closed group of professionals with a vested interest in validating its practices and existence. The very language of the discipline is disingenuous, as if conceived to mislead. The Annual Allowable Cut is not a limit never to be exceeded but a quota to be met. The Fall Down Effect, the planned decline in timber production as the old growth is depleted, is promoted as if it were a natural phenomenon when it is, in fact, a stunning admission that the forests have been drastically overcut every year since modern forestry was implemented in the 1940s. Multiple Use Forestry—which implies that the forests are managed for a variety of purposes, including recreation, tourism and wildlife—begins with a clearcut. Old growth is "harvested," though it was never planted and no one expects it to grow back. Ancient forests are "decadent" and "overmature," when by any ecological definition they are at their richest and most biologically diverse state.

The most misleading of these terms is "sustained yield," for it has led the public to believe that the trees are growing back as fast as they are being cut. But they are not. In British Columbia alone there are 3.5 million hectares of insufficiently restocked lands. We continue to cut at a rate of 270,000 hectares per year. Every year 2.5 million logging truck loads roll down the highways of the province. Lined up bumper to bumper, they would encircle the Earth twice. In practice, sustained-yield forestry remains an untested hypothesis: after three generations we are still cutting into our biological capital, the irreplaceable old-growth forests. As a scientific concept, sustained yield loses all relevance when applied to an ecological situation the basic parameters of which remain unknown. At best, sustained yield is a theoretical possibility; at worst, a semantic sleight of hand, intended only to deceive.

Anyone who has flown over Vancouver Island, or seen the endless clearcuts of the interior of the province, grows wary of the rhetoric and empty promises of the forest industry. Fishermen and women become skeptical when they learn that logging has driven 142 salmon stocks to extinction and left 624 others on the brink. Timber for British Columbia mills now comes from Manitoba. Truck drivers from Quesnel, a pulp-and-paper town in the centre of the province, haul loads hundreds of kilometres south from the Yukon. Just one of the clearcuts southeast of Prince George covers 500 square kilometres, five times the area of the City of Toronto. This, after sixty years of official commitment to sustained-yield forestry. The lament of the old-time foresters—

that if only the public understood, it would appreciate what we do—falls flat. The public understands but does not like what it sees.

Fortunately, this orthodoxy is now being challenged. Many in the Pacific Northwest, including the best and brightest of professional foresters, recognize the need to move beyond, to an era in which resource decisions are truly based on ecological imperatives, in which the goal of economic sustainability is transformed from a cliché into an article of faith. To make this transition will not be easy, and it will involve much more than tinkering with the edges of an industry that generates $15.9 billion a year in the province of British Columbia alone. Dispatching delegations to Europe to reassure customers, or devising new regulations that if implemented may mitigate some of the worst ecological impacts, will neither restore the public's confidence and trust nor address the underlying challenge of transforming the economy.

Any worker who has wielded a saw or ripped logs from a setting knows that in the end it all comes down to production. The enormous wealth generated over the last fifty years has been possible only because we have been willing to indulge egregious practices in the woods that have little to do with the actual promise of forestry. Spreading clearcuts ever deeper into the hinterland is a policy of the past, crude and anachronistic, certain to lead to a dramatic decline in the forestry sector and to bitterness and disappointment in the communities that rely upon the forests for both spiritual and material well-being. Revitalizing cutover lands with vibrant tree plantations, implementing intensive silviculture to increase yields, establishing the finest model of forest management on a finite land base—these are initiatives that will both allow communities to prosper and enable them to fulfil a moral obligation to leave to the future as healthy an environment as the one they inherited.

There is no better place to pursue a new way of thinking than in the temperate rain forests of the coast. At the moment, less than 6 per cent has been protected, the remainder is slated to be logged. If anything, this ratio should be reversed. These forests are as rare and endangered as any natural feature on the face of the Earth, as biologically significant as any terrestrial ecosystem that has ever existed. If, knowing this, we still allow them to be cut down, what will it say about us as a people? What will be the legacy of our times?

The truth is that in an increasingly complex and fragmented world, we need these ancient forests, alive and intact. For the children of the

Nisga'a and other Native groups, they are an image of the beginning of time, when Raven emerged from the darkness and young boys went in search of mysteries at the far reaches of the world. For my own two young girls, they echo with a shallower history but one that is nevertheless rich in the struggles of their great-grandparents, men and women who travelled halfway around the world to live in this place. Today, all peoples in this land are drawn together by a single thread of destiny. We live at the edge of the clearcut; our hands will determine the fate of these forests. If we do nothing, they will be lost within our lifetime, and we will be left to explain our inaction. If we preserve these ancient forests, they will stand for all generations and for all time as symbols of the geography of hope. They are called old growth not because they are frail but because they shelter all of our history and embrace all of our dreams.

THE END
OF THE WILD

S ome years ago at a symposium in Barbados, I was fortunate to share the podium with two extraordinary scientists. The first to speak was Richard Leakey, the renowned anthropologist who, with his mother and father, drew from the dust and ashes of Africa the story of the birth of our species. The meeting concluded with astronaut Story Musgrave, the first physician to walk in space. It was an odd and moving juxtaposition of the endpoints of the human experience. Dr. Musgrave recognized the irony, and it saddened him. He told of what it had been like to know the beauty of the Earth as seen from the heavens. There he was, suspended 320 kilometres miles above the Earth, travelling 29 000 kilometres per hour with the golden visor of his helmet illuminated by a single sight, a small and fragile blue planet, floating, as he recalled, "in the velvet void of space." To have experienced that vision, he said, a sight made possible only by the brilliance of human technology, and to remember the blindness with which we as a species abuse our only home, was to know the purest sensation of horror.

Many believe that this image of the Earth, first brought home to us but a generation ago, will have a more profound impact on human thought than did the Copernican revolution of the sixteenth century, which transformed the philosophical foundations of the Western world by revealing that our planet was not the centre of the universe. From space, we see not a limitless frontier nor the stunning products of man but a single interactive sphere of life, a living organism composed of air, water and soil. It is this transcendent vision which, more than any amount of scientific data, teaches us the Earth is a finite place that can endure our foolish ways for only so long.

225

In light of this new perspective, this new hope, the past and present deeds of human beings often appear inconceivably cruel and sordid. Shortly after leaving Barbados, while lecturing in the American Midwest, I visited two places that in a different, more sensitive world would surely be enshrined as memorials to the victims of the ecological catastrophes that occurred there. The first locality was the site of the last great nesting flock of passenger pigeons, a small stretch of woodland on the banks of the Green River near Mammoth Cave, Ohio. This story of extinction is well known. Yet until I stood in that cold, dark forest, I had never sensed the full weight of the disaster, the scale and violence of it.

At one time, passenger pigeons accounted for 40 per cent of the entire bird population of North America. In 1870, at a time when their numbers were already greatly diminished, a single column 1.5 kilometres wide and 500 kilometres long, containing an estimated two billion birds, passed over Cincinnati on the Ohio River. Imagine such a sight. Assuming that each bird ate 250 millilitres of seeds a day, a flock that size must have consumed each day over 500 million litres of grain. Such sightings were not unusual. In 1813 James Audubon was travelling in a wagon from his home on the Ohio River to Louisville, some 100 kilometres away, when a stream of passenger pigeons filled the sky so that the "light of the noonday sun was obscured as by an eclipse." He reached Louisville at sunset and the birds were still coming. He estimated that the flock contained over one billion birds, and it was but one of several columns of pigeons that blackened the sky that day.

Audubon visited roosting and nesting sites to find trees 60 centimetres in diameter broken off at the ground by the weight of birds. He saw dung so deep on the forest floor that he mistook it for snow. He once stood in the midst of a flock when the birds took flight and then landed. He compared the noise and confusion to that of a gale, the sound of their landing to thunder.

It is difficult now to imagine the ravages that over the course of half a century destroyed this creature. Throughout the nineteenth century, pigeon meat was a mainstay of the American diet, and merchants in the eastern cities sold as many as eighteen thousand birds a day. Pigeon hunting was a full-time job for thousands of people. The term "stool pigeon" derives from a standard killing technique of the era. A hunter would sew shut the eyes of a living bird, bind its feet to a pole driven into the ground and wait in the surrounding grass for flocks to respond to its cry. When the birds came, they arrived in such numbers that the hunter could simply bat them out of the air with a club. The more affluent classes slaughtered birds for recreation. It was not unusual for shooting clubs to go through fifty thousand birds in a weekend competition; hundreds of thousands of live birds were catapulted to their death before the diminishing supply forced skeet shooters to turn to clay pigeons.

By 1896, a mere fifty years after the first serious impact of man, there were only some 250,000 birds left. In April of that year, the birds came together for one last nesting flock in the forest outside of Bowling Green, Ohio. Telegraph wires hummed with the news, and the hunters converged. In a final orgy of slaughter, over 200,000 pigeons were killed, 40,000 mutilated, 100,000 chicks destroyed. A mere 5,000 birds survived. The entire kill was to be shipped east, but there was a derailment on the line and the dead birds rotted in their crates. On March 24,1900, the last passenger pigeon in the wild was shot by a young boy. On September 1,1914, as the Battle of the Marne consumed the flower of European youth, the world's last passenger pigeon died in captivity.

When I left the scene of this final and impossible slaughter, I travelled west to Sioux City, Iowa, to speak at Buena Vista College. There, I was fortunate to visit a remnant patch of tall grass prairie, a 75-hectare preserve that represents one of the largest remaining vestiges of an ecosystem that once carpeted North America from southern Canada to Texas. Again it was winter, and the cold wind blew through the coneflowers and the dozens of species of grass. The young biology student who was with me was familiar with every species in that extraordinary mosaic—they were like old friends to him. Yet as we walked through that tired field, my thoughts drifted from the plants to the horizon. I tried to imagine buffalo moving through the grass, the physics of waves as millions of animals crossed the prairie.

As late as 1871, buffalo outnumbered people in North America. In that year one could stand on a bluff in the Dakotas and see nothing but buffalo in every direction for 50 kilometres. Herds were so large that it took days for them to pass a single point. Wyatt Earp described one herd of a million animals stretching across a grazing area the size of Rhode Island. Within nine years of that sighting, buffalo had vanished from the plains.

The destruction of the buffalo resulted from a campaign of biological terrorism unparallelled in the history of the Americas. United States government policy was explicit. As General Philip Sheridan wrote at the time, "The buffalo hunters have done more in the past two years to settle the vexed Indian Question than the regular army has accomplished in the last thirty years. They are destroying the Indians' commissary. Send them powder and lead, and let them kill until they have exterminated the buffalo," Between 1850 and 1880, more than 75 million buffalo hides were sold to American dealers. No one knows how many more animals were slaughtered and left on the prairie. A decade after Native resistance collapsed, Sheridan advised Congress to mint a commemorative medal, with a dead buffalo on one side, a dead Indian on the other.

I thought of this history as I stood in that tall grass prairie near Sioux City. What disturbed me the most was to realize how effortlessly we have removed ourselves from this ecological tragedy. Today, the people of Iowa, good and decent folk, live contentedly in a landscape of cornfields that is claustrophobic in its monotony. The era of the tall grass prairie, like the time of the buffalo, is as distant from their lives as the fall of Rome or the siege of Troy. Yet the destruction occurred but a century ago, well within the lifetime of their grandparents.

This capacity to forget, this fluidity of memory, is a frightening human trait. Several years ago, I spent many months in Haiti, a country that as recently as the 1920s was 80 per cent forested. Today, less than 5 per cent of the forest cover remains. I remember standing with a Vodoun priest on a barren ridge, peering across a wasteland, a desolate valley of scrub and halfhearted trees. He waxed eloquent as if words alone might have squeezed beauty from that wretched sight. He could think only of angels, I of locusts. Though witness to an ecological holocaust that within this century had devastated his entire country, this man had managed to endure without losing his human dignity. Faced with nothing, he adorned his life with his imagination. This was inspiring but also terrifying. People appear to be able to tolerate and adapt to almost any degree of environmental degradation. As the farmers of Iowa today live without wild things, the people of Haiti scratch a living from soil that may never again know the comfort of shade.

From a distance, both in time and space, we can perceive these terrible and poignant events for what they were, unmitigated ecological disasters that robbed us and the future of something unimaginably precious in order to satisfy the immediate and mundane needs of the present. The luxury of hindsight, however, does little to cure the blindness with which we today overlook deeds of equal magnitude and folly.

In a manner that will be difficult for our descendants to comprehend, we drift toward a world in which people take for granted an impoverished environment, transformed by foolish negligence and reduced by expediency to a shadow of the glory that once was. In three generations, a moment in time, we have contaminated the water, air and soil, driven countless species to extinction, dammed the rivers, poisoned the rain, torn down the ancient forests and ripped holes in the heavens. As Harvard biologist E. O. Wilson reminds us, this century will be remembered not for its wars or technological advances but rather as the era in which men and women stood by and either passively endorsed or actively supported the massive destruction of biological diversity on the planet.

Nowhere is the crisis more intense, or the outcome more consequential, than in the tropical rain forests, home to the greatest concentration of biological wealth on Earth. When Joseph Conrad wrote that the jungle was less a forest than a primeval mob, a remnant of an ancient era when vegetation rioted and consumed the Earth, he referred to a time still known to our fathers and mothers, a time when the tropical rain forests of the world stood immense, inviolable, a mantle of green stretching across entire continents. Today, sadly, that era is no more. In many parts of the tropics, the clouds are of smoke, the scents are of grease and lube oil, and the sounds are of machinery, the buzz of chainsaws and the cacophony of enormous reptilian earth movers hissing and moaning with exertion. It is a violent overture, like the opening notes of an opera about war, a war between humans and the land, a wrenching terminal struggle to make the latter conform to the whims and designs of the former. The residue of this war darkens the landscapes of Borneo and Sumatra, Madagascar and the Congo, Costa Rica, Gabon, Indonesia and a dozen other lands once covered in forest. Now the conflict consumes the heart of the Amazon, and it is there that the ultimate fate of the world's tropical rain forests will be decided.

For more than three years, I travelled in South America, largely in the Northwest Amazon of Colombia, Ecuador and Peru, living among twenty or more indigenous groups to study their use of plants. As a young anthropologist, I had learned that the key to overcoming cultural barriers was to identify common ground, a mutual passion that might provide a window into the inner workings of a society. In the Canadian north, where I was raised among the seasonally nomadic Athabaskans, the obvious metaphor was the hunt. Unless you were able

229

to follow caribou over the tundra and track moose through the spruce, you would never dance to the rhythm of the culture. In the Northwest Amazon, a world of leaves, water and silence, where the forest canopy is so dense that some Indians do not distinguish the colour blue from the colour green, you cannot know a people without embracing their plants. Botany provides the perfect conduit to culture. I became an ethnobotanist because I could not imagine any other way of understanding the lives of the people of the forest.

Perhaps because of this interest in both ethnography and botany, I sensed even as a student the parallel between the erosion of biological diversity and the collapse of cultural diversity. This connection, so obvious today, eluded many in those early years when academics, though cognizant of the unfolding reality, nevertheless remained wary. I recall one evening at Harvard in the fall of 1979 when E. O. Wilson strode to the lectern in the Nash Lecture Hall to introduce Norman Myers, who had recently published *The Sinking Ark*, one of the first books to anticipate the biodiversity crisis. The lecture hall was almost empty. That same evening, across Oxford Street at Sanders Theater, His Holiness the Fourteenth Dalai Lama was making his first public appearance in the United States, an overtly political act that sparked the campaign for a free Tibet. Naturally, Sanders Theater was packed. The historic significance of the Dalai Lama's visit did not register with Wilson, who referred to the Tibetan leader in decidedly unflattering terms. If even Harvard students could not get their priorities right, he noted in apologizing to Myers for the sparse audience, what chance did biologists have of educating the public at large?

Today, Professor Wilson, a man of modesty, wisdom and immense generosity of spirit, would be the first to acknowledge his oversight and note that, in speaking for the Tibetan people, the Dalai Lama was campaigning for the preservation of a way of life, a unique culture as vital to human destiny as any element of nature's mosaic. When Wilson was born, five years before the birth of the Dalai Lama, there were fifteen thousand languages spoken on Earth. A language, of course, is not merely a cluster of words or a set of grammatical rules; it is a flash of the human spirit, the filter through which the soul of a people reaches into the material world. A language is as divine and mysterious as a living creature. Today, perhaps six thousand languages still are spoken. Every two weeks, somewhere on Earth one of these is lost. In another century, only a few hundred will survive.

If there is one lesson that I have drawn from my travels, it is that cultural and biological diversity are far more than the foundation of stability, they are an article of faith, a fundamental truth that indicates the way things are supposed to be. If diversity is a source of wonder, its opposite—the ubiquitous condensation to some blandly amorphous and singularly generic modern culture that I have witnessed in all parts of the world—is a source of dismay. Travel offers a unique perspective, for if done carefully it allows you to stretch history across space. With a little effort, you can place yourself at almost any moment in this historical progression. In the course of an afternoon, I have moved from an indigenous society first contacted peacefully a decade before, to a neighbouring tribe whose ranks have been ravaged by disease and exploitation for centuries. In eastern Ecuador, I lived in a Kofán village that was destroyed in a single season by the discovery of oil. When I returned a year later, the shaman I once worked with had died and his son had a job with Texaco. I have seen Waorani children playing with piles of DDT dispensed by government health officials, Tukano men reduced to coca-growing serfs, Chimane women in absurd missionary dress Servicing the military posts in eastern Bolivia, Bora hunting lands stripped of vegetation and infested with cattle. In Borneo, the Penan, the last nomads of Southeast Asia, today live in squalid settlements in wooden shacks built of planks ripped from the trees of their forests.

We are living in the midst of an ecological catastrophe every bit as tragic as that of the slaughter of the buffalo and the passenger pigeon. Wherever one looks, there are governmental policies that are equally blind, economic rationales equally compelling. All memory is convulsed in an upheaval of violence. There is a fire burning over the Earth, taking with it plants and animals, cultures, languages, ancient skills and visionary wisdom. Quelling this flame and reinventing the poetry of diversity is the most important challenge of our times.

Also available from Tauris Parke Paperbacks

Letters of Transit
Adventures and Encounters from America to the Pacific Isles
Matthew Stevenson

A beautifully crafted and exciting blend of travel, history, political observation and personal experience, *Letters of Transit* is the distillation of the colourful and eventful journeys Matthew Stevenson has made throughout the world for over 20 years. The perfect travelling companion, Stevenson takes the reader with him on a diverse range of fascinating travels to places such as Serbia, Afghanistan, Northern Ireland, South Africa, Korea and America. He describes his crossing of Poland by bicycle, a family holiday to Petra, bullfights in Mexico City, a visit to the battlefield at Guadalcanal, where his father fought and a trip to Palestinian refugee camps in Jordan. Written with humour, understanding and insight, *Letters of Transit* captures the imagination from the very first page.

Paperback
ISBN 978 1 84511 4541

> '*Matthew Stevenson is humane, percipient, witty and well-informed about a bewildering number of subjects. He also writes like a dream.*'
> Simon Hoggart, Guardian

TPP

www.taurisparkepaperbacks.com